SUMMARY
of
UNSHAKEABLE

A FastReads Summary with Key Takeaways & Analysis

NOTE: The purpose of this FastReads summary is to help you decide if it's worth the time, money and effort reading the original book (if you haven't already). FastReads has pulled out the essence with commentary and critique—but only to help you ascertain the value of the book for yourself. This summary is meant to be a supplement to, and not a replacement for the original book.

Follow <u>this link</u> to purchase a copy of the original book on Amazon.

TABLE OF CONTENTS

EXECUTIVE SUMMARY

In this book, Tony Robbins lays out the principles anyone can use to make order out of market chaos, create an actionable investment plan, and achieve financial freedom. He teams up with Peter Mallouk to create a step-by-step guide that both novice and professional investors can use to withstand and profit from market uncertainty.

The authors reiterate that when market corrections and crashes occur, emotions overwhelm logical reasoning and cost investors fortunes. In the mayhem, the so-called finance professionals lose sight of the one fact that has remained constant for over 200 years: the stock market always rises over the long term. The duo argues that if investors diversify their portfolios, minimize taxes and expenses, and stay in the market long enough, the power of compounding takes over and accelerates their journey to financial freedom.

Unshakeable gives readers the tools to financial freedom and, more than that, to true wealth. It outlines practical tips for acquiring a true wealth mindset and living in a state of gratitude and enjoyment, no matter the circumstances of one's life.

Tony Robbins is a sobering voice in the financial barnyard filled with Chicken Littles and snake-oil peddlers.

SECTION 1
WEALTH: THE RULE BOOK

CHAPTER 1: UNSHAKEABLE
Power and Peace of Mind in a World of Uncertainty

The ultimate human desire is to live in abundance.

Everyone aspires to have financial security—and the comfort and freedom that come with it—regardless of the dips and turns in the economy. Everyone wants to be unshakeable.

But being unshakeable is not just about achieving financial security; it is about having the confidence to withstand and take advantage of the uncertainty that follows major economic meltdowns. It is about having the mental fortitude to see through the financial fog and quickly get back on course when the miasma of loss knocks you down.

Building this fortitude can be taxing, especially for investors who have burned their fingers in the market before.

Eight years on, the fear and sense of loss that came with the 2008 financial crisis is still palpable. Policy changes that followed the crisis have done little to abate mass pessimism. Today, developed countries are experimenting with negative interest rates, and high-quality bonds are now offering yields as low as 0.001%. Current policy changes, it would seem, are only palliative.

As of 2016, the stock market had been on a bull run for two and half years in a row. Thanks to mass pessimism, rumors of an imminent fall have never been more widespread.

But even with all the uncertainty, astute investors are still winning the financial game. When you understand how elite players profit from anticipating market falls, you can benefit from the worst snowstorm and accelerate your journey to financial freedom.

Key Takeaways

• To be unshakeable is to acquire the financial literacy, confidence, and security that allows you to withstand and profit from the worst turns in the market. With the right insights, skills, and commitment, anyone can master the financial game.

• The best investors understand that market corrections and crashes occur regularly but never last. They anticipate the chaos that comes with these turns and profit from it.

CHAPTER 2: WINTER IS COMING … BUT WHEN?
These Seven Facts Will Free You from the Fear of Corrections and Crashes

Savvy investors understand that compounding has the power to turn a modest investment into a fortune.

Most people don't take advantage of the power of compounding because they believe they can earn their way to financial freedom. But no one really does.

The easiest way to build your freedom fund is to have your bank automatically deduct 15 or 20% of your income and inject it into an index fund or diversified portfolio. If you have too many obligations to commit 20% of your income to a long-term investment, start by saving 3% and gradually increase your savings over time. The most important thing is to take the first step, and to take it early.

The stock market comes highly recommended because it has consistently made millions of people rich. In the last two centuries or so, despite devastating crashes and corrections, the stock market has remained the single greatest value creator for long-term investors.

Notwithstanding this fact, most people choose to stay out of the stock market because they fear a bull run is nearing its end or a bear run will go on indefinitely.

The following seven facts can help you get over market anxiety, discover proven patterns, and develop a winning strategy. Note that a correction is when the market falls by at least 10% from its peak, and a bear market is when the market falls by at least 20% from its peak.

1. On average, market corrections occur about once every year. The Armageddon predictions TV "experts" make are nothing more than attention-seeking drama. Corrections are regular occurrences, most of which last less than two months. Since 1900, the market has fallen, on average, 13.5% during corrections. When you accept this fact, you gain the courage to withstand the discomfort of corrections.

2. Less than one in five corrections turns into bear a market. A decline of more than 10% in the stock market often creates a selling frenzy amid fears of a bear market. Experienced investors know that most corrections are slight inconveniences they can withstand.

3. Consistent stock market predictions are impossible to make. No investment banker, Wall Street analyst, or world-renowned investor can predict when the market will rise or fall. Those who make accurate predictions are only right by chance. Astute investors focus on what they know and what they can control.

4. Despite numerous short-term drops, the stock market rises over the long run. Between 1980 and 2015, the S&P 500 index fell, on average, about 14.5% a year. With everything that happened during that period—the Gulf wars, 9/11, Middle East crises, the 2008 financial crisis—investors realized positive returns in 27 out of those 36 years. As the population grows and productivity increases, the upward trend is certain to continue.

5. Bear markets only occur every three to five years. On average, the S&P 500 index makes a 33% drop when the market crashes, and crashes last between a month and two years. When mass fear sparks massive selling, savvy investors—who know the bear market won't last—take advantage of the chaos to get bargain prices on stocks.

"Sir John Templeton, who made a fortune buying cheap stocks in the midst of World War II, explained: 'The best opportunities come in times of maximum pessimism'" (Robbins, 38).

6. Bear markets ultimately give way to bull markets. After the stock market hit rock bottom in March 2009, the S&P 500 index rose by 69.5% over the next 12 months and an astounding 266% over the subsequent seven years. All bear markets from 1949 have given way to bull markets.

7. Being out of the stock market is the costliest mistake. Playing wait-and-see is a losing game because most of the best stock market days occur within weeks of the worst trading days. If you waited on the sidelines and missed 10 of the best trading days in the last 20 years, you would have forfeited almost half of the S&P 500 returns consistent investors accumulated. It doesn't matter if you enter the market on the worst day; if you stay in and do nothing for long enough, the power of compounding evens out your losses and rewards you with a substantial sum.

Key Takeaways

• Invest early. In a few years, the compound interest you earn adds more value to your investment than the installments you make.

• Corrections and bear markets are short-term occurrences and natural parts of the stock market. Most investors miss out on building wealth because they pull their money out at the first sign of trouble. Super-investors like Warren Buffet see opportunity in every downturn.

• A growing population, a growing economy, and increasing technological innovation and productivity mean that the US stock market will continue to rise in the long run. An all-time market high does not necessarily mean recession is imminent; almost everything today is priced at an all-time high.

• The capricious nature of the stock market makes it almost impossible for short-term traders to profit over the long run. Successful investors pursue a buy-and-hold strategy to harness the power of compounding.

CHAPTER 3: HIDDEN FEES AND HALF-TRUTHS
How Wall Street Fools You into Overpaying for Underperformance

Excessive fees can cost you as much as two-thirds of your investment returns. If you invest in a fund with annualized returns of 7% for 50 years, and your fund manager charges you 2% in fees, each dollar invested returns 10 dollars. Without the 2% fees, each dollar invested would return 30 dollars.

Mutual funds, which are actively managed, may be the go-to choice of investment for people daunted by the complexity or futility of picking individual stocks, but they make lousy returns.

Actively managed funds try to add value to the basket of stocks they manage by predicting companies that will perform well in the future and adding these stocks to their portfolio. Unfortunately, no one is good at predicting the future. Worse, the commissions brokerage firms charge for each transaction and the capital-gains tax the government collects on every stock sale make active trading very expensive. Fund managers have to make impossibly huge returns to cover commissions and taxes and still have sizeable returns for their investors.

By comparison, index funds cost less to manage and accumulate more returns. These funds buy all the stocks in an index, such as S&P 500, and hold them for years. Since they execute only a few trades, index funds incur low transaction costs, low fees, and low taxes. Unlike mutual funds—which reserve cash for potential opportunities and payoffs—index funds invest all their cash and, consequently, achieve even more returns.

Research on market activity between 1929 and 1999 has indicated that buy-and-hold strategies outperformed market-timing strategies 80% of the time. A study of 203 actively managed mutual funds with $100 million in assets or more revealed that between 1984 and 1998, only 4 of these funds beat the S&P 500.

The typical mutual fund firm knows it can't beat the market. But because index funds are not lucrative, it devises schemes to dupe the misinformed public. The firm opens and actively trade several funds, drops the ones that perform poorly, and hypes the few that outperform index funds by chance. As the super-fund frenzy catches on, it becomes easy, even for the experienced investor, to forget that he has a better chance of winning the Olympics than consistently outperforming the S&P 500.

Key Takeaways

• Despite their popularity, only a single-digit percentage of mutual funds outperform index funds. High transaction fees and taxes, coupled with human error, make actively managed funds only good for their managers.

• If you take your nest-egg from a mutual fund and invest it in an index fund, you save at least 1% in fees and gain at least 1% in added returns. This additional 2% returns compounds and adds up to 20 years' worth of income to your retirement package.

CHAPTER 4: RESCUING OUR RETIREMENT PLANS
What Your 401(k) Provider Doesn't Want You to Know

Until recently, the law did not require companies providing 401(k) plans to disclose how much they charged their customers.

Even with the enactment of the disclosure bill in 2012, providers continue to take advantage of their clients' ignorance and charge huge commissions and hidden charges. In one survey, a nonprofit organization found that 71% of Americans were unaware that they paid fees on their 401(k) plans. 91% did not know how much fees they paid.

A recent study found that 401(k) providers deduct 17 different fees from their clients' savings. These fees, which are usually obscured by vague terms like "contract asset charge" and "asset management charge" in disclosure documents, amount to nearly 2% a year. Coupled with the high fees charged by mutual funds in the typical 401(k), unsuspecting contributors may be losing as much as 5% in costs a year.

It gets worse for nurses, teachers, and nonprofit employees who contribute to 403(b) plans. These plans charge as much as 6% "sales charge" on deposits, up to 2% in management fees, and about 1% in mutual fund expenses. In the first year of contribution, a teacher is already down 9%.

401(k) plans are prone to abuse from all fronts. Almost all of the well-known 401(k) providers receive payments from mutual fund firms in exchange for inclusion in the list of mutual funds available to employees. These funds are not only expensive, but also serial underperformers.

Over the years, providers have devised schemes that preclude employees from escaping the pervasive savings drain. Most providers only offer the option of investing in index funds to employees with sizeable plans. Providers who offer index funds to smaller plans often charge huge sales loads or exorbitant annual markups. Even providers who give customers the privilege of self-directing their own 401(k) plans charge as much as 2% in annual fees for this privilege.

Fortunately, a new breed of providers now offers slashed fees and inexpensive index funds to contributors. America's Best 401k (ABk)—which bundles its fees to promote transparency—charges, in total, just 0.65% a year.

For employers who wish to take their employees off the 401(k) rip-off, the first step is to benchmark their broker and provider fees against competitor rates using online services such as ShowMeTheFees.com. The service analyzes plans and calculates how much users can save by switching.

Employers have a fiduciary duty to ensure the plans they sponsor charge reasonable fees. Employees can sue their companies if they offer plans with excessive fees, and employers are liable to fines of up to $600,000 for enrolling employees in illegal plans.

Key Takeaways

• The exorbitant management fees that most 401(k) providers charge, coupled with the high management and transaction fees mutual funds charge, easily waste away two thirds of employees' retirement returns.

• Using online services, employees can benchmark their 401(k) provider fees against market rates and pressure their sponsors to switch plans. An informed switch can save more than 50% in fees.

CHAPTER 5: WHO CAN YOU REALLY TRUST?
Pulling Back the Curtain on the Tricks of the Trade

An independent and competent financial advisor can help you articulate your financial goals, rebalance a skewed portfolio, lower investment expenses, brave volatility, and, ultimately, increase your chances of achieving financial freedom.

Out of this realization, perhaps, the number of Americans using financial advisory services doubled between 2010 and 2015. As of 2016, 40% of Americans were consulting financial advisors.

Ironically, about 60% of the US population has admitted it doesn't trust that financial advisors are looking after their clients' best interests. These sentiments are understandable, especially when one considers that the biggest financial institutions in the country have had to make multimillion-dollar settlements for misusing customer assets or manipulating rates.

It's difficult to find someone to trust in an industry that prioritizes the interests of shareholders, incentivizes employees to put their interests second, and pushes customer interests to a distant third.

"Regardless of the title, what you really need to know is that 90% of the roughly 310,000 financial advisors in America are actually just brokers. In other words, they're paid to sell financial products to customers like you and me in return for a fee" (Robbins, 76).

To know if you can trust your financial advisor, find out which of the three categories of advisors he falls into.

• **Brokers**, who make up about 90% of all advisors, receive fees or commissions for selling products. They have a vested interest in selling you mutual funds and other expensive products, regardless of whether you need them or not, to meet their contractual obligations. They don't have to recommend the best product for you; the law merely requires them to recommend *suitable* products.

• **Registered investment advisors (RIAs)**, who make up the remaining 10% of financial advisors, have a fiduciary duty to *always* act in the best interest of their clients. RIAs must disclose to their clients any conflict of interest and explain the fees they charge. RIAs are fewer than brokers because they don't take commissions and, consequently, don't make as much money as brokers. Most people who seek financial advice from brokers are unaware of the existence of RIAs.

• **Dually registered advisors** play both broker and registered investment advisor. They can hawk expensive products and get fat commissions one moment and promise you full disclosure the next moment.

Of the 310,000 financial advisors in the US, only 1.6% are pure RIAs. These fiduciaries are your best bet for solid financial advice.

Even so, independent advisors may lure you into crafty but legal schemes to milk more money from you. A registered investment advisor, for example, may recommend proprietary mutual funds operated by a second arm of his advisory firm. Alternatively, a sly RIA may agree to recommend a company's mutual funds to his clients in exchange for a "consultation fee" because he is legally barred from accepting commissions.

More commonly, the RIA recommends a "model portfolio" which has an additional fee above the asset management fee you are already paying. When you subscribe to this model, you pay your advisor twice for doing the job you hired him to do.

Before using the services of a registered financial advisor, ask him if he is affiliated with a broker-dealer, if his firm runs separately managed funds, and if he receives third-party compensation for recommending products. Find out if he shares your financial philosophy and ensure you relate on a personal level.

Key Takeaways

• About 90% of all financial advisors are brokers who have huge incentives to hawk overpriced substandard products. They don't have any legal obligation to put your interest first, and they don't have to disclose any conflict of interest.

• Hire a competent registered investment advisor to get the best financial advice. Check your advisor's professional credentials and ensure he or she has experience working with people like you.

SECTION 2:
THE UNSHAKEABLE PLAYBOOK

CHAPTER 6: THE CORE FOUR
The Key Principles That Can Help Guide Every Investment Decision You Make

Success is not a function of luck. It is a combination of functional beliefs, purposeful strategy, and deliberate effort. Successful people simply play the financial game differently from everyone else.

Although the most successful investors have unique investing styles, they use four core principles, almost obsessively, to make investment decisions:

1. Don't lose money.

While everyone else is figuring out how to maximize returns, super-investors are figuring out how to avoid losing.

"But the best investors are obsessed with avoiding losses. Why? Because they understand a simple but profound fact: the more money you lose, the harder it is to get back to where you started." (Kindle Locations 1978-1980).

Most people overlook the simple math: If you lose 50% of your investment, you'll need to *double* your remaining investment to be whole again. Billionaire investor Paul Tudor Jones considers capping the downside to be 10 times more important than capturing returns.

Successful investors guard against the risk of unexpected events and mitigate the risk of being wrong. They know that no matter how smart or successful they are, they don't know what the markets will do tomorrow. They design portfolios with a diversified mix of investments to mitigate their downside when the unexpected occurs.

2. Reduce risks, maximize returns

Smart investors don't accept that they have to take big risks to get high returns; they look for investment opportunities with minimal risks and huge rewards.

Paul Tudor Jones invests in opportunities that, ideally, have a 1:5 risk/reward ratio. With this ratio, he could lose everything in 4 out of 5 investments and still break even, if the fifth investment works out. If two investments turn out as expected, he doubles his money. Since opportunities with a 1:5 risk/reward ratio are difficult to come by, he often settles for a risk/reward ratio of 1:3.

The common investor can always to find opportunities to buy undervalued stocks with potentially high returns during periods of economic uncertainty and mass pessimism.

3. Increase tax efficiency

If you sell an investment within the year of purchase, your profits are subject to the ordinary tax rate of 50%. If you hold the same investment for a year or more, you only pay 20% long-term capital gains tax when you sell it.

The short-term gains mutual funds make are subject to the ordinary tax income. If you deduct 50% tax and about 2% management fees and account for inflation, the 8% annualized pre-tax returns mutual fund managers tout easily drop to a measly 1%.

Successful investors are smart about their taxes because they know tax burdens can erode the money they have for reinvesting and spending. Part of being tax-smart is investing in index funds—which accrue less tax because they are not actively managed—instead of mutual funds, and maximizing contributions to a 401(k) or other tax-deferred investment.

4. Diversify

A well-designed portfolio diversifies within asset classes, across asset classes, across markets and countries, and across time.

Diversification protects against the urge to overinvest in one approach or investment that "works". It lowers risks and increases returns at no extra cost. Diversification is a critical strategy because every asset class is cyclical. What works today is almost certain to lose as much as 50% of its value in the future.

Key Takeaways

• Elite investors build wealth by capping their downsides, hunting opportunities with asymmetric risk/reward ratios, keeping their tax liability to the bare minimum, and diversifying their investments.

• Split your money among 15 or more good but uncorrelated investments to mitigate risk and increase returns. Hold your investments for the long-term to increase tax-efficiency and realize even more returns.

CHAPTER 7: SLAY THE BEAR
How to Navigate Crashes and Corrections to Accelerate Your Financial Freedom

Savvy investors see the best opportunities in bear markets and mass pessimism. They know that the S&P 500 index always soars in the twelve months that follow the lowest point of a crash or correction. The knowledge that bear markets always turn to bull markets, regardless of how bleak the outlook is, gives them the courage to endure uncertainty and fear less.

On the flipside, smart investors prepare for the storm while the skies are still clear. They know market corrections and crashes are never far off.

Diversifying lowers risk and increases returns because economic changes affect asset classes differently. In 2008, for example, investment grade bonds rose 5.24% as the S&P 500 index fell 38%.

A well-balanced portfolio diversifies within and across the major asset classes:

Stocks

Stocks have, over the last 100 years, earned investors average returns of 9 to 10%. A devastating decline in the stock market occurs once every four years or so, but there's almost always a positive trend in 10 years or more. A good portfolio should have a large chunk of cash on stocks, but not too much to force you to sell when a bear market puts pressure on your personal finances.

Bonds

Compared to stocks, bonds have lower risks and fewer returns. Including bonds in your portfolio allows you to meet any financial needs that may arise while you are still invested in the stock market. Smart investors sell bonds during bear markets and invest the proceeds in undervalued stock.

Alternative Investments

Although most alternative investments are illiquid, tax inefficient, and expensive, they are vital components of a diversified portfolio because they are unrelated to the stock and bond market.

• **Real Estate Investment Trusts (REITs)** allow you to own a piece of residential properties at a low cost and minimal hassle. The value of your investment increases when the value of the underlying property appreciates, and you get to receive regular income from a share of the profits.

• **Private Equity Funds** pool money and use it to buy a company or part of it. They add value to the investment by making the target company more efficient. These funds are potentially lucrative, but they are risky and charge high fees.

• **Master Limited Partnerships** invest in energy infrastructure and pay their investors income from the tolls they collect. They offer low risk, good returns, and tax efficiency on long-term investments.

Some investors consider gold a safe cushion against stock market caprice, but bonds and the abovementioned alternative investments always outperform the metal. Hedge funds would be good alternative investments if they did not charge exorbitant fees and almost always lag behind the S&P 500.

There is no single best way to combine investments and design the perfect asset allocation. Still, the approach you take to diversification should match your needs, not your age or your tolerance for risk. The financial advisor who helps you with this process should ascertain your financial goals and propose an asset allocation customized for you. Whatever portfolio you create, include index funds to maximize diversification.

Key Takeaways

• The people who survive a bear market are those who prepare for the crash while markets are still doing well. They take time to build the emotional fortitude that enables them to withstand the uncertainty that comes with falling markets.

• The right balance of stocks, bonds, and alternative investments, diversified across multiple markets, minimizes investment risks and accelerates the journey to financial freedom.

• Invest in bonds, dividend-paying stocks, and other income-generating asset classes to cushion your finances and allow the value of your stocks to increase undisturbed.

SECTION 3:
THE PSYCHOLOGY OF WEALTH

CHAPTER 8: SILENCING THE ENEMY WITHIN
The Six Money Mistakes Investors Make and How You Can Avoid Them

According to neuroscientists, the human brain processes financial losses using the same parts that process mortal threats.

It makes sense, then, that people panic and sell everything (the equivalent of running when confronted by mortal danger) when markets plummet. Before the typical investor has had a chance to realize or remember that bear markets are buying opportunities, this automatic response has already kicked in.

Knowing what to invest in, how to minimize fees and taxes, and how to diversify is only part of the journey to financial freedom. Mastering your psychology is the biggest hurdle you have to overcome.

Simple systems can help you prevent self-sabotage by encouraging you to question and counter the beliefs that activate your fight-or-flight mechanism. A system of checks is as important for you as an investor as it is for a pilot; it ensures you know what to do when something happens and provides a safeguard against botched execution.

A good system has checks for each of the common mistakes investors make:

Confirmation bias.

The human brain is hardwired to seek and believe information that validates its current beliefs. To check this bias, experienced investors actively seek divergent interpretations of market patterns from competent people before they invest. They find out what they don't know and where they could go wrong.

Recency bias.

Most people take recent events to signal ongoing or long-term trends and, subsequently, get in or out of the wrong market at the worst time possible. Recency bias is at the root of the biggest mistake small investors make: buying rising stocks and selling falling stocks under the assumptions that the current trend will continue. To mitigate against the risk of buying high and selling low, decide beforehand how you will diversify your portfolio and make a commitment to rebalance once every year.

Overconfidence.

It's human nature to overestimate one's knowledge, skills, and abilities. Most investors either assume they will be as skilled at investing as they are in another area of their life or acquire a false sense of confidence from optimistic finance "professionals." To keep overconfidence and the subsequent tendency to overtrade in check, admit to yourself that you have no special edge over the market. Buy and hold safe and low-cost investments like index funds.

Greed.

It's easy to forget that successful investors got where they are by compounding small, incremental changes over years. Greed increases risk exposure and, consequently, contravenes the first principle of investing: do not lose money.

"Wall Street wins by getting you to be more active, but you win by patiently staying in the game for decades. Remember, as Warren Buffett says, 'The stock market is a device for transferring money from the impatient to the patient'" (Robbins, 155).

To check against greed, feed your mind with long-term thoughts. Substitute finance shows on TV with literature by patient investors like Warren Buffet. Check your portfolio only once a year.

Home bias.

Sticking with the familiar is efficient and works well in other areas of life, but not so much for investing. Investing too heavily in your company's stock, industry, or country increases your risk exposure and caps your upside. Talk to your advisor about diversifying broadly across geographic markets.

Negativity bias.

As part of its survival mechanism, the human brain recalls negative events more vividly than positive events. Investors who know that the best opportunities come from periods of mass pessimism may fail to act on this knowledge because they focus too much on negative experiences from the past.

To check against this bias, prepare for the emotional toll that comes with market chaos by designing the right asset allocation. Write your motives and goals for investing in each asset class and refer to these notes whenever you feel like you need to cash out.

Key Takeaways

• Your mind is your biggest obstacle to your financial well-being. Knowing how and what to invest is only beneficial if you take the time to weed out unconscious beliefs and limit your brain's tendency to exaggerate danger and seek pleasure.

• A checklist limits self-sabotage by compensating for faulty memory and attention. Design a checklist for each market pattern and include checks for common mental biases. Use it to vet current and potential investments.

CHAPTER 9: REAL WEALTH
Making the Most Important Decision of Your Life

Financial freedom is a great ideal to attain, but it is only part of being wealthy. Real wealth includes emotional, psychological and spiritual freedom.

The psychological aspect of wealth is as important—perhaps more important—than the financial aspect because the positive feelings you associate with money don't come from the money itself. They come from the sense of freedom and comfort that comes from knowing you have enough.

An Extraordinary Life

The ultimate human goal is to live an extraordinary life. Depending on whom you ask, this could mean building a billion-dollar empire, getting closer to God, living in a beach-house, or raising wonderful children. Whatever an extraordinary life means to you, it begins with the mastery of achievement and fulfillment skills.

Whatever you set out to achieve, the prerequisites are focus, massive action, and grace. When you single-mindedly focus on your goal, your attention and energy flow to actions that help you get there. However, focus means nothing if you don't get started. You have to execute, model people who have succeeded in a similar path, and take massive and consistent action. Through all these processes, you have to acknowledge the power of grace in your life—whether for you grace means luck or God.

Achievement is only the capacity to master the external world. You could achieve everything you ever wanted, but it would mean nothing if you are not fulfilled. To be content and sustainably happy, you have to master your internal self. Fulfillment becomes a part of you when you keep growing and keep giving.

On Suffering

Suffering—be it in form of stress, worry, frustration, or other negative emotion—comes from your interpretation of the things that happen to you.

No situation has the capacity to make you suffer; suffering begins and ends with your thoughts. You suffer when you think you lost or will lose something you value, when you think you have or will have less, or when you think you'll never have something you value. Suffering becomes your reality when you believe these thoughts.

You can choose to live in a beautiful state full of gratitude, curiosity, love, and joy regardless of your circumstances in life.

This beautiful state starts with a steadfast commitment to enjoy life and be happy no matter what happens; no matter what desire or expectation you or someone else fails to meet. This is the most important decision you can make in your life.

When you start to feel worried, stressed, or angry, take a deep breath, identify the thoughts behind your suffering, and question their validity. Once you realize that you don't have to believe these thoughts, take a moment to find something to appreciate around you. When you shift your thoughts from what is wrong to what is worth appreciating, and when you do this consistently enough, you override your natural tendency to focus on *loss, less,* and *never.*

Gratitude is such a powerful emotion that when you are experiencing it, it is impossible to experience a negative emotion.

You can align your mind and heart and make true abundance a habit by practicing gratitude meditation. Close your eyes, place both of your hands on your heart, and feel it pumping. Breathe. As you feel the gift of your heart beating, step into three experiences for which you are most grateful and let the gratitude fill you. Explore each experience for at least 30 seconds.

"It's so simple and yet so profound: appreciation, enjoyment, and love are nothing less than the antidotes to suffering. It's all about shifting your focus away from the illusion of loss, less, or never, and engaging your gratitude, appreciation, and love for what you already have in your life!" (Robbins, 184).

Key Takeaways

• Fame and fortune mean nothing if you don't invite the joy of fulfillment into your life. Make personal growth a lifelong pursuit and give—no matter how little you have—to nurture an abundance mindset.

• Your thoughts and decisions create your reality. Take some time to appreciate what you have, the people in your life, and the experiences you've lived through to overwhelm the thoughts of loss, less, and never that create suffering.

• Ultimately, to have true wealth is to live in a beautiful state. You can choose to possess the freedom and abundance that comes with this state now, no matter the circumstances of your life, by practicing gratitude meditation.

EDITORIAL REVIEW

In 1973, Princeton economist Burton Malkiel published his seminal work on market efficiency and, with his book *A Random Walk Down Wall Street*, popularized what is arguably one of the most overlooked hypotheses in finance. Malkiel argued that asset prices move in random patterns—the implication being that no one can consistently outperform market averages. He analyzed market prediction strategies and concluded that their returns are almost always less than the returns achieved by passive buy-and-hold strategies.

John C. Bogle presumably built on this hypothesis to create the first index mutual fund in 1975. While marketing what later came to be known as the Vanguard 500 Index Fund, Bogle admitted that the fund would not outperform the market, but he promised investors that it would not underperform the market either. Wall Street analysts mocked the idea, called it "un-American," and wondered aloud if there was any investor who would settle for "average" returns. Four decades on, the Vanguard group manages approximately $4 trillion in assets. Its returns are still average, but it has consistently outperformed actively managed funds over the years.

But even with the rise and rise of the index fund, TV pundits and Wall Street analysts remain adamant that with the right analysis, consistent profits can be made from stock picking.

If there has been anything consistent about the behavior of the stock market in the last 100 years, it is this: the market rises and falls on a regular basis, biased towards the uptrend. There is no telling if or when individual stocks will rise or fall. Yesterday's hot picks are almost always tomorrow's junk.

Tony Robbins comes to remind readers this fundamental truth: markets correct and crash, but the patient investor who has capped his downside need not live in fear. He reiterates that the combination of low costs, low risk, and diversity makes index funds the only investment that adequately takes advantage of the market's upward bias. Index funds are still an investor's best bet for building wealth.

In *Unshakeable: Your Financial Freedom Playbook* Robbins condenses financial freedom insights from his New York Times bestseller *Money:*

Master the Game and adds new practical tips for conquering market uncertainty and creating real wealth. His argument is simple: the most efficient way to build financial wealth is to invest in low-cost and low-risk index funds, diversify with bonds and alternative investments, minimize fees and taxes, and hold investments for the long term.

He concedes that market corrections and crashes come with a lot of uncertainty. However, he notes, investors can embrace and profit from these occurrences when they discover that crashes are regular occurrences and harmless for investors with diversified portfolios.

The book delivers on its promise to help readers build mental fortitude for the economic volatility and uncertainty that lies ahead. A selection of irrefutable facts put the stock market in perspective, and, with layman explanations, Robbins helps the reader understand that there is nothing to fear if he or she knows what to expect and prepares for it.

However, the book falls short on its promise to help readers design asset allocation and create an actionable financial plan. Peter Mallouk, the co-author, samples asset classes and principles for creating a good portfolio. In what is perhaps the book's biggest letdown, he fails to offer specific advice about creating a customized portfolio. Instead, he advises readers to consult a competent financial advisor.

In what comes out as an overt marketing ploy, the book makes numerous references to the services offered by a financial advisory company that Robbins and Mallouk have a sizeable stake in. The references are a little off-putting and suspicious, especially when one considers that the book is supposed to offer impartial financial advice. Robbins also makes periodic references to his previous book *Money: Master the Game*. Inadvertently, perhaps, he makes the reader who hasn't read the book feel like he or she is missing out.

All the same, *Unshakeable* offers practical advice that any investor can use to find value deals, minimize expenses, and build mental fortitude. It comes highly recommended for the reader who is just starting out his or her investment journey.

ABOUT THE AUTHORS

Tony Robbins is an investor, entrepreneur, and a world-renowned life and business strategist. He has coached some of the most successful personalities in the world, including former president Bill Clinton, tennis superstar Serena Williams, and award-winning actor Leonardo diCaprio. He has authored four best-selling books covering topics from overcoming fears to mastering finances. His sensational personality and pragmatic personal development seminars have touched and changed the lives of millions of people across the globe.

Peter Mallouk is a certified financial planner and the president of Creative Planning, Inc, a financial advisory and wealth management firm that manages more than $23 billion in assets. Barron's magazine named Mallouk the leading independent advisor in America in 2013, 2014, and 2015. Including *Unshakeable*, Mallouk has authored two New York Times bestselling books about investing.

END

If you enjoyed this summary, please leave an honest review on Amazon.com! It'd mean a lot to us!

If you haven't already, we encourage you to purchase a copy of the original book.

KNIGHT of the TEMPLE

Stuart J Dimmock

Note for Librarians: A cataloguing record for this book is available from Library and Archives
Canada at www.collectionscanada.ca/amicus/index-e.html
ISBN 1-4120-6317-5

*Printed in Victoria, BC, Canada. Printed on paper with minimum 30% recycled fibre. Trafford's print shop
runs on "green energy" from solar, wind and other environmentally-friendly power sources.*

Offices in Canada, USA, Ireland and UK

This book was published *on-demand* in cooperation with Trafford Publishing. On-demand
publishing is a unique process and service of making a book available for retail sale to the
public taking advantage of on-demand manufacturing and Internet marketing. On-demand
publishing includes promotions, retail sales, manufacturing, order fulfilment, accounting and
collecting royalties on behalf of the author.

Book sales for North America and international:
Trafford Publishing, 6E–2333 Government St.,
Victoria, BC v8t 4p4 CANADA
phone 250 383 6864 (toll-free 1 888 232 4444)
fax 250 383 6804; email to orders@trafford.com
Book sales in Europe:
Trafford Publishing (uk) Ltd., Enterprise House, Wistaston Road Business Centre,
Wistaston Road, Crewe, Cheshire cw2 7rp UNITED KINGDOM
phone 01270 251 396 (local rate 0845 230 9601)
facsimile 01270 254 983; orders.uk@trafford.com
Order online at:
trafford.com/05-1228

10 9 8 7 6 5 4 3 2

To Stanley William, a fearless caballero
on whom Fortuna ceased to smile.

Acknowledgements

My thanks to Patricia, my wife, for her steadfast
support and hard work in producing this book and to
my good friend, Peter Coltman, for reading the
manuscript and offering valuable comment.

Cover design: P A Dimmock, 2005

About the author

Stuart Dimmock's first degree is in history and education. He worked initially as a university teacher and then as a senior executive in the public service. First novel, *Tracer*, was published in 1990. His previous work has generally been non-fiction.

He and his wife sailed their boat from England to the Mediterranean in 2000. They live now in southern Spain.

A Note for Readers

The following four pages contain:-

1. Map of 13th century Spain, showing Christian and Muslim kingdoms and the route of the Camino de Santiago.

2. Glossary of medieval and Spanish terms used. These are printed in italic in the text.

3. Description of the Templars' day, i.e. prescribed times of services, meals etc.

Christian Spain and the Camino de Santiago in the early 13th Century

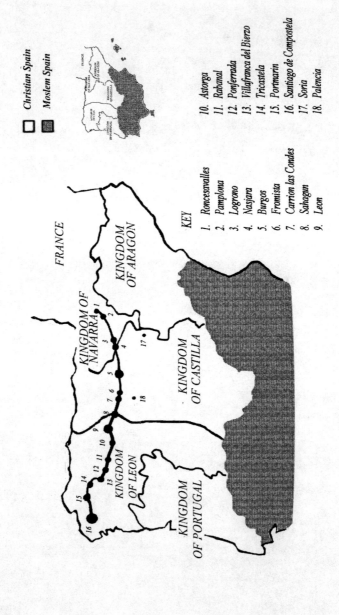

☐ Christian Spain

▦ Moslem Spain

FRANCE

KINGDOM OF NAVARRA

KINGDOM OF ARAGON

KINGDOM OF CASTILLA

KINGDOM OF LEON

KINGDOM OF PORTUGAL

KEY

1. Roncesvalles
2. Pamplona
3. Logroño
4. Nasjara
5. Burgos
6. Fromista
7. Carrion las Condes
8. Sahagun
9. Leon
10. Astorga
11. Rabanal
12. Ponferrada
13. Villafranca del Bierzo
14. Tricastela
15. Portmarin
16. Santiago de Compostela
17. Soria
18. Palencia

GLOSSARY

Affray	mock battle at a tourney
Bandido	bandit
Barrio	neighbourhood
Bodega	winery, wine cellar
Broigne	jacket, sometimes sleeveless, made of thick leather treated with beeswax, worn by squires and men-at-arms
Burnous	hooded cloak
Caballero	knight
Camino	road
Casa mayor	large house
Casque	iron or steel helmet in shape of pointed bowl
Cathar	medieval European heresy that spread from Balkans in the tenth century. Cathars believed the world was under Satan's dominion: men and women would be reincarnated constantly unless united, through Cathar faith, with Christ.
Chausses	mail leggings worn by knight
Confrere	fellow member
El Campeador	'the battler'; nickname of the Spanish hero El Cid
Ferdinands	coins minted by Ferdinand I of Castile
Francos	privileged foreigners, generally French, who settled in Sahagun in the tenth and eleventh centuries and granted tax and trade exemptions by its great Clunaic monastery of San Benito
Franks	crusaders, generally French and from the nobility, who acquired titles and lands and lived in the Holy Land after its conquest by the First Crusade
Hauberk	chain mail shirt, generally extending down to the knees, worn by knight
Hostal	hotel, guesthouse

GLOSSARY continued

Langue d'oc	language spoken in medieval France in region south of the River Loire
Langue d'oil	language spoken in medieval France in region north of the River Loire
Lauds	see 'The Medieval Day'
League	approximately 3 miles or 5 kilometres
Mark	target (term still used today by confidence tricksters)
Matins	see 'The Medieval Day'
Meseta	high tableland of central Spain
Noones	see 'The Medieval Day'
Oblate	person dedicated to a monastic life
Outreamer	the Holy Land (literally 'overseas')
Paladins	Peers of Charlemagne's court, said to have been slain in a legendary battle with the infidel giant Aigolando close by Sahagun. The dead Christian knights' spears blossomed into palms in recognition of their martyrdom
Plaza mayor	main square
Quintain	target attached to pole, often rotating; used for practising jousting
Reconquista	reconquest of Moorish Spain
Renegardo	renegade, outcast
Senori	senior male citizens with a voice in the government of town or city
Servien	servant
Sext	see 'The Medieval Day'
Solar	small private room
Taberna	tavern, pub
Taifa	Moorish kingdom
Terce	see 'The Medieval Day'
Vespers	see 'The Medieval Day'

THE MEDIEVAL DAY AND THE TEMPLAR RULE

The Medieval Day
The periods of daylight and night were divided by twelve. Therefore in summer an hour of daylight was longer than in winter.

The Templar Day According to the Rule
The Templar Rule followed closely the 'Rule of St. Benedict', introduced in the sixth century and followed by Benedictine monasteries.

At night		Matins		
6am	(1st hour)	Prime		
		Mass (or after Sext)		
9am	(3rd hour)	Terce		
12noon	(6th hour)	Sext		
		Mass (if not heard earlier)	-	Lunch
3pm	(9th hour)	Noones		
		Vespers for the dead		
		Vigils for the dead		
Dusk		Vespers	-	Supper
		Compline	-	A drink
Dark			-	Retire to bed (light kept burning in dormitories)

- Times would vary according to the seasons.

- Services were held in the chapel or in hall if a commandery had no chapel.

- On active service knights and sergeants were required to say Paternoster (Our Father) hourly.

- Only one meal a day during Lent and other times of fasting.

- Benedictine monasteries observed an additional service, Lauds, which was held at first light.

1

We mortals can never know why Fortuna chanced William Stanley's destiny on the Wheel of Fate. We can say however that his involvement with the 'Prisciliano heresy' began when he was summoned to attend Robert Montagnac in the Master's quarters on the day after the Feast of the Assumption, in the year of Our Lord, 1206. William was lancing against a *quintain* on the training ground outside Ponferrada's walls and on receipt of the order he returned to the castle where he gave his horse into the care of his squire. He thought to go to the dormitory to change into his knight's robe, but given the urgency of the summons he decided to go directly to Montagnac's *solar* in the north tower.

The first floor of the north tower was a storeroom: the air was cool — a welcome relief from the August sun — and once his eyes had accustomed to the gloom he started up the steep spiral steps that led the top. He was uneasy. He had been surprised by Montagnac's order because it breached his ban against seeing anyone in his quarters and he did not seem to be the sort who would break his own rules. William could think of no reason for this extraordinary summons, but he decided that whatever the cause he would watch his tongue. He climbed steadily; taking brief rests to catch his breath, enjoying the draught that was funnelling up the dark, narrow stair. He would be thirty-seven at Michaelmas — old by a fighting man's standards — and he wanted to have plenty of wind when he reached the Master's solar on the third floor.

****

Robert Montagnac, knight of the Order of the Temple of Jerusalem and its new Master of Ponferrada since Holy Week, had been sitting on the stone window seat of his solar in the hours since *Prime* considering a difficult problem. If he handled it well it could mean promotion away from Ponferrada; handling it badly could leave him guarding pilgrims for the rest of his days. The Master's principal responsibility was to ensure safe passage on the road to Santiago for a distance of seventy *leagues*: all the way from Sahagun on the eastern border of Leon to the sacred walls of the Holy City. It was not the promotion he would have chosen for himself, but like all knights of the Temple he was sworn to obedience and since Easter he had set to and reorganised his command and increased the number of patrols. Ponferrada and its outlying commanderies were efficient now for the first time in years and he yearned for the opportunity to apply his skills to a higher purpose. He shifted his position to ease the pain in his crippled leg: the price paid for his sobriquet, 'Montagnac the Brave'. He needed someone to scour the country. He could not, because his injury prevented him sitting a horse for any length of time, and his duties required his presence at Ponferrada. One of his knights would have to do it. But who should he chose? His knights totalled fourteen. Sergeants were more plentiful and there was a virtual abundance of serving brothers, but the possibility of choosing anyone from the lower ranks never crossed his mind.

His preference was for a fellow countryman and there were two French knights in his command: one of the *langue d'oil*, the other of *langue d'oc*. But they were based in commanderies that were over three days ride away: choosing either would entail a lengthy delay and his superiors might accuse him of being dilatory. To guard against such an accusation meant picking a knight from the castle's garrison. Since his reorganisation only four knights were garrisoned permanently at Ponferrada: the Infirmarer, an elderly German who was part blind; two Castilians, both young and untried and an English *confrere*.

It was clear immediately to Montagnac that the English confrere, William Stanley, was the only choice. He was not dismayed: at his first chapter meeting he had ordered every knight and sergeant to say a little about their history and he had marked Stanley as being different from the rest. He had fought in the Holy Land and been posted to reinforce the Temple's forces in Spain after the Battle of Alarcos. He knew the Camino territory well and although he was English he had an ear for different tongues and could speak Castilian, langue d'oc and langue d'oil fluently. In character he appeared to be pious — but not overly so. In Montagnac's opinion men of great piety were seldom effective in achieving God's purpose. He was short of speech, although on the few occasions he'd spoken in chapter his comments were sound. Montagnac wanted a man who could think for himself, but not one who was clever enough to think independently.

The sound of footsteps on the tower's stairs broke in on Montagnac's thoughts. Turning away from the window he saw Stanley standing at the solar's threshold and when he saw what the knight was wearing he was incensed. Instead of his long white robe, as stipulated in the Order's Rule, Stanley was dressed in his linen under breeches, old leather boots and a sleeveless *broigne* — the garb of a common foot soldier. Montagnac was astonished at such effrontery. Stanley wasn't a novice; he knew the Rule required knights to wear their robe inside a commandery: insolence like this couldn't be excused. Montagnac glared at Stanley's bare arms, unsure whether to proceed with the meeting in the way he'd planned, or to castigate the knight for his dress.

"You sent for me, Master," said William.

The room was quite dark and he couldn't see the anger on Montagnac's face, only his outline against the window. There was a long moment's silence. Montagnac knew that to begin the meeting with angry words was a mistake, nevertheless it was shameful to be treated thus. He managed, finally, to rein in his temper; he would put Stanley's disgraceful behaviour to one side, but he would neither forgive nor forget it. He pointed at the seat, on the opposite side of the window.

"Sit down. I want to speak to you."

He watched Stanley as he walked across to the window, noting his self-confident carriage and his sense of authority and pride. The broigne accentuated his leanness of waist, breadth of shoulder and muscular arms. Seeing himself, as he had once been, his dislike of Stanley was enhanced by envy.

At the May chapter meeting, when Stanley had given a brief account of his record, Montagnac had fixed his age at some years past thirty. Looking at him afresh, he was surprised to see how well he bore them. His violet blue eyes were clear, his teeth were good and his face, though tanned and lined by sun and weather, was free of pocks and warts. Only the grey in his beard and dark hair spoke of a man of seasoned maturity. If Montagnac had found Stanley handsome he could not have borne it. But the knight's mouth was too wide, his nose too long and his brow too low for Montagnac's taste. In fact he relished the thought that Stanley's feature spoke of commoners' blood in his lineage.

"Why were you sentenced to serve in the Order?" Montagnac asked abruptly, in a tone that intimated his dislike. He hadn't cared to ask in the chapter meeting but it was important now to know something of the man who sat opposite him.

"I killed a knight at a tourney in Flanders. The Bishop of Bruges said it was murder, but before I was condemned, news came of Saladin's victory at the Battle of Hattin and I was sentenced to fight in the Holy Land as a knight in the Order."

"Did you do murder?" demanded Montagnac, continuing to stare at Stanley.

"It was long time ago, Master."

William knew he hadn't answered the question, and he wasn't going to. Montagnac wasn't his confessor and since his public scourging in the Bishop's Court he hadn't even spoken to God on the matter.

"Did you?"

"The Bishop judged me guilty. I confessed my sin and entered the Order. Since then I have tried to serve Christ and our Lady."

Montagnac heard the finality in the knight's answer and his sense of resignation. He leaned back and rubbed his crippled leg gently to ease the pain. In spite of his dislike of Stanley he was impressed by his straightforward replies. A foolish man would have said more.

Sensing that he had passed some sort of test, William leaned back too and rested his shoulders against the sill of the turret window. He was sure that Montagnac hadn't summoned him to hear his lifestory. So, what was the reason? Had he done wrong? Was he to be disciplined? Was that the reason for the sharpness of Montagnac's questions? He glanced around the solar, bare now of the few comforts that had lightened the burden of the previous Master's old age. A cot with a single thin blanket stood in one corner, a chest for clothes in another and a small crucifix hung from a nail in the wall. Why hadn't Montagnac chosen to take up quarters elsewhere? Why would a crippled man climb regularly to the top of a tower? thought William, unless he wanted to be known as a stoic. He had guessed, at their first meeting in Holy Week that Montagnac was a careerist; the type of officer he disliked most. Seeing him at close quarters however — his unbending leg and twisted shoulder, eyes sunk deep in their sockets, the grey pallor of his face, lined prematurely by pain — William felt sudden pity for the man. But he knew better than to let sympathy be his guide.
"Why did you want to see me, Master?"
Was there arrogance in his tone? Montagnac looked at him closely. He might not like the knight, but he also knew that there was no one else he could choose.
"Go down and wait for me on the first floor," he snapped, struggling to get to his feet.

It took time for Montagnac to descend the steps from his solar so William waited at the tower's open door, watching a gang of serving brothers mixing a lime and pebble mortar to reinforce the north wall. It was hot work and although they had stripped off their brown woollen robes they were still sweating profusely.
"Come with me," said Montagnac once he'd reached the bottom step.
He limped off into the shadows behind the sacks of grain and barrels of oil, wine and salted pork that were piled high across the boarded floor, with William following behind.
"What do you make of that?" asked Montagnac, when they came to a space in the stacks of stores on the far side of the room.
William stopped in surprise. In front of him, in a patch of light from a high window, was the stone bath they used for pickling meat. The body of a very fat man was lying inside it. He was naked, his chest bore the livid scar of a blade wound and his thick, fleshy throat had been cut from ear to ear.
"A group of pilgrims brought him in this morning, after *Matins*," said Montagnac. "He's been murdered," he added, superfluously.

2

Montagnac took a small roll of blood stained parchment out of his robe's pocket and thrust it at William. "Can you read Latin?"

William shook his head. He had learned it as a boy, but it was years since he'd had reason to use it and he thought it wiser to stay silent in case he'd lost the skill.

"It's a letter of introduction," said Montagnac. It was a short letter and he'd read the legible bit so many times he could recite it by heart. "It's addressed to any Christian lord, spiritual or temporal. It says he's Rolfe Cardiaye, Deputy Prior of the Abbey of Cluny. He holds a Papal commission and is to be given any assistance he may require," he paused, "and it's signed and sealed by His Holiness, Innocent III."

William whistled softly.

"Precisely," said Montagnac, dryly. "It's not every day you see a letter signed by the Pope."

William pointed at the roll of parchment. "What was his commission?"

"Obliterated by his blood unfortunately. All we know is that he was killed at Foncebadon. The pilgrims who brought him here said he was travelling alone. They stayed at our refuge in Rabanal on the night before last and set off together yesterday at dawn. They were on foot, he was on a horse and he'd soon left them behind. They'd stopped by Foncebadon's cross to catch their breath when their dog started kicking up a rumpus. They went to see what the matter was." Montagnac pointed at the corpse. "It was digging him up."

"Digging him up?"

"Yes, strange isn't it? The pilgrims said it was a very shallow grave, covered by rocks and a few branches that had been hacked off the trees." He turned and looked up at William. "Have you ever heard of *bandidos* burying anybody?"

"No, never. They leave even their own dead for the wolves."

Montagnac pointed at the corpse. "Then why should they bury him?"

William shrugged. "Because they didn't want him found, I suppose."

"That's what I think. And he was killed quietly too. The pilgrims didn't hear or see a thing. No one passed them on the trail, no shouts, no cries for help, not even the sound of horses' hooves — nothing." He shook his finger at the dead man. "I've been thinking about this since dawn and I don't think he was killed by bandidos. I think he was killed for a reason: someone wanted him dead. Does that make sense to you?"

William thought about Montagnac's proposition for a few moments.

"Yes, that makes sense."

Montagnac nodded, glad that Stanley agreed with his theory. It strengthened his resolve to investigate Cardiaye's death.

William stared at Cardiaye — a man who'd taken a vow of poverty — disgusted by the sight of his gluttonously bloated body. "Did the pilgrims find anything else on him?"

"No, he'd been stripped bare. Not that he carried much. The pilgrims said his only possessions were a rosary and a leather saddle pouch. I assume there was money in it. I think his killers must have dropped the letter by mistake. And they'd taken his palfrey too. It was a good horse by all accounts — a chestnut mare — so it should fetch a fair price." Montagnac turned and grasped William's forearm. "We need to do something about this. Cardiaye was an important man, on a mission for His Holiness. I've no idea why he was on the *Camino*, but I do know he was murdered on our territory and in broad daylight. And people — other important people — will want to know how we could let it happen."

"We can't be everywhere, Master. We don't have the men."

"Do you think anyone will take cognisance of that?" hissed Montagnac, exasperated at the thought of fortune's sudden turn against him. He pointed at the corpse. "The poor wretch was killed less than a league from our post at Rabanal. Christ strike me! You could piss from Foncebadon's cross to the spot where they found him!" He sighed wearily. "You served in *Outreamer* for over five years. Surely I don't need to tell you how the world works? Our Order is going to be blamed for this, and that means us here, at Ponferrada. The Knights of Santiago are forever whining to the King about how much land we hold and how little we do for it. By God! They'll have a field day with this. The Order has given up one castle to the Calatravans already, before we know it the damn Santiagos will be asking the King to give them Ponferrada. Well, I'm damned if we're going to sit on our arses and wait for it to happen, not on my watch. That's why I sent for you. We're going to investigate this murder, and I want you to do it. Is that clear?"

"Yes, Master," said William

He'd had several confrontations over the years with knights from the Spanish military orders and he too was suspicious of their motives.

Montagnac sniffed the air. "He'll have to be buried, and soon. Come on, let's get out of here."

Pushing past William, he limped around the piles of sacks and barrels to the tower's open door. They stood in silence for a few moments and breathed in the fresh air.

"Cardiaye's palfrey bore Cluny's brand apparently," said Montagnac. "Even so, I can't believe his killers would have slaughtered it. Can you?"

William shook his head. "No, it's far too valuable."

"Then as far as I can see, our only hope is to track it down. If we can, we might be able to get our hands on these villains. You've patrolled this country for what — ten years? Where would you sell a stolen horse?"

"You could sell it privately, but if it bore a brand and you couldn't show a bill of sale you'd get next to nothing for it. To get a good price you'd have to auction it at one of the less scrupulous chartered markets. There are more markets to the east than the west," said William, weighing the possibilities. "And the going's a lot easier to the east. Getting past our refuge at Rabanal wouldn't be a problem, you'd just swing south off the trail and pick it up again near Astorga."

"And sell it there, or in Leon," Montagnac concluded.

William shook his head. "Not in Astorga. Selling a horse there without a bill of sale is far too risky. The Bishop rules the city with a rod of iron. His Court hangs horse thieves as a matter of course, and buyers too, if the magistrate thinks they knew the horse was stolen. The Office of the King's Constable regulates Leon's market and sellers have to show a proper bill of sale before the auction. You could bribe an official I suppose, but that would cut your profit and he might still arrest you once he'd got your money."

"Then where?" interrupted Montagnac, testily, irritated by his lack of local knowledge.

"I'd take it to Sahagun," said William, heedless of Montagnac's interjection. "The monastery of San Benito holds the charters for Sahagun's markets, but the big merchants run them. The Benedictines are only interested in collecting their taxes."

"But Sahagun is four days ride away!"

Montagnac turned away from William to lean against the tower's doorway. He sighed. He felt tired, from worrying over what to do about Cardiaye and his ever-present pain. Perhaps he should have acted on his first thought: to keep Cardiaye's death secret, to bury him in an unmarked grave and say nothing. The pilgrims who'd brought in his body knew he was a cleric, but they didn't know his name: as far as the world was concerned he would have just disappeared. People did disappear on the trail. The idea had a lot of appeal; he wouldn't have to make long reports to his superiors, more important, he couldn't be blamed. He had decided against it because he'd reasoned that although the pilgrims didn't know Cardiaye's identity it wouldn't stop them babbling about their find in every *taberna* and *hostal* along the Way. Questions would be asked when Cardiaye was posted missing — Cluny might even offer a reward — and if some damn bounty hunter linked his disappearance to the pilgrims' story about finding a dead cleric on the trail he might be called to account. It was at this point that he had decided the safest course was to report Cardiaye's murder and set up a formal investigation. And he couldn't back out of it, not now, not after sharing the facts with Stanley. He didn't believe in his heart that the killers would ever be found — the territory was too big and the law too weak. Nevertheless he was determined that his investigation would appear to reach a satisfactory conclusion. At the very least he would have to convince the Provincial Commander that it was based on fact and sound reason: sending Stanley to Sahagun could look like a wild goose chase. But where in this God forsaken wilderness should he look for the killers? He had little local knowledge himself, but Stanley knew the territory and what he'd said had been plausible. It could certainly provide the basis for a credible rationale.

He offered a swift, silent prayer for success — he'd gamble on Stanley's intuition. And to be on the safe side he'd send a patrol to the west as far as Portmarin. He'd lead it too; at least he'd lead it as far as Villafranca. It was only four leagues from Ponferrada: he could sit a horse for that distance. He'd rest in its monastery of Santa Maria overnight and return next day to the castle. He straightened up, feeling a new sense of confidence now that he'd made a decision.

"Right!" he said, authoritatively, turning to face Stanley. "You're promoted to acting captain. Take two, no three, good horses from the stables and ride like the Devil to Sahagun. And be discreet. You'll have to tell Simon de Sevry some of the story but keep the Pope's letter to yourself. And if you need any men, use ours — even if you have to strip the garrison. We need to keep this in the Order; we don't want the damn Santiagos to know we're in the dung. I'll have to report it to Leon of course, I can delay a little, but not much more than seven days." Seized by a sudden inspiration he pointed at the broigne. "Keep that that damned thing on and get the armourer to give you a *casque*, then nobody will take you for a knight of the Temple. Now get your equipment together and draw your rations and attend me in the hall in a quarter hour."

When William entered the hall Montagnac was sitting in the Master's place at the top of the long table.
"Here's your warrant," he said, handing William a small scroll bearing the Order's seal — two knights astride a single horse — and Ponferrada's crest. "It says you're a captain, with my authority to act in the name of the Order." He slid a small leather purse across the table to William together with a slip of paper. "That should be sufficient for any necessary expenses." He pointed to the paper. "Make your mark on the receipt." He watched William sign his name. "You can write *langue d'oil* I see. That's good, because I want you to keep a note of what you spend. Nothing elaborate, just a simple record, so that I can make a proper account to our treasury. Are you ready to leave?"
"My squire is saddling the horses now Master and —"

"You're not intending to take a squire?" interrupted Montagnac, in a sudden temper. Hasn't this damned knight understood what I've said about the need for discretion, he thought, angry at the very idea of bringing a squire — a paid servant who wasn't even a member of the Order — into the investigation.

"No my lord," replied William calmly, realising that Montagnac's quick temper was probably caused by his pain. "I'm going by myself. As you ordered."

Montagnac relaxed and his anger left him with an audible sigh.

"You better be off then. And make no mistake Brother: the aim of your mission is to protect the good name of our Order. Find Cardiaye's killers, if you can, and bring them back here, dead or alive."

3

William arrived outside the gate of Sahagun's commandery in the second hour before dawn on the third day after he'd left Ponferrada. The horses were on their last legs and so was he: his body ached, his head was throbbing, mind and senses were dulled by fatigue. He struggled for some time over the simple task of getting out of the saddle and once both feet were on the ground he had to grab the horse's mane to stop from falling over. He clung to the beast, head pressed against its sweating withers, summoning the energy required to walk the few steps to the commandery's gate. Taking a deep breath he launched himself at it, found a rope and yanked hard, making the bell clang long and loud.

The sleepy eyed serving brother who opened it recognised William immediately in the light from his torch's flame. He was surprised to a see a knight dressed like a common soldier however. He saluted and held the gate wide so that William and his three exhausted horses could pass through and after shutting and barring it he illuminated the way across the courtyard. Once they reached the stables he ignored William's mumblings about seeing the horses bedded down and led them inside himself. When he reappeared, moment's later, with William's saddlebags, he found the knight leaning against the jamb of the stable door on the verge of sleep. He took hold of William's arm and shook it
"I want to see Simon de Sevry," William muttered.
"The commander's out on a patrol, your honour, but he'll be back before *Sext*. Why don't you go to the knights' dormitory? Your honour needs to sleep now." The brother slipped the saddlebags over William's shoulder and pushed him gently towards the glimmering light of a torch on the far side of the yard, which illuminated the steps that led up from the courtyard to the living quarters on the first floor. "Your honour's the only knight here; you won't disturb anybody."
Following the brother's bidding, William lurched across the courtyard, up the steps, through the house's main door and down its long, dim corridor. After passing the refectory he turned to his left and stumbled along the short passageway that led to the knights' dormitory. He barged inside and crashed about in the dark until he bumped into a cot and tumbled, full-length, on to it. He was asleep almost instantly.

It was the hour before noon when he awoke. He lay on his back, squinting in the bright light that shone through the dormitory's unshuttered windows, trying to remember where he was and it was several moments before he could gather his fuddled thoughts. He was still tired and the muscles in his back and thighs ached, but his head was clear and his mind was soon busy with thoughts about his mission. He couldn't stay abed when there was work to be done and after easing himself off the low cot he knelt to pray. He could tell by the sun that he had missed *Terce* and in its stead he said seven Paternosters, the substitute prescribed by the Rule for those on active service. He said them slowly and carefully, his mind's eye on the painting of Mary and the Baby Jesus in the tiny church on his family's estate. His duty to God discharged; he pushed weariness aside and performed the exercises he did every morning to keep his body strong and supple.

He was very hungry. Nevertheless, missing Terce whilst in a commandery required an act of contrition and he decided to observe the Rule: he would drink but he wouldn't eat until the noon meal. The most important task in the meantime was to go to the stables and inspect his horses. He was sure that the serving brothers were already gossiping about his unexpected arrival; once they saw his attire they'd be clacking like geese, so before leaving the dormitory he fished his knight's robe out of his saddlebag and slipped it on over his broigne and breeches.

As he had expected, his mounts were in poor condition and he spent some time assuring himself that the brother who served as the commandery's stableman, veterinary and blacksmith was skilled in the care of horseflesh. Then he went to the chapter room to wait for de Sevry. Its windows were kept half shuttered in summer and William relished the chance to escape from the sun. The room had been used as a banqueting hall in earlier times and was furnished still with its original long table and benches. Their previous owner, a wealthy merchant without heirs, had bequeathed his house to the Order on condition that prayers be said thrice yearly for his soul. The Order had agreed and so gained a commandery in the northeast *barrio*, away from the crowds on the noisy west side.

It reminded William of his family's fortified manor in England and he liked its atmosphere. One of Sahagun's oldest *casa mayors,* it had been constructed at a time when defence was the first consideration. Built of stone it stood around a square cobbled courtyard: store rooms and kitchen, the armoury, laundry, stables and smithy occupied the ground floor, while the first floor accommodated the chapter room, dormitories, refectory and an intimate little chapel with a retable showing Christ and His Apostles. A stout gatehouse and heavy oak gate protected the only way in. There were no external windows and a battlement walkway ran along the top of its roof. It wasn't a castle, but it would serve as a stronghold if manned adequately. However, like all of Montagnac's commanderies, its fighting complement, of de Sevry and four sergeants, was well below strength.

4

De Sevry, dressed in his knight's white robe, entered the chapter room a little before noon. He greeted William and after he had sat down on the opposite side of the long table William passed over his warrant. De Sevry could not read Latin and he scrutinised merely the seals before giving it back.

"I need your help," said William, before explaining the reason for his visit in the way Montagnac had commanded.

After he'd finished speaking De Sevrey stared at him quizzically. He couldn't believe that Montagnac had sent Stanley all the way to Sahagun to search for a stolen horse, even if it had belonged to the Deputy Prior of Cluny.

"The Master seems to be making a lot of fuss over one dead monk," he said, eventually. "We bury at least half a dozen pilgrims on this stretch of the trail every season. God knows how many die between here and Santiago."

"We don't think this was a random killing."

De Sevry shrugged. If Stanley chose not to tell the whole story about Cardiaye's murder, so be it. Stanley held a captain's warrant and he was sworn to obey a superior's orders: he would give the English knight all the help he could. Besides, he didn't like people from Ponferrada sniffing around his commandery and giving Stanley his full co-operation was the quickest way of getting rid of him.

"The Thursday market's the best place to sell a horse," said de Sevry. "The town's packed; peasants come in from leagues around."

William had lost all track of time. "When's that?"

De Sevry raised his eyebrows. "Tomorrow. They've moved the livestock market since you were last here to make way for the new church. It's held now on that patch of open ground by the monastery's east wall."

"The Benedictines agreed to that? What about the noise?"

De Sevry shrugged. "I suppose they're willing to suffer it once a week for their market taxes. Which they've increased," he added.

"What about the sheriff? Is he still taking bribes?"

"Flies eat dung, don't they? You won't get any help from him, he never does anything that might upset the *francos*. I'm sure you know how things work here, Brother William; the sheriff's appointed by the Town Council, the Council's controlled by the small merchants and traders and it does what the French families tell it. They're the people who run Sahagun. The sheriff arrests the petty thieves and tricksters who prey on pilgrims; they're bad for everyone's business. But he wouldn't dare do anything about the gambling dens or the brothels because he knows the francos own them. You can't really blame him; he and his deputies are no match for their mercenaries. Only San Benito has the power to stand up to them. The Benedictines gave the French their privileges after all: they could rescind them if they wanted and call on the King's assistance if the francos resisted. But they don't seem to know, or care about what goes on. And until they do the French are tucked up in their casa mayors, safe and sound with their old privileges, taking a profit from every dirty business in town."

"What about the horse dealers? The francos don't run them."
"They pay the sheriff to look the other way. It's the talk of the town. And I wonder whether news of it has reached Leon. Last month the King's Constable sent a magistrate with a company of soldiers to inspect the horse market and every livery stable. No one knew they were coming and by the time they left they'd hanged half a dozen horse thieves and several dealers." He smiled briefly at William. "So you're lucky, there aren't so many rascals to choose from."

"Where should I look first?"
"Without doubt Jesus Porcelus would have been your man, until the King's magistrate hanged him. Now — if the horse is in Sahagun — I'd say that Carlos Noriega is your best bet. He's the biggest buyer of stolen horses now, or so they say. Buys from the thieves, changes their brands and sells them on with a forged bill of sale — it's a profitable business. If Noriega has bought Cardiaye's palfrey he'll want to be rid of it as soon as possible and it's quicker to sell it at tomorrow's auction than make a private sale. Noriega's brother-in-law is on the Town Council by the way so you can bet that he's got the sheriff in his pocket, one way or another."
"It looks like Noriega's the man I've got to see."
De Sevry nodded. "The dealers haven't moved, they're still in the west barrio on the other side of the *plaza mayor*." He rose from the table. "I'll detail a couple of sergeants to show you to Noriega's stables. They're young and green but they'll back you up if you need it. Look to Noriega's henchman; he's a bruiser and Noriega's a back-stabber. Will you go now or stay for Sext?"
"I'll stay and I'd like to eat in the refectory afterwards. But don't go," said William, motioning de Sevry to sit down. "The bell's not yet chimed and there's something else I want to ask."

5

William waited until de Sevry had resumed his seat. The Aquitaine knight had been in the Leon command for less than a year and William had always thought there was a slyness about him.

"Tell me," he said, staring into de Sevry's dark eyes, "who's the young wench I saw outside the kitchen when I was in the courtyard this morning?"

"A wench?" said de Sevry, innocently, but he could not hold William's gaze.

"Who is she?"

"Oh, you must mean Isabella," said de Sevry, carelessly. "Her father was one of our local benefactors. He died some months back. She's an orphan now, so I put her to work in the kitchen. Only temporarily of course, until I can arrange something more permanent. She milks our livestock too. We're very short-handed here Brother, we need all the help we can get." He shrugged. "She's only a child."

"Don't play the fool with me! A child is a girl who plays with dolls. This Isabella is a young woman, and comely too."

De Sevry hesitated. He knew that Montagnac had issued strict orders against women entering his commanderies, but he also expected the commanderies to manage their own affairs. And his order, in de Sevry's view, was an overly strict interpretation of the Rule: women were allowed into Templar houses, if circumstances warranted it. The girl came from a good family; he'd known her father and he'd asked de Sevry, as head of the Sahagun commandery, to ensure she would be taken care of after his death. There would be time enough to send her off to her family in Burgos once she had accepted her loss, and he was convinced that she'd overcome her grief more easily in the familiar surroundings of Sahagun. Meanwhile she could work in the commandery. It wasn't as if she lived there. Indeed, he had arranged lodgings for her personally in a young widow's house nearby.

It was a pack of lies, but de Sevry had rehearsed it many times and he thought that it sounded plausible. In truth, Isabella's father had expected that de Sevry would escort her safely to her cousin's family in Burgos immediately after his burial; he had never dreamed she would be taken into the commandery. But she was sixteen and pretty and de Sevry ached to have her. He had vowed to be chaste, but his lust was unquenchable, even though he prayed constantly for strength to overcome it. Desire for Isabella ran through him like fire and he'd set her to work in the commandery so she would be near him, so that he could be kind to her and gradually gain her trust, and then, when the time was ripe, he would have her. He glanced up at Stanley, angry with himself for allowing Isabella to work in the commandery while he was out on patrol. Damn the bloody knight's eyes for seeing her, he thought, conscious of the Englishman's reputation for piety and self-discipline. If he was to succeed in his plan to deflower her he had to see off Stanley's accusation.

"Bless me, Brother William," he said, mockingly. "A captain for three days and you are judging me already?"

"I'd say these things to you Brother Simon, be I captain, or no. You know Montagnac's orders. He's forbidden women entering our houses."

"She doesn't live here Brother William. She works here and she lodges in the town. And Montagnac's order is not the Rule. I believe for example that the castle of Monzon in Aragon employs a milkmaid and women often came into our house at La Rochelle, and I've heard they're allowed in English houses too."

"I don't give a damn about what happens in either Aragon or France. This is Leon and we are under Montagnac's orders."

"I am in command here, Brother William, not you. She's only here in the hours of daylight. She doesn't sleep here. She has lost her father, the only person she had in the world. She needs time to grieve and she'll be safer here than roaming Sahagun's streets. I'm sure you know what happens to street children in this town."

The bell tolling for Sext interrupted him. He rose from his bench. "Shall we go?"

William nodded, stood up and followed de Sevry to the door, but as the Aquitaine knight reached out to open it William swung him round and slapped his face so hard that he fell backwards onto the floor. William brought the heel of his boot down onto de Sevry's breastbone.

"Do all the brothers have her, or just you?" he asked, quietly.

"God blind you! I command this house and it runs in the manner I say! What gives you the right to question my orders in my commandery? Have you never thought to look to the needs of a defenceless woman?"

"To protect a woman from harm is one thing, to seduce a virgin when you've sworn a vow of chastity is a sin."

"Who in Hell are you to preach to me? You damn penitent! I'm not a prisoner in the Order, I joined of my own free will!"

"All the more reason for you to honour your vows then. And if you can't, you should leave before you bring disgrace down on us."

William stepped back so that de Sevry could get up. As he rose from the floor de Sevry launched himself at William intending to butt him in the stomach. But he moved swiftly to one side and seizing de Sevry's lowered head in both hands he ran him pell mell into the room's heavy oak door. As de Sevry's skull cracked against it William kicked the knight's feet out from under him so that he crashed face first onto the floor.

"Tell me the truth about you and this wench and tell me now!" William jabbed de Sevry in the ribs with his boot. "Or tell it to Montagnac and spend the next year living off the floor at Ponferrada. You'll soon forget this Isabella when you're fighting the dogs for food." He kicked de Sevry again. "Come on Brother Simon, speak out!"

De Sevry's spirit to resist faltered and died. The thought of facing Montagnac's ferocity sent a tremor through his guts.
"I've not laid down with her," he panted. "I swear it by the Virgin."
"But it was your intention?"
"Yes, may God forgive me."
"It is said by some of our brethren that you were whipped for tupping a woman at La Rochelle. Is that true?"
"I was whipped, it's true, but I never had her."
De Sevry flushed with shame still whenever he remembered the moment his old Master and several knights had entered the hay barn at La Rochelle and seized his feet and dragged him off a willing and eager young girl who worked in a nearby tavern. They would have let her go scot free, had she not been saucy to the Master. He had taken a switch to her there and then and flayed the skin off her back. They had made him watch the beating. Afterwards they had tied him by his ankles and dragged him behind the Master's horse to the commandery where he'd been locked up without food and water for three days. On the fourth he'd been taken from his cell to the chapel where, in front of all, he'd been stripped, and whipped by the Master until he could no longer stand. Once he had regained his strength he had been posted to Spain.
"Is this girl completely alone in the world?"
"No, she has family at Burgos."
William shook his head. "Detail an escort to take her there, today."
"Will you report it to Montagnac?"
"I won't speak of the matter again — unless you give me cause — but I think you should talk about your sin to one of our chaplains." William offered de Sevry his hand. "Now get on your feet; we're late for Sext."

6

It wanted another half-hour to the start of siesta when William dressed in his white robe and the two young sergeants, in their *hauberks* and black surcoats, set out for Noriega's stables. The mid-day meal of broth, stewed goat, beans and bread had been good; his weariness had gone and he was eager to get on with his mission. Both sergeants were little more than boys and he had decided from the outset that once they had taken him to Noriega's stables they could make themselves scarce. If it came to a fight — which he did not intend — they would be more hindrance than help.

They were soon in the west barrio's narrow streets, shouldering their way through the hot, sweaty crush of pilgrims and traders, babbling and bellowing in a scramble of buying and selling. Sahagun was a boomtown and William hated it: set in the middle of nowhere its only purpose was to service the needs of pilgrims. Once upon a time — before Cluny Abbey had produced the Codex Calixtinus — it had been nothing more than a collection of hovels outside the walls of San Benito. Now, thanks to the Codex, it was the eighth 'official stop' on the Way. Written as a guide for the pilgrims from France, the Codex gave advice about places to stop and the churches and shrines to pray. It promoted the pilgrimage across Christendom and once Pope Alexander offered a plenary indulgence to those who made the journey; they flocked to Santiago and to all the other 'stops' along the Camino.

The trail was long and arduous; from Roncesvalles, in the Pyrenees, to Santiago was a hundred and fifty leagues. Pilgrims had come with money and it turned poor pueblos into prosperous towns and gave Christianity the means to settle the wilderness, but its blessings were mixed. The Codex warned against those who took to the trail to commit crime and, in William's opinion, the advice was as good now as it had ever been. Camino towns opened their gates to both the good and the wicked, but none could match the evil done in Sahagun, which, like Sodom, seemed to wallow in its sin.

"Noriega's stables are round the next turning, opposite the *Dos Leones* taberna." It was Juan, the older of the two sergeants, who was speaking.
"What does Noriega look like?" asked William.
"Short and thin, a long nose like a rat and one eye," said the younger one. "And his bodyguard Gomez is a bull of a man."
William nodded. "Thanks for showing me. You needn't wait, I can find my own way back."
"But Brother Simon said we were to stay with you," protested Juan. "And you haven't brought your sword, " he added, unbuckling his own. He offered it to William. "You'd better have mine."

"Thank you for your concern, but I won't need it. There's not going to be any trouble; I just want to look round Noreiga's stable. I'm not expecting a fight." He patted Juan's shoulder. "Don't worry, I'll be fine."

Once they were out of view William stripped off his knight's robe and, grabbing the wrist of a *gamberro* who was passing by, he held up a coin in the street urchin's dirty face.
"Do you want to earn this?"
 The boy nodded with a wolfish grin and William gave him his robe.
"Then look after this until I come back. The coin's worth more than the robe: remember that."
"Don't worry, your honour, I'll be here when you get back".
Although not yet ten, he knew the price of everything and he knew that the coin would buy three robes like William's. More important, it would buy him all the food he could eat for a week. Hugging the robe in his arms he sat on a doorstep in the shade and watched William walk the few paces to the corner and turn into the next street.

7

William generally avoided the town's tumultuous west barrio if he could; it was the first time he had been in the *Calle de Caballo* and he sauntered along it slowly to get the lie of the land. It was narrow and the absence of passageways between its houses made it seem gloomy and cramped. Its name — 'Horse Street' — was apt. There were saddlers, farriers, livery stables, horse doctors and dealers: every business, apart from the Two Lions taberna, was concerned with horses. Horse dung was piled up in heaps outside stables and the gutters overflowed with piss. Even the air was rank with their stink. During business hours it would be a hive of activity, but most had shuttered their doors for siesta; nobody was about and what noise that there was came from the taberna. William stopped outside to study the layout of Noriega's stable. Built on two storeys and fitted with hefty doors and strong locks, it was one of the largest in the street. It looked as if the hayloft's door was kept open permanently, but it was three times his height from the ground. It would be damned difficult to break in and it could be done only at night, after the taberna had closed.

For the first time since leaving Ponferrada he was uncertain about what to do. He had no authority to arrest, or even question a citizen of the town — that was the sheriff's job and he was on Noriega's side. Nevertheless he had to search the stable and time was slipping away. Noriega was still open for business but he'd be shutting for siesta at any moment and once he'd locked up there was no easy way in. William came to a snap decision. A frontal assault was his only option. He unhooked the thong that secured his dagger in its sheath and, after calling on the Virgin for protection, he took a deep breath and walked inside.

It was gloomy and the first thing he noticed was a heavy block and tackle secured to a beam above his head. To his left he counted eight stalls, horses were standing in five of them, but a chestnut palfrey wasn't among them. The wall on the right was taken up with bundles of bridles, reins and ropes, and a sturdy ladder that gave access to the hayloft. Its trap door was open and the daylight that shone through showed a tall slatted fence, which divided off the rear part of the stable. The fence had a boarded gate, it was partially open and as he strained to see what lay in the darkness beyond it a man's gruff voice called out: "What do yer want?"
A man appeared at the gate. He walked over to William and looked him up and down.
"I said what do yer want, soldier?"
He was short and thin and William guessed that he was not yet thirty. His long hair and straggly beard were greasy, his nose was long and pointed and he was in want of an eye. It was Noriega.

"I'm looking for a horse."

Noriega's single eye gazed at him shrewdly.

"Then yer've come to the right place. 'Ow much yer got to spend?"

"That depends what you've got to sell?"

"Look fer yerself." Noriega stood to one side and gestured towards the five horses that were standing quietly in their stalls. "Watch out for the grey gelding, he's a bit skittish. Needs a good rider to 'andle 'im."

Taking his time and feigning interest in Noriega's brief commentary on their pedigrees and history William commenced a careful scrutiny of each horse. "You've got proper bills of sale for these I suppose?"

"Of course I got bills of sale. I'm a trusted man of business. The premier 'orse dealer in Sahagun, that's me. Ask anyone, they'll tell yer, I only sell the finest 'orses and I always give my customers a good deal. Now which of these beauties are yer interested in?"

William finished his inspection and returned to where Noriega was standing. "These are broken down nags and you know it. Have you nothing else?" He nodded towards the rear of the stables. "What's back there? I'll pay a fair price for a good horse, and ask no questions."

Noriega gave William a long hard stare, hawked up phlegm and spat it onto the floor in front of his feet.

"A pox on yer mother."

"That's a pity. I was looking for a palfrey," William said calmly. "A chestnut mare, in fact."

Noriega took a step backwards.

"I've told yer! Now get out of here before I slit yer tongue!"

"A chestnut mare with an 'AC' brand? You know? 'AC'? As in the Abbey of Cluny?" There was no threat in his voice.

"Gomez!" Noriega called, over his shoulder, as he took another step backwards. "'ere! Now!"

A man appeared almost instantly from the rear of the stables and stood beside Noriega. William was surprised that someone of his bulk could move so quickly; instinctively, he took Gomez's measure. He was a head taller, his legs were trunks of muscle, his chest and shoulders were as broad as a bull's and his brutish face had a pair of small, deeply set eyes that gave no hint of sense or feeling. William had no doubt that a single punch from one of Gomez's huge fists would destroy him.

Noriega pointed at William. "Send this piece of shit to the Devil!"

Gomez came at William without hesitation. He knew he had one chance only. He feinted to his left, ducked under Gomez's swinging fist and jerked his head upwards, hitting the colossus on the point of his chin. At the same moment he groped for the giant's groin and, grasping hold of his target, he squeezed them. Gomez let out an agonised bellow. William squeezed harder and he kept squeezing until the man sank to his knees. When, at last,

William released him, Gomez flopped, face down on the ground, like a dead fish. The instant Gomez hit the ground William turned on Noriega, who was standing stock still, paralysed with disbelief, staring at his champion's prone figure. William punched him once, under the heart, and he dropped to the floor, robbed of all breath.

Using ropes that were hanging on the wall William worked quickly to lash each man's hands and feet and he gagged Gomez with a sleeve torn from his shirt. Neither of them offered any resistance: Gomez had fainted and Noriega was still intent on sucking air into his lungs. The moment he'd finished William ran over to the stable door and peered out. The street was empty although the noise from the taberna was noticeably louder. Did Noriega spend his siestas there? If he did, his friends were bound to miss him sooner or later and they might come over and see what was keeping him. William closed the doors and looped them together with rope to guard against any possible interruption. Then he made his way to the rear of the stables. It was almost pitch dark beyond the slatted fence and he discovered the horse more by its sounds than by sight. He loosed its tether and led it out of the darkness and into the beam of daylight that was shining through the loft's trap door. He prayed he had found Cardiaye's horse and when he saw its colour and that it bore Cluny's brand he gave thanks to the Virgin.

As he finished praying, he noticed Noriega trying to get to his feet. He stayed by the mare, stroking and patting her withers and the moment Noriega succeeded William kicked his legs from under him. Noriega, his hands tied behind his back, went down like a felled tree and hit the floor with a thump that knocked the air out of him once more. William felt no pity for him. He was a knave who traded stolen horses with bandidos and William had seen for himself how they went about their business. About a year ago his patrol had come across a small group of unescorted pilgrims who had been waylaid by bandidos: the men castrated, their eyes gouged; the women raped and mutilated and left to bleed to death in the scorching sun. Animals like Noriega grew rich on their plunder. He deserved no mercy. As for Gomez, William checked his bonds and gag then hit him behind the ear with the pommel of his dagger to quiet him.

Then he went back to Noriega, who was lying directly under the stable's heavy block and tackle. William pulled the ropes to check the movement of the block's pulleys and he was pleased to see they were well greased and that the ropes ran smoothly. After fashioning a harness from one end of the tackle, he secured it to Cardiaye's palfrey. Then he tied a noose in the other end and slipped it over Noriega's head.

"What in Christ's name are yer doing?" wheezed Noriega, as William pulled him to his feet. "Who are yer? For the love of Jesus, what in 'ell do you want?"

"Blasphemy's a sin," said William, coldly, adjusting the rope so that the noose nestled against Noriega's left ear.

He nudged the mare forwards until the rope was taut. The pulley wheels squeaked and the rope stretched a little before it began to bite into the Noriega's throat. The dealer opened his mouth to shout, but William jerked the mare, choking off Noriega's cry for help.

William pointed at the mare. "Who sold you this horse?"

"God blind yer, son of a whore!"

William moved the mare forwards until Noriega was forced onto his toes and kept him there until the pain in the dealer's legs had become unbearable, then he nudged the mare again, gently. It stepped one pace forwards and Noriega was off the ground, gurgling and choking, his feet in the air, scrabbling and straining to find a toehold.

"Who sold you this horse?"

He eased the mare backward until Noriega could stand just on the tips of his toes.

"Yer want money? Is that what yer want? I've got money!" Noriega sobbed. "Let me down and I'll give yer all the money yer want."

"I don't want money. Just tell me who sold you this horse."

"Yer must want money, everybody wants money!"

"Who sold you the horse?"

Noriega managed to swivel his head so that he could see William with his good eye.

"And if I tell yer, yer'll still 'ang me," he croaked. "'ow can I trust yer?"

"You can't, but it's the only chance you've got. Now tell me, who sold you this horse?"

Terrified, Noriega stared at William, desperate to see any sign of pity in his face.

"Swear, on Christ and the Virgin that you won't 'ang me!"

"I swear I won't hang you," said William, solemnly.

"Swear in Their names!"

"I swear in the name of Christ and the Virgin that I won't hang you, and may my soul go straight to Hell if I break this vow. Now, who sold you the horse?"

"You promise?" Noriega begged.

William pulled the mare forwards until the tips of Noriega's toes were off the ground and he was kicking out, trying to touch earth.

"Who sold you the horse?"

William released the tension on the rope until Noriega's toes could just support his weight. He stood alongside the mare for a moment or two watching Noriega trying desperately to keep his balance. Then he stepped away and took his armoured mittens out of his belt.

"All right, have it your way," he said, preparing to bring them down onto the mare's rump.

"The Moor. I don't know his name. I just knows him as 'the Moor'," Noriega babbled. "That's what everyone calls 'im. He's black and as tall as you and he's only got 'alf an ear."

"Where do I find this Moor?"

"I don't know. He's not from Sahagun. He only comes 'ere when he's got 'orses to sell. They say he lives with the Maragatos, somewhere out in the desert between 'ere and Astorga. That's all I know. I swear it on the Cross. Please, your 'onour, let me down," whimpered Noriega.

It sounded convincing. "All right, my friend, you can relax," said William, reassuringly. "I'll keep my promise, I won't hang you."

"Oh, sweet Jesus," breathed Noriega, as William slackened the rope.

But the moment the soles of his feet touched the floor William swung him around and grabbing a hank of his hair he pulled back Noriega's head and cut his throat from ear to ear.

8

When William entered the commandery's gate on Cardiaye's mare, de Sevry, in company with the two sergeants, was just setting out to look for him. De Sevry didn't ask questions until he and William were sitting together in the chapter room, when he requested a full account. He sat in silence for several moments when William had finished.

"Did you really kill Noriega?" he said, at last.

William nodded.

"With respect, Brother: that's murder."

William shook his head. "What happened to Cardiaye was murder. I executed a wicked man."

"So you let him confess his sins?"

"There wasn't time for that. You know very well that pilgrims are killed for their horses and that men like Noriega get rich on it. The sheriff wouldn't have arrested him — you said so yourself. We are knights, Brother Simon. When we gained our spurs we took a vow to protect the weak and innocent; if the law won't do it, then we must."

"I don't think Noriega's brother-in-law or the Town Council will see it that way. The sheriff will turn Sahagun upside down. Dammit Brother! The sergeants know you went to Noriega's stables. Have you thought of that? May God keep us! What do I say if the sheriff comes here?"

"He won't. I've told you, nobody saw me, apart from Gomez, and I doubt if he'll recognise me. Besides, I was wearing a broigne: they'll be looking for a common soldier, not a Templar."

De Sevry sighed. "For the sake of everyone, let's hope you're right. But to be on the safe side I'll give the two sergeants the job of escorting Isabella to Burgos. And they'd better stay there in our commandery for the next few weeks. Hopefully things will have died down by then."

"And what will you say if the sheriff comes knocking at the gate?"

De Sevry stared into William's eyes.

"I'm a knight of the Temple, same as you. I won't betray you, if that's what you mean. I'll say nothing to the sheriff. But I tell you truly, Brother, what you did was wrong. You told me that I should talk to a priest, but after what you've just told me I think you should too."

Both men fell silent, each dwelling on his own thoughts.

Eventually, William asked, "Have you heard of this bandido they call 'the Moor'?"

De Sevry shook his head.

"Then I'll have to ask the Maragatos."

"How do you know they'll talk to you? They don't like strangers. Can you speak their tongue?"

"No, but they're Christians and I'm sure we'll find a way to get along."

"You're mad, Bother William. Do you really think you can find this man?"

"I'm under orders to try."

De Sevry sighed. "Well, if you insist on going off into the wilderness I suggest you take young Pero Colasa with you."

"Who's he?"

"He works with the carpenter. He's a half-breed Maragato and he speaks their tongue. He's still a lad — about ten or eleven I suppose — but you won't have to worry about him; he can take care of himself. He's a runt, but he's tough. Once you've finished with him, drop him off at a village on the trail. He'll find his way back."

William's first thought was to say no; the last thing he wanted was to have a brat in tow. On the other hand de Sevry had a point — if he couldn't converse with the Maragatos he'd have little chance of finding the Moor.

"Thank you, Brother Simon. I'll take him. And I need a fresh horse and field rations for four days. I'll give you a receipt so you can charge it to Ponferrada, and you'd better include the cost of feed and medicines for my horses while they're here. I want to be on my way within the hour."

"Don't you worry, Brother, you'll be gone by *Noones*," said de Sevry, coldly. "I want you out of here as soon as possible."

9

The bell was summoning the brothers to Noones when William rode out of the commandery's gate. He was mounted on a strong young stallion; the boy, Pero, was sitting behind him, clutching his belt. Cardiaye's mare, her rein secured to his saddle's pommel, was trotting alongside. He was pleased with himself: he had found the palfrey and, with the Virgin as his guide, he believed he would find the Moor. Montagnac had promised to delay his report on Cardiaye's death for a week, which meant he still had four days left to find the Moor and take him back to Ponferrada. It was difficult, but not impossible with Her help. But while he was satisfied with the progress of his mission he was angry and perplexed over de Sevry's accusation. Angry, because a man like de Sevry, who had ignored Montagnac's orders in the hope of seducing a virgin, believed he had the right to judge him. And perplexed, because he could not understand how de Sevry could take such a view. Indeed William wished now that he had challenged him to substantiate his judgement. As he left Sahagun and headed west on the pilgrims' trail, passing the field of blooming spears that witnessed the martyrdom of Charlemagne's *paladins*; de Sevry's comment about him needing a confessor was still playing on his mind.

It was eleven leagues from Sahagun to Leon — the ninth official stop on the trail. Pilgrims who had set out from Sahagun that morning were already well on their way when William left and it wasn't until early evening that he began to overtake groups of stragglers — mostly elderly or sick — who were struggling to reach civilisation before dark. Riding the mare and stallion in rotation William was able to make good time and they arrived at the little walled town of Mansilla las Mulas — five leagues from Leon — shortly before sunset. The average distance between most of the official stops was about ten leagues — a day's ride. Pilgrims with transport, who were concerned to reach Santiago as soon as possible, could reckon to set out at dawn, rest in the hottest hour of the day and reach the next official stop by sundown. But they were few: the great majority travelled on foot, many were sick or infirm and most left the trail at various points to visit important shrines. It might take three days or more to cover ten leagues and towns like Mansilla, which stood by a bridge on the banks of the Esla, offered a night's safe haven.

They arrived to find its three hospices full and William went to one of the town's privately run hostals. It was a mean place, run for profit and he paid an exorbitant price for an evening meal and a tiny room. After supping on coarse brown bread smeared with pig's fat and a jug of cheap wine William said Compline. They lay down on the same hard bed and Pero was soon snoring softly. But William could not get de Sevry's words out of his mind and sleep eluded him for a long time.

They rose when it was still dark and began the day with prayers. Then, after tending to the horses and filling their water skins they rode away from the hostal in dawn's first glow. A little way outside Mansilla they turned off the Camino onto a track that led them south and west towards the Maragateria — the country of the Maragatos.

After eight years in the deserts and marshes of the Holy Land William had travelled to Spain, expecting to find woods and green hills. Initially, as he'd followed the pilgrim's trail through the mountains of Navarre, he had not been disappointed. Indeed, its lush valleys reminded him of England. But then, past the forest of Oca, to the north east of Burgos, the landscape had suddenly changed: it was no longer verdant but stern and forbidding, with rough hewn mountains and wide plains that cropped only stones, scrub and stunted pines. A land that was dust dry in summer, cold in winter, devoid of life and silent.

As they rode deeper into the Maragateria the land itself seemed to give off a sense of desolate melancholy. It's parched, stony soil provided meagre sustenance and from the time before memory its people had earned their bread from trade. They were carriers and their mule trains criss-crossed the wilderness delivering goods to every corner of Spain. Unable to fill their bellies the land nurtured their character: self reliant, ferocious if attacked, honest and grave, the Maragatos lived by their customs and shunned strangers.

They halted at noon, to rest in the shade by one of the Maragateria's rare streams. There had been no opportunity for William to have a sluice down in nearly a month and once they had watered the horses he had stripped and washed in the shallow river. Washing wasn't forbidden by the Rule, but many saw it as ungodly and the zealots believed it was sinful. In the Holy Land however William had soon come to the conclusion that living in its fierce heat and dust was intolerable unless, like many of the Frank nobles and a few long serving Templars, one adopted some of the Saracen's customs. From that time on he had bathed whenever he had the opportunity. He was rubbing himself down with his *surcoat* when he noticed the boy staring at him, curiously.
"What's the matter with you lad?"
"I told you before, my name's Pero" said the boy, defiantly.
William smiled. It had been the first thing the boy had said when they had met at the Sahagun commandery. Since then, he had done as he'd been bidden and apart from saying their prayers they'd hardly spoken a word.

William wasn't sure whether his habit of silence had been learned in the Temple's service or from the Maragatos. He had certainly inherited their looks: small for his age, he was thin and sinewy, with dark eyes and prominent cheeks and a thatch of black hair.

"Well then Pero, what's troubling you?"

"Aren't you afraid of catching a chill?"

William laughed. "In this heat?"

"But washing harms you. Everybody knows that."

"The Moors bathe, it doesn't do them any harm".

"But they're different to us!"

"How so?"

"They're not Christian."

"No, but they're men, just like us. And in some things they know more than we do."

Pero stared at William in surprise. "That's not true."

"Yes it is," said William, climbing into his linen breeches. "They don't believe that Jesus is the Son of God, that's true, but their weapons are made of better steel, their doctors heal wounds that we can't and they seem to know more about the world than we do."

Pero pointed at the scar that William carried on his right side, below his ribs. "Did you get that in the Holy Land?"

"Yes, and if I hadn't been treated by a Saracen doctor I would be dead. He taught me the importance of cleanliness, so don't believe people when they say you shouldn't wash."

"What about the scars on your back? Did you get those in the Holy Land too?"

"No. Now stop your questions and get the horses."

They walked their horses for over a league before either spoke again.

"Why aren't you dressed as a knight?" asked Pero.

"Because I was told not to."

Pero was aching to ask who had told him to wear a broigne and the reason, but he had learned from the carpenter very early in his apprenticeship that he must always respect his betters and that knights were to be treated as gods. Moreover, if he spoke out of turn to one he'd likely get a cuff, if not from the knight then the carpenter.

"It must be hot inside your armour," he said instead, hoping that a more adroit approach might lead the knight to answer his question unwittingly.

"Hotter than a loaf in a baker's oven," replied William cheerfully.

"It must be very heavy too," said Pero.

He helped the armourer occasionally and the first time he'd handled a knight's hauberk and *chausses* he'd been astounded by their weight; he couldn't think how a man could bear to spend most of his life inside them.

William realised suddenly that Pero was trying still to get an answer to his original question; he decided that a question of his own was the best way to disrupt the boy's stratagem.

"How did you come to be a *servien* in the Order, Pero?"

"I was on the trail, with my mother, when a Templar patrol found us. She was dying and she begged the knight in charge to look after me. It was her last wish. He took me to Sahagun and I was given to the brother carpenter to learn his trade."

"Do you know the name of the knight?"

"Philipe de Tankerville, I think."

"Philipe de Tankerville?" William said in surprise. "Are you sure? When was this?"

"A long time ago. I'm not sure when, maybe when I was six or seven."

"And how old are you now?"

"I think ten maybe, or eleven."

According to William's reckoning de Tankerville must have found the boy on the trail sometime around 1202 to 1203. The last time he'd seen Philipe was at the siege of Acre in '91. Philipe's hand had been crushed by a Saracen's axe: the Infirmarer had declared him unfit for military duties and once his cauterised stump had healed he'd been posted to the Paris Temple. William had been posted to Spain in '97 and there'd been no report of Philipe staying at any of the commanderies along the Camino since then — so what had his friend been doing in Sahagun?

10

In the second hour after noon they reached the top of a long, gently sloping hill and a Maragato village came into view. Alone in the landscape under a vaulting blue sky it stood at the crossing of two mule roads: east to west, from Barcelona to Porto, and north to south, from Leon to Toledo. William knew only its approximate location and he was relieved that he'd found it. The Maragatos weren't the only travellers in their land; bandidos moved across it too and he hadn't relished the prospect of spending a night camped out under the stars with the protection of only a single sword.

"Now listen to me, Pero," William said, after he'd reined in the horses. "We're going to the village's taberna. Once we get there stay close, stand behind me, keep your eyes on the floor and don't speak unless I tell you. I know very little of their tongue and I want you to translate for me. Do you understand?"

Pero nodded. "Don't worry, Brother William, I won't let you down."

They trotted down the hillside and joined the Barcelona to Porto road, where they slowed and walked the horses into the eastern end of the little village. Its handful of single storey, brown stone buildings were drawn up in a long, neat line along both sides of the street. Every door and shutter was closed, not a living thing stirred in the fierce afternoon heat and the only sound was their horses' hooves. They found the taberna at the western edge of the village. The gates to its shady courtyard were open and a few mules and horses stood inside, tethered to a post.

The instant William entered the taberna, all talk ceased: wine pitchers stopped pouring, beakers were set down on tables, and men, with their backs to the door, turned on their stools to join in the collective stare. William ignored them and walked up to the long wooden counter, with Pero close on his heels.

"Wine and water for me and the boy," he said, in corrupt Maragato, staring directly at the barkeeper, who had the prominent cheeks and dark eyes that were typical of his breed.

He gave William a hostile stare for several moments. Then he turned away and filled two earthen pitchers with equal measures of water and wine. As he placed them and two beakers on the counter, his clientele's steely looks lost their edge; eyes turned away and talk began once more. William poured water and wine into the beakers, passed the weaker mix to Pero and drank his own straight down. Then, after refilling his beaker, he leaned with his back against the bar and looked around the room.

About twenty men were sitting around eight of its ten tables. There were two doors at the rear and watching a man come in through one of them convinced him that it led to the outside privy. He guessed that the other led to the rooms for boarders and the taberna's whores. He heard the barman speak and turning round to face him he nodded to Pero to translate

"He said where have we come from and where are we going," said Pero.

William jerked his thumb backward over his shoulder towards the east then he pointed to the west. The barkeeper nodded.

"Tell him I want to speak to the headman," William said to Pero.

They spoke quickly and he didn't understand a word until the Maragato pointed to a small group of men sitting round a table.

"The headman is called Zancudo," said Pero, nodding in the same direction. "He's sitting over there, with his sons."

"Remember what I told you, Pero," said William, and picking up his beaker he walked across the cobbled floor to the headman's table.

The four Maragatos at the table were dressed in similar fashion; black jerkins, knee length boots, wide, bell-bottomed breeches and hats with exceptionally wide brims. As he arrived at their table they stopped talking and looked up at him from under their hats' brims. Three of them were young, he guessed between eighteen, and five and twenty. The fourth man was much older; his beard was grey, his bearing grave and his eyes were tired and wise.

"What is it that your honour wants of me?" he asked, in formal Castilian.

William offered a silent prayer of thanks to the Virgin—if he and the headman could talk directly to each other it would be a lot easier.

"Information," said William, "if it would please your honour to be so kind."

The Maragato pointed at the empty stool, on the opposite side of the table to him.

"Information is precious. Sit down, your honour, and tell me what it is you think I can speak of."

William pulled up the extra stool and as he sat down Zancudo turned his gaze on Pero.

"Tell me boy, were your parents Maragato?" asked Zancudo, speaking still in Castilian.

"Yes, your honour."

"And what is your name?"

"Pero Colasa. It was my mother's name."

Zancudo stared at Pero. "I see. And you live with the Knights Templars in Sahagun. Is this not true?"

Pero nodded.

"Then why come here Pero Colasa?"

"He came with me, your honour," William interrupted. "I needed someone who could speak your tongue."

"As you can see boy," said Zancudo, turning his attention back to Pero. "I speak Castilian. This gentleman does not need you. Go and sit over there."

31

He gestured towards a stool by the large empty stone fireplace before turning once more to face William. "You said you wanted information?"

"I'm looking for a man, your honour. I believe he lives in the Maragateria. I don't know his name, except that people call him 'the Moor'," said William, speaking slowly in order to match the tempo of Zancudo's slow drawl. "They say he is tall, with black skin and that he is in need of an ear."
"Why is your honour looking for this man?"
William glanced at Zancudo's three sons. Each was armed with two daggers and a short sword and they looked like they knew how to use them. He had known, when he was still at Sahagun, that this question would be asked and that he wouldn't know whether the man, who asked it, was friend or enemy to the Moor.
"He killed a man and stole his horse," he said, gazing steadily at Zancudo.
"I see," said Zancudo, nodding gravely. "And this man you say the Moor killed, he was your honour's kinsman, or perhaps your honour's friend?"
William shook his head. "He was neither."
"Then there is a price on the Moor's head? You hunt him for the bounty perhaps?"
"No," said William, emphatically. "He killed a holy man, a man of God. I've been given the job of bringing him to justice."
Zancudo was silent for a few moments.
"Ramone. Ramone al Madena," he said, eventually. "This is the man you seek. He is a bad man your honour; a thief and a cut-throat, a man without family, friends or honour. A half-breed: his father was a Moor and his mother was Maragata. After she gave birth to her bastard she was branded a whore and banished." He shook his head sadly. "The son of Moor and a whore. I think this is not the best way for a man to begin his life."
"Where will I find him?"
"He does not live in the Maragateria, but in *las tierras del mal* — the badlands — a day's ride from here. You follow the mule road that goes south to Toledo. Half a day's ride down the Toledo road you will come to a large rock surrounded by trees. You will see it a long way off. Turn off the road there and go towards the south west. After another half a day's ride you will find a water hole. The trees that grow round it will show you where it is. That is where you will find Ramone's cabin."
"Do you think he'll be there?" asked William.

Zancudo nodded towards the barkeeper. "Mateo brings harlots here from Sahagun. Many travellers pass through and he and the girls make good money." He shrugged. "Your honour must understand, we Maragatos do not approve of this, but it keeps our own women from being molested." He pointed over his shoulder, with his thumb, towards the rear of the bar room. "One of the whores who works here is Ramone's woman, when he's at his cabin she goes to him. Nobody knows how he tells her when he will be there. It is a mystery."

He turned and called, in his own tongue, to Mateo and after a short conversation he turned again to William. "Mateo says the whore left here this morning. She goes to Ramone. She has no horse, so it will take her two days to walk to the water hole. I think that is where your honour will find him tomorrow night."

William offered another silent prayer to the Virgin for helping him find the path.

"Now, if your honour permits," said Zancudo, "I would like to ask your honour a question. You say you hunt the Moor because he killed a holy man and you wear the leather coat of a *soldado grosero*, but I do not think you are a common soldier. So I ask your honour, who are you?"

"He's a knight of the Order of the Temple," a voice boomed out, over the noise of the bar room chatter. William spun around on his stool to see a heavily built man wearing a light, loose fitting cloak over a short hauberk. The voice was familiar but it was several moments before he recognised Philipe de Tankerville. He leapt off his stool and turned to face his old friend and, after a moment's hesitation, they clasped hands and kissed each other's cheeks. He felt the formal coolness of de Tankerville's greeting however, but he hadn't expected Philipe would be overflowing with joy to see him.

De Tankerville bowed, briefly but respectfully to Zancudo. "Excuse us, your honour, but if you have finished your business my friend and I have much to talk about."

"I believe we have finished," replied Zancudo. "But may it please your honour to remember that the mule train for Toledo will be here soon."

De Tankerville nodded and led William to an empty table and called for two large pitchers of wine and a small one of water.

11

"How is the Order treating you, Will?" asked de Tankerville, speaking in the tongue of northern France, once they'd sat down.

"What are you doing here?" William was incredulous at meeting his old friend.

"I'm a courier for the Paris Temple. We have a contract with Zancudo to carry our goods in Spain. I'm on my way to Toledo. I've passed through here several times in the last few years."

"But I've never heard word of you. Why don't you stay at our houses?"

"Tush, Will," de Tankerville said, archly. "In matters such as these our Order prefers secrecy. We hide in out of the way places and practice anonymity. Why do you think I'm not dressed as a Templar? We live in a wicked world. You must have learned that from your Masters, surely?"

William was about to reply when the barkeeper came and placed pitchers of wine and water and two clean beakers on their table.

"You're moving gold," he said, once the man was out hearing.

De Tankerville filled his beaker to the brim with wine and leaning forward he wagged the forefinger of his only hand at William.

"Be careful," he mocked, "careless words could cost me my life. Worse still, Paris might lose some of its gold."

He gulped down his wine and refilled his beaker while William was pouring a measure of water.

He was shocked by Philipe's appearance: his grey eyes, once clear as crystal, were bloodshot and rheumy and his face bore the flush of a heavy drinker; his hair was thin; his beard grey and several teeth were missing. In his prime he'd moved with an agile grace, but he'd grown flesh and he was no longer light on his feet. He'd always had a sardonic humour, but it had sourness now and he sounded melancholic, careworn and bitter. William watched as his old friend drained down a second beaker of strong wine as if it were water.

"So what are you doing here, dressed in a soldier's jerkin?" asked Philipe, as he refilled his beaker.

"I'm on an errand for the Master at Ponferrada, Robert Montagnac."

"Robert Montagnac," Philipe sneered. "Ha!"

"Do you know him?"

"Served with him in Paris for a couple of years. Stupid and ambitious, and willing to do anything to please his superiors — that's Robert. He'd always got his nose up the Master's arse. He was desperate to make his name in Outreamer, never stopped bleating about it, but they sent him to Castile instead. Poor bastard — he was terribly disappointed. So, he's at Ponferrada is he? Jesus Christ! He won't be happy about that. How in God's name does he come to be in an out of the way place like Ponferrada? Did he do wrong?"

"He arrived from Aragon at Easter," said William, noting Philipe's disparagement of Ponferrada. Did people say the same of him? he wondered. "The previous Master was sick for several years before he died and he let things slip. He was a good man though — a knight of the old school. Montagnac's got the job of licking the command into shape and he's been kicking our rumps from the moment he arrived. We're in much better order now but the sense of fellowship has gone."

"I can believe it. He was my senior in Paris and I admit I feared him. Mind you, he was a damn fine horseman."

"Not any more. He was crippled at the Battle of Alarcos; leading the rearguard action that saved the King of Castile's life. He proved his mettle, but he'll never take the field again." He paused. "Philipe, you drink too much."

De Tankerville glared at Stanley — his friend — the man who had killed the first born son of the Count of Flanders and earned them a sentence of twenty years. He'd spent nearly half his life being punished for a crime he hadn't committed and he still didn't know whether Balleranche's death had been an accident or murder. Stanley had refused to plead murder in the Bishop's court although Philipe knew he was capable of it. When they'd been boys in training Stanley had turned on a squire who'd been slandering his mother. He'd given him a ferocious thrashing and Philipe had no doubts that his friend would have killed the squire if he hadn't stepped in. If he'd been at Stanley's side in the tourney's *affray* he would have tried certainly to stop him killing Balleranche. But they had become separated in the melee and when the affray was over he'd found himself suddenly arrested and accused of murder.

He had protested his innocence at the trial and Stanley, to his credit, had sworn on oath that he had played no part in Balleranche's death. It did no good: Stanley and he were known widely as fast friends and the Bishop would hear none of it. He'd been found guilty of conspiracy to murder and the plans he'd made for himself had vanished forever. He'd been forced to swear oaths of obedience, poverty and chastity to the Templars. Oaths, which since he was innocent, he never intended to keep and he'd held Stanley accountable for his fate. He'd recognised immediately that it was Stanley sitting at Zancudo's table and seeing him after so many years had re-ignited his smouldering rage. He could have borne the sight of him better if he'd been old and bowed. But his appearance had hardly changed. Christ's Wounds! The whore's son seemed to have thrived on a Templar's life! There was grey in his hair and wrinkles on his face, but he had still those handsome looks that had stolen the women's hearts. While he in contrast— Philipe de Tankerville, son of a Count — had to break his vows of chastity with common harlots that he paid with money stolen from the Temple.

De Tankerville swallowed on his anger, raised his beaker and took a long draft.

"As drunk as a Templar — isn't that what people say of us, Will?" He drank down the wine, emptied what was left in the first pitcher into his beaker and started on the second jug. "And how come you're at Ponferrada? Did you argue with another King in front of his army and the Master of Jerusalem?"

"How did you know about that? You were laid out in the Infirmary?"

"Mother of God, William. Everybody in Outreamer knew about it; the news spread far and wide. You didn't expect anything different, did you? What did Robert de Sable say about it?"

William shook his head and smiled grimly. "He wasn't especially pleased."

"I should think not. Where would we be if lowly knights of the Temple shouted their displeasure in the faces of their betters?"

"It was the right thing to do. They were committing sin."

"What in Hell had that got to do with you?"

"Jesus Christ, Philipe! They were bringing dishonour on every man there, surely you can see that!"

"Of course they were," said de Tankerville, as if it were a matter of fact. "And guess who paid for it," he added, quietly. "So tell me Will, how long have you been in Spain? You weren't in that bloody mess at Alarcos, were you?"

"No, I was posted here a long time after the Battle, in '97, with other replacements from the Holy Land. My God, things were bad, there wasn't a family in Castile that didn't lose someone. It's a miracle the Moors didn't march north and mop up what was left."

"Too anxious to get back to their hot arsed houris in Cordoba, I expect." De Tankerville leaned forwards across the table, determined suddenly to see if he could shock Stanley. "Speaking of which," he said in a hoarse whisper. "What about the women in this country. Aren't they beauties? Not like those Holy Land hags, eh? Sweet Jesus, Mary and Joseph, I could have every one of them, couldn't you?" He seized Stanley's arm. "Have you? Have you tupped any of these little dark eyed bitches?" He nodded towards the rear of the bar. "One of the whores back there is just the sort you like, long legs, small tits. We could have her together. Remember? Like the old days, one of us in her mouth, the other in her cunny." He drained his beaker and slammed it down on the table.

William was speechless. In the past — before they were Templars — he'd often seen de Tankerville drunk. Indeed, as young knights, they'd often been drunk together, but he'd never seen him like this.

"Philipe," he said sternly. "Get a hold of yourself! Have you no pride? We're Templars for God's sake!"

De Tankerville leaned back and gazed at him with eyes that could no longer focus.

"You never cease to amaze me. Do you know that? I've never met anybody who could adjust to situations as quickly as you: when the Bishop sentenced us to serve as Templars you turned from madcap Will Stanley, the virgin ravisher, into a psalm singing, po faced brother before I could blink. I swear to Christ, when you go to Hell you'll be friends with the Devil in less than a week. Listen to yourself. You've buckled down like a good boy and done everything they've told you. All the preaching about defending the Holy Land and fighting the Infidel for God's Glory. You think its true, don't you?"

"Now listen Philipe!"

"No! You listen! I know something of the world, not like you, stuck in a dunghole like Ponferrada. We may win here, in Spain, but believe me we'll lose the Holy Land sooner or later. The *Franks* are always squabbling and falling out over trifles and even if they did pull together they don't have the men to stand up to someone who can unite the Saracens, like Saladin. Christendom's kings won't commit the money and men needed to hold on to it — they're too busy fighting among themselves. Didn't you learn anything when you were there with your King Richard? Why we didn't conquer Jerusalem for instance? I'll tell you why. Because even if we'd taken the bloody city we'd have lost it again the moment Richard and his armies had packed up and gone home." Philipe held up the stump of his right arm. "You're a believer Will, so tell me, what's my reward for this? I'm not a knight anymore. I'm a clerk. A bloody clerk! And the Order's a bank. That's what we do in Paris. We hoard money and lend it to kings at a profit. I'll tell you true, there are times when I've thought about stealing it." He drank off the wine in his beaker and leaned over the table. "We're getting old William," he said morosely, exhausted suddenly by his tirade and the wine that had dulled his senses. "I want to be my own man again, buy some land, get a wife, have children and continue my seed before it's too late." He picked up the second pitcher and drank deeply from it.

William stared at Philipe trying to see the man he thought he knew. They'd lived together, as boys, through their years of training. Once knighted they'd followed the tourneys across France and beyond; won prizes, wooed ladies and bedded whores. Life had been good. But that life had ended when they'd been tried for murder at Bruges. He'd protested Philipe's innocence long and loudly, but to no avail. Philipe had been wronged it was true. But that was his fate: he would gain nothing by moaning about it. For his part, he would never have sworn an oath to fight for the Bishop. But his vows and Philipe's had been given to the Templars: knights like themselves, and they were bound in honour to keep them. He'd accepted his lot; he was serving his penance and he was disappointed with Philipe for lacking the necessary fortitude and pride. He had sullied his honour, his most precious possession, for which any true knight would readily die.

"Have you spoken to your confessor about your transgressions, Philipe?" He was lost for words and it was the first thing he thought to say. "I know it's hard, but we gave our word to serve as Templars."

"I'll not be bound by words I gave to a damn bishop!"

"You didn't swear your oath to a bishop. You gave your word to fellow knights, to fight and endure alongside them, as a brother."

De Tankerville seized the empty wine pitcher and threw it against the wall.

"You pious son of a whore!" he shouted. "Is that all you can say to me? You ruined my life when you killed Balleranche. Do you know that? You might not have had prospects, but I had. I could have married my cousin. She had land. I could have had children with her, done anything, if it hadn't been for you. Ever since it happened, I've wanted to know the truth. You were envious of Balleranche, weren't you? He had everything you wanted — he was rich, he came from a family of the Blood, he had power, influence, everything. And he was going to have Elizabeth too, wasn't he? She was going to marry him, not you. She might have flirted with you, but when it came to the real thing, she wanted him, not some ragged arse knight from the English shires, with nothing to offer save the honour of winning a tourney. Is that why you murdered Balleranche? Because Elizabeth chose him instead of you?"

"I didn't murder him!" shouted William. "He should have asked for quarter!"

"He didn't have to! It was a tourney for Christ's sake! Not war! You bastard! I always knew you meant to kill him!"

William hit de Tankerville across his cheek as hard as he could with the back of his hand knocking him off his stool and as he hit the floor William was on his feet, drawing his sword. He would have killed too, but suddenly Zancudo's three sons were around him, crowding and pushing him away from de Tankerville.

"My lord!" said Zancudo, loudly and sharply, abandoning his slow, soft drawl. "The knight is drunk, there is no virtue in this. Please, your honour." He put his hand on William's sword arm. "Your honour, please put away your sword."

His words cooled the red heat of William's temper; he relaxed and slid his half-drawn sword back into its scabbard. Zancudo nodded to his sons and they hauled de Tankerville to his feet and hustled him out the taberna's door.

"I fear your honour's friend is sick in his soul," said Zancudo. "But we know him, and we will make sure no harm befalls him."

William wanted to say something about his past friendship with Philipe but his emotions were in turmoil and he couldn't bring himself to speak.

Zancudo pointed towards Pero, who was still sitting on his stool, shocked by the sudden violence and unaware that William had struck the man who had been his saviour.

"Your honour will take the boy with you when you leave. It is not safe for him here."

"How so? I was going to send him back to Sahagun."

"A woman of the Maragatos may not marry an outsider and remain with our people. A girl will run off with a stranger sometimes of course." He shrugged. "Life is life, it happens. But if a Maragata who is married should lie down with another man she is damned and it is her husband's duty to kill her."

William nodded towards Pero. "Was that the boy's fate?"

"Yes. After his mother married she had a secret passion with a stranger. He gave her a son and she hid the truth that the boy was a bastard. Then her husband discovered her lie. He killed the man of course, but the affair brought great dishonour that could only be righted by spilling her blood. He wanted to kill the boy too, but that is against our law—a child has no part in its own creation."

"I believe my friend found him and his mother on the pilgrims' trail," interjected William.

"This is true. She was fleeing with the boy. She was dying from her wounds when your friend found them."

"Did my friend stop the husband from killing the boy?"

Zancudo shook his head. "No your honour, I did. It was my duty; this boy Pero is my nephew, his mother was married to my younger brother. He came to hate me for saving the boy's life and we had a bitter quarrel. He renounced his family and has become a *renegado* and if he discovers the boy is in the Maragateria he will kill him. So please your honour, take him with you."

12

Montagnac had not been in so much pain since he had lain in the surgeon's tent on the day after Alarcos. But he had stayed in the saddle and kept going, doggedly on, in pursuit of a gang of ruffians he had been hunting for the past three days. Setting out from Ponferrada on the morning after Stanley had left for Sahagun, he had intended to go no farther than Villafranca del Bierzo. On the first day he had ridden to Concabelos, some two and a half leagues down the trail and spent the night at its refuge. Before setting out on the second day he had ordered a sergeant to ride ahead to Villafranca and reserve him a guestroom at its monastery of Santa Maria, one of his favourite stopping places on the Camino. Built over a hundred years earlier by monks from Cluny, it stood near the confluence of the Burbia and Valcarce and as you lay abed at night, you could hear the soft gurgling of both rivers.

He had supped in the company of its abbot and was on the point of taking his leave when Brother Pedro, his senior sergeant, brought news that a troupe of players, en route to Santiago, had performed in the town's square on the previous afternoon. More to the point, they had a horse with them and many of the sergeant's informants were convinced it was stolen. They were divided as to whether or not it was a mare, but all were sure that its colour was chestnut. Lying on his cot in one of the monastery's small guestrooms, listening to the monks singing Matins, Montagnac was convinced this news was Heaven sent.

Accordingly, instead of returning to Ponferrada the next morning he had led his men across the bridge over the Burbia and headed north on the Way to Santiago. The trail ran alongside the Valcarce for the first league or so; the going was easy and they made steady progress. Thereafter it left the river and climbed steeply into the mountains. It was hard going: his horse began to slip and slide on rocks and shale and he was soon in considerable pain. The path that ascended from Villafranca to the Cordilla Mountains and through the passes at Perdrafita, Cebreiro and Poio was the most dreaded stretch on the Camino. Some swore that demons and werewolves haunted its forests; sceptics however had more tangible fears. The weather was no friend: summer's air was scorching, except when north-westerlies brought tempest and chilling rain; in winter Cebreiro bore the brunt of freezing blizzards and those who travelled unprepared were often found, frozen. But the greater threat came from bandidos who lived among its peaks and as Montagnac and his men climbed higher they had their first taste of fear.

The patrol reached the refuge at Cebreiro in the last of day's light. Eleven hours had passed since they'd ridden over the Burbia and Montagnac knew his infirmities had slowed them. Cebreiro's refuge — a little Benedictine monastery — had but one guestroom. A French noblewoman, en route home from Santiago had prior claim to that and Montagnac had to sleep in the cloister with his men. Thick blankets were provided to protect against the chill, but as the effect of supper's strong wine declined his pains returned and he began to shiver.

He'd learned at supper that the troupe had passed by on Wednesday in the early afternoon and the abbot had been sure that Linares was their immediate destination. The noblewoman agreed: passing through Linares, late, on the same afternoon she had seen a group of men in its little square erecting a makeshift stage. She knew too that Tricastela, only two leagues further down the trail, was expecting a group of travelling players to perform there on Saturday, at their saint's festival.

When the patrol left on Thursday in the first hour after dawn Montagnac knew that he must keep a faster pace. While saying his morning prayers he had come to the firm conclusion that the players had killed Cardiaye and if he could maintain a reasonable speed he would catch them at Linares, or if not, at Tricastela on the morrow's afternoon. An hour later, when the patrol lost sight of the monastery in the morning mist and his horse was struggling up the steep and narrow path to the Poio pass he was telling himself that he alone would solve Cardiaye's murder. It was a wonderful prospect and, in combination with the monks' fortified wine, it helped to ease his pain.

13

"Why did you strike that man, Brother William?" asked Pero.
They had been travelling since dawn and had reached the large rock on the Toledo road. Now they were heading south-west into the tierras del mal, a silent, desolate wilderness that gave refuge to the gangs of bandidos who roamed the lands between Christian and Muslim Spain.

They had stayed at the taberna the previous night and William insisted they sleep in its stable, away from the sight and sound of its whores. During his initial years in the Order he'd spent many a night remembering women he'd pleasured and, when he was not actively campaigning in Outreamer, he was tempted often by the sight of a pretty maiden. The Frank's noblewomen were exceedingly handsome and their attitudes towards men and their role in the world were far more forthright and bold than their sisters in France. He had enjoyed dalliances with several although, mindful of his vow of chastity, they had never passed beyond playful flirtation. It was a new experience: he'd disdained the gentle nuances of courtly love 'til then, but by the time he'd left Outreamer he'd begun to appreciate and enjoy the ecstasy of unconsummated passion. His posting to Spain removed him from such temptation and, as time passed by at Ponferrada, the nature of life—spent beyond female company, under the Rule's strict and unchanging regime—had gradually gelded his carnal desires until, finally, he had embraced celibacy. The sight of a beautiful face could catch him off guard still, or memories of ladies might sometimes come to mind, but they no longer stirred him. Indeed, he had come almost to dislike women. Thus the thought of spending a night next to the harlots' rooms, hearing the sounds of them whoring, disgusted him.

Pero had wanted to sleep in a bed, but the air in the stable was cooler. Its straw was comfortable too and the boy was soon snoring. William in contrast dozed fitfully, his mind flying hither and thither over images from the past and when at last he had fallen asleep he'd dreamed of Elizabeth's enticing smile and the fear in Balleranche's eyes when he'd killed him. Waking in a panic he'd spent the rest of the night grappling with both Philipe's and de Sevry's accusations. He could not overcome them and he'd fallen into a melancholy that prayers would not dispel.

"He was drunk," William said, over his shoulder, to Pero. "He spoke foolishly and I lost my temper."
"I thought you were going to kill him."
"No, I was just angry."
But he knew that he would have killed Philipe if Zancudo's sons had not intervened and it troubled him deeply.

"What do you remember of the time before you were apprenticed to the carpenter?" he asked, as a way of diverting Pero's questions.

"I was happy. I remember my mother used to hug and kiss me. My father had a beard and he was very strong. He was often away, but when he came home he let me ride the mules. Then everything changed. I remember my father shouting and hitting my mother. She was crying and screaming, but he kept hitting her and I was frightened she would fall onto the fire. Then we were running in the dark—I don't remember any more."

Except to say their hourly prayers, they didn't speak again until they saw a clump of trees outlined against the sun on the western horizon. Throughout the day they had walked and ridden their horses in rotation and William guessed they'd covered a distance of about twelve leagues. From the time they had rested in the late afternoon William had been considering the best way of assaulting the Moor's cabin; surprise was the only means of success and he would need the cover of night to achieve it.

They were five hundred paces from the oasis and the moon was well on the rise when they dismounted to say their prayers. After William had said *Vespers*, they ate their last ration of bread and sun dried grapes before drinking what remained of their water. Once they had eaten William told Pero his plan. They would cut strips off their bedrolls and use them to muffle their horses' hooves. Then, when it was dark, they would walk with the horses, by the light of the moon, to a piece of low ground some two hundred paces short of the oasis. Pero would stay there while he went in search of the Moor and when he'd found and captured him he would call out for Pero to bring up the horses.

"Do you think it'll work?" asked Pero.

William heard the boy's scepticism and, in truth, he shared it. There wasn't a scrap of cover between the oasis and the spot where he'd leave Pero, and if the Moor were on guard and carrying a bow he'd be bristling with arrows before he could reach it.

"Of course it'll work!" hissed William. "Have more faith in our Lady."

They set to and once they'd muffled the horses they sat without speaking until dark with Pero saying his prayers and William thinking about events in his past.

They set out in the second hour of night in the light of a full moon and it seemed a long time before they arrived at the shallow depression where Pero would stay with their horses.

"Remember now, don't move from here until I call you," whispered William, putting the casque's linen arming cap on his head and tying its straps under his chin.

He raised his head over the top of the depression and scanned the flat, stony ground that lay between them and the oasis. The darkness under its trees was deep and impenetrable. In contrast, the open ground before it was as clear as day. He spat on the iron casque and smeared it with earth to dull its sheen.

"I'll have to go slowly so as not to make any noise," he said softly, cramming it on his head. "So don't worry if you have to wait a long time. Just come when I call."

"What happens if you don't call?"

"Then I'll be dead." He passed Pero his dagger. "If I am killed get away from here as fast as you can. Take the horses back to Sahagun and tell Simon de Sevry everything that's happened. Now, say your prayers and wait for my call."

He crawled for most of the way, stopping now and then, straining to catch any sound. With fifty paces to go he stood up and scampered for the nearest trees, dropping onto his belly the moment he reached them. Scenting wood smoke he strained for a sight of the Moor's cabin and found it in the centre of the oasis on a patch of open ground. It was small, probably just one room and roughly built in stone. There was no sound and the only sign of life was a horse, standing quietly, in an adjacent corral. He had crawled to within twenty paces of the cabin when he caught the sound of a man speaking. He lay still, straining to hear what was being said. Suddenly a woman screamed. William froze. She screamed again and in a rush of blood he got to his feet and ran towards the cabin. He came up against its wall with a crash and stood, breathing heavily, his back pressed against its still warm stones. Its door was close by, it was ajar and he pushed it gently with the point of his sword. It swung inwards, grating softly on its hinges. He braced himself, expecting the man he'd heard to make a sally, but no one came out and except for a woman's moaning there wasn't another sound. Calling on the Virgin to protect him he stepped away from the wall and dived headfirst through the open door. Rolling forwards on his back he came up onto his feet with sword en guarde. No one came from the shadows beyond the firelight to attack him but he was shocked by what he'd found.

A woman, tied by her wrists to a hook in a roof beam, was hanging over the fire. She was naked and the soles of her feet were slowly toasting in its flames. On the earth floor beside it a man, dark skinned, was lying face down. Seeing his congealed blood William knew he was dead and that he had found the Moor. A blanket that had hung over the cabin's rear window had been torn off its nails and William guessed that the man he'd heard talking had escaped through it. Scattering the fire with his feet he looked for a stool. Seeing one, he placed it by the woman and stood on it and, supporting her weight, he cut her down. She had taken a fearsome battering, but she was breathing still and he carried her over to the bed and laid her gently on it. He was covering her with the blanket when he heard the sound. Horses approaching! Snatching up his sword and readying himself to make a stand he moved towards the cabin's door.

"I told you to wait until I called!" William shouted angrily to Pero, as he reined in the horses outside the cabin. He pulled the boy off Cardiaye's palfrey. "In Christ's name lad, do as you're told!"
"I'm sorry, I heard the screams and when you didn't call I was frightened."
"Disobey me again and I'll thrash you," said William, shoving him towards the cabin's door.
He heard the arrow's hiss the instant before it struck, knocking Pero to the ground. A rider with sword raised high, burst out of the shadows and galloped towards him. William waited; watching the glistening sword, standing his ground as the horse came on. Then, at the very last moment he tucked his chin into his chest and rolled forwards, towards the horse and to the right of its hooves. He rose, thrusting his blade point upwards into the rider's face as the rider's sword came down, striking William's head with a force that snapped his casque's chinstrap, sending it spinning across the ground and him sprawling. Gathering what wits that were left to him, he forced himself to stand and face a second charge. But there was no second charge: the rider had gone. He dropped his sword, staggered for several paces and then fell, senseless to the ground.

14

The sun was high when he awoke. His tongue was parched, his head pounding and until he saw Pero lying beside him he had no recollection. After a while he crawled over to the waterhole and doused his head and, feeling a little better, he set about examining the boy. The arrow had entered his shoulder below the collarbone. He had lost a lot of blood but he was breathing, although he would die if it were not removed. Examining Pero's back William was relieved to see an exit wound with the greater part of the arrowhead protruding. Like any warrior who had seen war, he knew what was needed even though he lacked a surgeon's speed and skill.

He was still groggy and it took longer than he expected to lay Pero on his bedroll, light a fire, fill an earthen pitcher with water, wash his hands and clean his dagger. Once he was ready he said a prayer to the Virgin and began a surgical procedure that he had often seen done in the Holy Land. First, he placed the dagger's blade in the hottest part of the fire. When it was hot he cut through the arrow's shaft, leaving a stump of sufficient length to be grasped firmly. After putting the knife back into the fire he washed Pero's shoulder. Speed was essential and the moment the dagger's blade began to glow he straddled Pero and, gripping the foreshortened shaft, he pushed the arrowhead out through the exit wound. Then he seized the exposed arrowhead and pulled the shaft out through the exit wound too. Pero awoke at William's first push and he screamed without ceasing until he laid the blade on his wounds, when he fainted. After pouring water on Pero's burns he left him in the shade and went to see if there was anything he could do for the woman.

From the moment he knelt down beside her he could see she was dying. She was no more than eighteen and he guessed that she'd been pretty.
"Is that you Ramone?" she whispered, suddenly in Castilian. "Are you there? I can't see you."
William moistened her bruised lips with water. "Shush child, you're safe now."
"You are not Ramone," she whimpered, looking towards him with eyes that were so badly bruised she could not see. "Oh God save us! Are you he?"
"No, he has gone."
"Are you a priest?"
"I am your confessor my child," he said, truthfully. "Tell me what happened so that God may forgive you. What is your name?"
There was a long pause before she spoke again.
"Maria — after Our Lady — He came for Ramone — Ramone had sold a horse — He said it was a bad thing — He wanted something from Ramone

— but Ramone wanted more gold. They fought — he killed Ramone — then he turned on me."

She was slipping away. William trickled more water onto her lips.

"Maria, who is the man who came to see Ramone?" he whispered her ear. "For the sake of your soul, you must tell me his name."

"I know Ramone's secret place," she breathed, "but I didn't tell him. He is the Devil!"

She whispered something that he couldn't hear.

"Maria!" he said in her ear, loudly and sternly. "Tell me his name!"

"The fire is hot — bless me Father — 'the fisherman'," she murmured, and died.

William sat beside her for a little time, saying prayers. He asked the Virgin to intercede for her, for God to make Pero well, and His forgiveness for not keeping the boy safe. Then he lay down to sleep.

15

Montagnac's patrol had caught up with the troupe at the San Xil crossroad an hour before sunset on Saturday. He had known they would be resting there from the reports he'd received at Tricastela a few hours earlier and he made sure, before they set off for San Xil, that his men knew the plan. He'd thought of several stratagems for capturing the players, but he had only eight men and he had decided that the simplest way was to ride up to the crossroad at the gallop and surround them. To capture the whole troupe required a swift deployment and he knew his infirmities would jeopardise his sergeants' chances of success. Consequently, before they were in sight of the crossroad he handed over command, temporarily, to his senior sergeant: Brother Pedro would lead the charge and he would follow on its heels as fast as he could.

The troupe, numbering ten men and four women had chosen to fight rather than stand to and he'd heard their shouts and screams as he'd trotted up to the crossroad. By the time he arrived the skirmish was over. Seeing two of his sergeants — Brothers Pedro and Jaime — lying dead, Montagnac cursed himself for being a cripple, for he knew that if he could have fought the outcome would have been different. Of the players, eight men and two women were dead. The rest had surrendered, they were unharmed and under guard. He would have accepted the loss of two sergeants more readily if they'd died in a worthy cause. However, the prize for their lives was not Cardiaye's chestnut mare, but a nag, broken down and half-starved.

Bitterly disappointed by the failure of his expedition he urged his horse over to the spot at the side of the path where the survivors were sitting. His whole being seethed with anger: against Cardiaye, for getting himself murdered; against Brother Pedro and Heaven for misleading him; but most of all against this bloody gang of villains who'd caused him to suffer such crucifying pain. His stomach churned at the mere thought of the journey back to Ponferrada. Champing on his anger he reined in his horse and looked down at the players. They stopped talking and looked up at him, but he'd caught a word or two of their conversation and he knew that, like him, they hailed from the Languedoc. He was sure too from what little he'd heard that they came from Albi, a town notorious for its allegiance to the *Cathar* heresy.

"Why didn't you surrender when ordered?" he demanded in their tongue.

"Please my lord, we thought you were bandidos," said one of the men.

Montagnac pointed at the sergeants. "Are you blind? Can't you see we're Templars!"

"But my lord. Your men rode up with swords drawn and attacked us!"

"It's true what he says, my lord," a woman interrupted.

"Hold your tongue you whore!" Montagnac shouted. He spoke to the man:
"Have you got a bill of sale for this horse? Or did you steal it? "
"No my lord, but it's been with us for years. It carries our costumes and props. Look at it, it's old. Why should we steal it?"

Montagnac turned to Brother Tomaso who, with Pedro dead, was now senior sergeant.
"We'll keep heading north on the Camino until we reach the path to the Abbey of Samos. It's not far. We can stay there overnight and bury our dead in its cemetery. I'll ride on ahead. Catch up with me as soon as you've finished here."
"What shall I do with these people, Master?" asked Tomaso, who, in common with the other sergeants came from Castile. None of them could speak langue d'oc and they were ignorant of what had passed between their Master and the players.
Montagnac pointed to the gnarled old oak that the players were sitting under.
"Hang them, they're horse thieves."
"And their horse?"
"Kill it. It's of no use to me."

16

William woke in mid afternoon with a pounding headache. His first act was to examine Pero; the boy was still sleeping, his breathing was regular, blood had returned to his cheeks and his deathly pallor had gone. He would mend with God's grace. After eating some of the Moor's bread and cheese he set about digging a grave for the woman. An axe and iron cooking pot were the only implements available and the ground was hard and stony. He could dig only a shallow grave and he had to cover her with a blanket, a few scrapes of earth and some heavy stones. After saying a prayer over her he set about a more difficult task: his orders were to take back Cardiaye's killer to Ponferrada, alive or dead and that meant lifting the Moor's body onto his horse. It was late afternoon by the time he finished, Pero was awake and he gave him food.

While carrying out his tasks he had been thinking about what the girl Maria had said. Montagnac had been right about Cardiaye's death — he had been murdered for a reason — and the course of events seemed clear. The Moor had been paid to kill and steal something from him by someone called the 'fisherman'. Ramone had done the deed but then he'd refused to hand it over without more gold. A fight had ensued and the 'fisherman' had killed him. Then this 'fisherman' character had turned on the girl in case she knew its whereabouts. She did, but although he'd beaten and tortured her she hadn't revealed her secret. What had this 'fisherman' wanted? The pilgrims who'd found Cardiaye said that his only possessions were a rosary and leather saddle pouch. Rosaries were ten a penny: it must be the pouch or its contents that the 'fisherman' wanted. The Moor had hidden it — William was sure of it — and he guessed it had to be somewhere close by. It was already late in the afternoon and looking at the sun's position he reckoned there was less than two hours of daylight left to find it.

He began his search in the Moor's cabin. It didn't take long to rifle through the contents of his clothes chest, turn over the wooden table, upend two stools, rip open the straw mattress and peer into a few pots and pans. Then he got onto his hands and knees and examined every bit of the earth floor. He could find no sign that its soil had been turned, there was no chimney, only a hole in the roof and there were no hiding places among the roof beams, or in the nooks and crannies in the cabin's walls. Dusk was fast approaching and William was pacing up and down, kicking pots and pans out of his path. Where in Hell would the Moor have hidden it? Perhaps it was buried outside. William kicked the fire's dead embers across the room and stamped angrily on the hearthstone. It moved slightly.
"The fire is hot," Maria had said before she had died.

Drawing his dagger from its sheath William dropped to his knees and prised up the hearthstone. Underneath was a deep hole with an old iron box at the bottom of it. He snatched its rope handles and pulled it out and, quivering with excitement, he broke its lock, threw back the lid and looked. Nestling inside was a leather saddle pouch.

17

They had set out for Ponferrada at sunrise the next morning: William in the lead, Pero — weak and in pain — on Cardiaye's mare and the Moor's horse, carrying its dead master, tied to the palfrey's tail. William had considered staying at the oasis for another day to give Pero more time to recover. He soon realised however that staying there could put them in greater jeopardy. There was food enough only for Pero for a single day, the grazing was poor and the Moor's stock of fodder was meagre; barely sufficient to give one feed to the horses. He knew by the blood on his sword that he'd wounded the 'fisherman': he did not think the man would return, but the Moor might have friends and Pero and he would be in mortal danger if they should pay a visit.

He planned to travel due north until they reached the Camino. Then they would turn west and follow it to Rabanal. Pero would stay at its pilgrims' refuge until his wound healed and he would push on to Ponferrada. He guessed it was about twelve leagues to the trail, a further three to Rabanal and five more to Ponferrada. They would have full water skins, both theirs and the Moor's and Maria's, and although they would be travelling across semi-arid plain, Zancudo had said that several streams flowed through it, so they should find more water along the way. He hoped to cover seven or eight leagues a day; if they could, they'd arrive at Rabanal in two days. It would be damned hot out there, with precious little shade, and it would be hard going for Pero, but he could see no alternative. He was worried too about their horses. His stallion was young and strong and if he walked and led it for part of each day it should keep its condition. Pero was too weak to walk: the palfrey would have to carry him. Though the mare was a good horse she would be suffering by the end of the day. The Moor's horse was the freshest of the bunch and it needed to be: he'd struggled for an hour or more getting its dead master across its back and he'd have to stay there until they reached Rabanal.

Zancudo's assurances about water were true and nine hours after setting out they came across a slow moving stream. Once they and their horses had drunk their fill Pero and he bathed. Pero was very tired and weak. He didn't want food, but William insisted and once the boy had eaten their rations he lay down to sleep. William was tired too, but he was anxious to examine in detail what he'd found in Cardiaye's saddle pouch and he spent the remaining hours of daylight going through it. When he'd opened it in the Moor's cabin he had expected to find something of value. Instead he'd found quills and ink and thirty sheets of paper of which twenty had been written on in a neat hand. Sitting with his back against a rock next to Pero, he began to examine the pages methodically. Twenty pages of Latin script: hardly a reason to kill for, but someone had thought so, and he thought he should see whether he could read it. It was a long time since he'd had reason to use Latin, nevertheless he managed to sort the pages into sequence and then he scanned each one, noting the words he could understand. He did it carefully, checking every detail. The sun had gone down and it was barely light enough to see by when he finished. Elated, he lay on his back looking at the stars, his mind buzzing with speculation. He hadn't read it — he could decipher barely one word in ten — he believed nevertheless that he'd found Cardiaye's journal and he was convinced it contained clues to the monk's murder, perhaps even the identity of his killer.

18

William promised Pero at dawn on the second day that they would reach Rabanal by late afternoon, where they'd sup on soup, bread and meat followed by quince and honey. They set off, in convoy, with William leading, Pero following and the Moor's horse hitched to the palfrey's tail, bringing up the rear. Three hours later, he called a halt and they stopped for a break and water.

"How are you feeling?" asked William, offering Pero his water skin.

Pero drank only a little before returning it and as he took it back William looked at the boy carefully, examining him for telltale signs. He'd seen wounded soldiers in a similar condition refuse water in the Holy Land and he knew it was often an omen that they'd lost their will to survive. He could see in a trice that the boy was suffering: his eyes were sunk inside their sockets; the skin around them was blotchy and dark; he was listless and his pallor had returned. Observing Pero, head drooping and swaying a little in the saddle, he determined that the little Maragato would not die and the best way to do that was to keep him awake and find ways to occupy his mind.

"Ever been to Gloucestershire?" he asked, once they had set off again.

"Where's that?" asked Pero, dully.

"In England, where I was born."

"Please be quiet, Brother William. Don't you know idle chatter is forbidden by the Rule?"

"Damn the Rule." He crossed himself automatically, as penance for his small blasphemy. "So, you haven't been there? Well then, I'll have to tell you about it."

And he began telling Pero about his boyhood. He talked about England's greenness and the smell of its rich, fertile earth after rain; its teeming wildlife; warm summer days, autumn mists, cold winter nights and snow. About growing up on his family's estate with his older brothers and sisters and going to school in the local Benedictine priory. He'd attended it from the age of seven to eleven and whereas his three older brothers had begrudged every moment of their studies he'd been an enthusiastic pupil, quick to learn arithmetic and Latin grammar.

On his eleventh birthday he had been sent to France to train as a knight in the service of the Count de Tankerville, his mother's second cousin, whose estates were in the lower Seine. In the first winter he was away his mother had died of a fever and his father had followed her quickly to his grave. William had never returned home to England again. As far as he could see there was nothing to be gained from it: he was fourth in line and he knew, even as a child, that unless his three brothers died he wouldn't inherit his father's estate. He would have to make his own way in the world like most of nobility's younger sons and he could see already that there were more opportunities in France than in England's narrow confines. He told Pero of his friendship with Philipe, the Count's youngest son and of the times they'd spent together as young knights competing in tourneys, in France and elsewhere. Some things were not spoken of: for instance, he didn't mention his rage against God for letting his father and mother die; nor did he speak of fornicating with the Count's prettiest serving maids. And while he spoke of his love of the tourney he said nothing about his conviction for murdering Edmund Balleranche.

Pero only listened at first but William gradually coaxed him into a conversation and when next they paused for water he looked a little brighter. "How far now?" asked Pero, as he was pushing the stopper back into his water skin.
"It's about another league to the Camino, I think."
William had looped his own water skin around the pommel of his saddle and he was bending to check the bindings on the Moor's horse when he noticed a small cloud of dust on the southeastern horizon: a sign of horses travelling swiftly. Saying nothing to Pero — there was no point yet in alerting him — he mounted his stallion without haste and, after letting the palfrey and the Moor's horse pass by, he took up position at the end of the line.

A little while later the riders' shimmering outlines were clearly visible within the dust cloud. He counted three. They were heading straight for him and he estimated that at their present rate of progress they would catch up within the quarter hour, he guessed too that they were bandidos. Trying to quell his alarm he scanned the terrain, searching for any natural feature that might offer some advantage. They were travelling through flat scrubland and as far as he could see there was only one defensive position — a clump of bushes atop a small conical hill some five hundred paces to the west. Spurring his horse he headed towards it, shouting for Pero to follow.

It was only a small hill, but it was better than being caught on the open plain and after riding around it he knew where he would make his stand. The bushes that clung to it were clumped closely together around the top of the summit. As high as his horse's shoulder and bristling with sharp spines they formed an almost impenetrable thicket. There was a small clearing at its centre, of sufficient size to accommodate Pero and the horses, and the only easy way in was by a path on its south side. It was some thirty paces long and wide enough to allow for the passage of two horses, but not wide enough to enable their riders to fight two abreast.

"What's the matter?" asked Pero, as he came up the hill.

William pointed to the dust cloud and dismounted. The three men who were riding them down could be seen clearly now.

"Holy Mother of God, bandidos!" wailed Pero.

"Come on, we haven't got much time!"

William helped Pero off the palfrey. Then, going down on one knee, he clutched the boy's good arm and stared into his frightened eyes.

"I want you to lead your's and the Moor's horse down the path behind you to the little clearing in the middle of these bushes and tether them there. Choose a sturdy branch and make sure you tie them properly, if it comes to a fight we don't want them breaking free and trampling us." He slipped the Moor's bow and sheaf of arrows off his shoulder and notched an arrow into the bowstring. "Take care of this, it's ready to shoot. Now, no matter what happens you're to stay in the clearing."

"Where will you be?"

"I'll stand a little way inside the path where it's narrowest. That way I'll have an advantage. But it may not come to a fight," he added, although he didn't believe it.

Pero turned and stared at the riders who now were less than three hundred paces away.

"Can't I fight with you Brother William? My right arm is good and I have the Moor's dagger."

William admired the boy's spirit but he shook his head. "You're my squire Pero. You will stand with the horses while I do the fighting." He kissed the boy and hugged him gently. "Now do as you are told and pray to Our Lady to deliver us from evil."

William waited until Pero had reached the little clearing then he remounted his stallion and backed it down the path until he had reached the narrowest spot, about a dozen paces inside the thicket. The bandidos' had odds of three to one in their favour and he hoped they'd be overconfident and ride two abreast along the path before realising there was insufficient space to swing their swords. There would be a moment of confusion as they jostled each other for advantage and that would be the moment when he'd attack and kill them. He slipped the securing thong off the hilt of his dagger, then, after shaking out his bedroll blanket and laying it across his lap, he drew his sword and rested the flat of its blade against his right shoulder. Patting his stallion's neck and saying soothing sounds to steady it he watched the riders close in on his position.

The three men pulled up their horses in a swirl of dust at the foot of the hill's south side, about thirty paces from William. One was wearing a long riding cloak and a broad brimmed Maragato hat that cast a deep shadow across his face. The other two were dressed in short cloaks, baggy pants and high pointed steel caps of the sort worn by Moorish cavalry. None of them was equipped with bow or shield and William gave thanks to see it. The one in the Maragato hat pointed left and right and his companions spurred their horses and galloped off around the base of the hill, in opposite directions, while he and William sat astride their steeds, staring at each other. His compadres rejoined him moments later. He said something to them and they shook their heads and William guessed they were telling him there was only one way in. Watching them muttering quietly and exchanging glances he prayed to the Virgin to give him strength. The one in the Maragato hat nodded in his direction and the other two nodded their agreement. Their muttering ceased, all three drew their swords and, urging their panting horses gently forwards, they started up the slope towards him.

19

The Maragato came to the front as they entered the path and his companions formed up, side by side, behind him. They came on, their horses blowing heavily and panting until he was within two sword's length of William. He reined in his mount and they exchanged a long stony stare. At this distance William could discern the face under the hat's wide brim and its resemblance to Zancudo was plain to see. William glanced past him at his companions. They were young — neither looked older than twenty — with a wild look in their eyes and William guessed they were landless half-breeds, who made their way by killing.

You have something I want, Templar," the Maragato said, in fluent Castilian. William wasn't surprised they knew his identity; news of strangers travelled quickly in the Maragateria.

"And what might that be, your honour?"

"I came to make a bargain. Everyone knows the Templars love gold." The Maragato pointed past William's shoulder to where Pero was standing with the horses. "I will give you gold for him."

"Pero Colasa is a servien in the Order of the Temple," said William solemnly. "He is under the authority of the Temple's commander at Sahagun, who has vouchsafed him to my protection. Now go about your business."

The half-breeds laughed and the Maragato nudged his horse a pace forwards.

"You know me, Templar?"

William spoke softly so that Pero wouldn't hear: "I know you're the boy's father."

The Maragato flushed with anger.

"He is not my son! He is bastardo! Now give him to me or I'll kill you!"

William snatched up his blanket and threw into the face of the Maragato's horse. It reared in fright and William spurred his stallion forwards, forcing the horse backwards and trapping the Maragato's sword arm against the bushes. Fighting desperately to regain control he had no defence against William's blow. His blade came down on the Maragato's neck; half severing his head, spraying blood and pitching him off his horse and onto the tops of the bushes. William spurred his stallion forwards: trained for combat, it charged the Maragato's horse once more. With insufficient space to turn, the beast backed sideways at speed into the half-breeds' shying horses. William pulled hard on the stallion's reins, keeping it free of the melee of terrified horseflesh that he had created. The opportunity he was hoping for came a moment later. The horse of the nearer bandido wheeled and reared in fright and the half-breed threw himself forwards onto its neck, desperately gathering in reins and half standing in his stirrups. William charged forwards and plunged his sword into the man's back, through ribs and lung until its point struck bone. He withdrew and the bandido slid backwards out of his saddle and fell under the horses, screaming.

The second half-breed broke free from the tangle, spurred his horse around and galloped down the hill and away in the direction from which he had come, with the rider-less horses cantering after him. William called for Pero to bring him the bow. The boy ran down the path and leaning out of his saddle, he took the loaded bow that Pero held up to him, wheeled his horse around and set off after the fleeing bandido. William's stallion was much fresher and its blood was up; he was within bow shot after a hundred paces, at two hundred he was holding the reins between his teeth, and at three hundred he loosed the arrow into the bandido's back. It struck between his shoulder blades, piercing the heart and killing him instantly. His horse slackened its pace; William grabbed its reins, pulled it up, pushed the bandido out of the saddle and returned to the thicket without a backward look.

On reaching the top of the hill he dismounted. The half-breed was alive still, spluttering frothy blood and gurgling for mercy. William didn't know whether he was Christian, nevertheless he said a brief prayer for his soul before killing him. The Maragato was dead already and seizing his ankles he dragged him off the bushes. He fell with a thud on the bloody earth and William heaved him over onto his belly so that Pero wouldn't see his face. He didn't know whether the boy would recognise him after all this time or if he knew the truth of his pedigree, but he would gain nothing by knowing that the dead Maragato was the man he'd once called 'father'.

Pero was staring at William with a mixture of awe and horror when he came into the clearing. He hadn't heard the words between William and the Maragato, but he'd seen him bring his sword down in an explosion of blood and the thrust that had brought the other man low. And he'd run and stood at the end of the path to watch him shoot down the third bandido. But what had shocked him most was the ruthless ferocity and breathtaking speed with which William had killed them. He had witnessed something that few serving brothers would ever see and he understood now why the serving brothers were so respectful of the knights and sergeants. He, the carpenter and his fellow serving brothers might live alongside them and join together in chapel to say their prayers, but the knights and sergeants were a different breed: their trade was killing.

"Have you killed many?" asked Pero hesitantly, watching William washing blood off himself and his sword with water squeezed from his drinking skin.

He returned Pero's stare for a moment, but he didn't answer until, after resheathing his sword in its scabbard, he walked across the clearing and knelt in front of him.

"I am a knight, boy; it's what I have been trained to do. It's my sworn duty to protect the weak and innocent from evil. Now, get on your knees with me and give thanks to Our Lady."

20

They reached the Camino a little after noon. There was always more traffic in the long days of summer and as they rode towards Rabanal they passed several groups of pilgrims on their way to Santiago. Finding the trail acted like a tonic on Pero and they covered the last few leagues in good time, arriving at the Order's refuge in late afternoon. Built of stone; it stood in its own walled courtyard and its gate was only a few steps away from Rabanal's little Romanesque church. Its kitchen and refectory were downstairs, women and men's dormitories were on the floor above and the sergeants who guarded it slept in a small dormitory at the rear. In addition there were three private rooms, discreetly tucked away, that were reserved for church dignitaries, nobles and others of the laity who could afford them. The Order demanded a high price of those who sought sanctuary from the common herd — far more than the cost of a room in one of Astorga's premier hostals — and it used the profits to defray the charge made to poorer pilgrims.

Alfonso, the refuge keeper, was short and stout with a fat red face. He received only a small stipend for his duties together with board and lodging. He rode a good horse nevertheless and was supposed to own several cheap hostals in Astorga. How he'd come by sufficient funds was unknown, although some said he'd bought them with money he'd made from overcharging wealthy pilgrims and serving poor ones short helpings of food. He had recognised William the moment he'd ridden into the yard, although he was surprised by the knight's unconventional appearance.

"It would be highly irregular. I'm sure the Master wouldn't approve," he said when William asked that he give Pero a private room. "Those rooms are reserved for special people. I'm sure you know that, Brother William." He pointed at Pero. "He's just a common boy. I'm sorry, he'll have to stay in the men's dormitory."

"The boy's wounded: he needs a bed of his own, peace and quiet and good food," replied William quietly. "He needs a private room."

Alfonso sighed. "I've already told you, he can't have a private room. Anyway, they're already reserved; I'm expecting three French churchmen tonight. I can't ask one of them to sleep in the dormitory — it wouldn't be right. The boy will be better off with his own kind, I'm sure. Won't you lad?" he added, encouragingly to Pero.

William grabbed Alfonso's tunic collar with both hands and hoisted the refuge keeper up onto his toes.

"I don't give a damn about your churchmen. If they're too high and mighty to sleep in the dormitory they can sleep in the yard. Show me to a private room and bring me hot water and clean linen so I can dress the boy's wound. After that I want food. And I don't want the pigs' swill you give to ordinary pilgrims. I want him to have what you're serving the clerics — bread, soup, good meat and vegetables. And I promised him quince and honey too. Can you manage that?"

Alfonso nodded vigorously.

"Then do it!" William ordered, before letting him go.

It was in the first hour after daybreak when William entered Ponferrada castle. He had set out from Rabanal the previous evening with Cardiaye's palfrey and the horse he'd captured, carrying the Moor. And before leaving he had promised Alfonso a thrashing if he moved Pero from his private room. They had shared a good supper and the lad had been much perkier once his belly was full of food. His wounds were healing and once he was better the senior sergeant would send him back to Sahagun in the company of pilgrims returning from Santiago. Despite his tiredness William had been anxious to get back to Ponferrada and he'd urged the horses past Foncebadon and up to the top of Monte Irago in the light of the moon. Dismounting at its summit, he had walked them down the northern slope and, on reaching the floor of the valley, he'd remounted and ridden the last league. It was eight days since he'd set out and he hoped to be in time to brief Montagnac before he sent his report to Leon.

He was proud of himself. He'd carried out his orders to the letter and in so doing had achieved what most men would have thought impossible. The years he'd spent in Spain, long years with little action save the dreary routine of guarding pilgrims had sapped his self-confidence. Hunting down the Moor had given him a chance to prove he was still able and resourceful and he was sure that even a hard taskmaster like Montagnac would recognise and acknowledge what he'd achieved. He hoped too that Montagnac would employ him henceforward on more exacting duties than shepherding people along the Camino.

Once inside the castle he rode directly to the stables and after dismounting he cut the cords that secured the Moor's carcass to the captured horse and pulled it to the ground. After calling for his squire to see to the horses he went to find Montagnac. He had crossed the courtyard and reached the top step outside the north tower's door when Hugh Bescanson, the young French knight who commanded the small garrison at Portmarin, opened it.
"Brother William!" said Bescanson, in surprise. "I'd almost given you up. Where in Hell have you been?"
"Carrying out Montagnac's orders." William pointed to the top of the tower. "Is he in his quarters?"
"Of course not! He's at Samos. He took a bad fall while he was leading a patrol."
William leaned against the tower's wall, stunned by Bescanson's news. "When did it happen?"
"Two days ago. They'd caught a group of horse thieves north of Tricastela. The sergeants were clearing up and he'd set off for Samos by himself apparently. His horse must have stumbled. Who knows? Anyway, he was

thrown off. They thought he was dead at first. He wasn't, so they decided to take him on to Samos." Bescanson paused for a moment to stare at William. "What in God's name are you wearing? Why aren't you in uniform?" He waved away William's explanation. "I was leading a patrol from Portmarin to Cebreiro and we'd stopped overnight at Samos. We were in the Abbey when they rode in with him. He was slipping in and out of consciousness all night: I doubt if he'll live. During a time when he was awake he ordered me to Ponferrada, to take temporary command."

"Did he mention my mission?"

"He said something about the Order being in trouble over some monk from Cluny, but he was babbling, I couldn't make any sense of it and frankly, I don't think there is any sense in it. Anyway, I've got enough on my plate as it is without worrying about a dead monk. But he gave strict orders that you were to report to him as soon as possible. He's probably dead by now of course, but orders are orders and if he lives and I've disobeyed him he'll kick my arse, so you better report to Samos. You're to come straight back though. If he is dead I need you to take over here while I go to Leon to report it and get further orders."

Bescanson pushed past William and clattered down the steps.

"And put your uniform on; you're improperly dressed," he called, over his shoulder as he hurried away across the courtyard.

William wondered whether he should call him back and brief him. He decided against it; Bescanson had many knightly qualities, but subtlety of thought wasn't among them. He was a young man who made up his mind quickly and if he'd already decided that there was nothing untoward about Cardiaye's death he would dismiss William's report as nothing more than an old man's tale of derring do. Everything that William had done since leaving Ponferrada seemed now to count for nothing. Indeed, if Montagnac was dead and the Provincial Commander confirmed Bescanson as Master it would count for nothing. William's sense of elation evaporated. He sat down, heavily, on the tower's stone steps. He felt old suddenly, and tired and depressed. After a while he got wearily to his feet and went to find the carpenter to ask him to make a coffin for the Moor and bury him in unconsecrated ground outside the castle walls. Then he went to the dormitory, donned his armour and surcoat and visited the chapel, where he gave thanks to the Virgin for his and Pero's deliverance and said his Paternosters. Within an hour of his arrival he was riding a fresh horse out of the gates, with two days' rations, Cardiaye's pouch in his saddlebag and a prayer on his lips that he would find Montagnac alive.

22

The Abbot of Samos learned back in his chair and, clasping his hands together over his ample belly, he fixed William with a piercing stare. "How did you find your Master?"

William sighed. "Not well, my lord. I fear he will die."

Indeed, when William had arrived earlier in the day at the Abbey's door he had expected to find that Montagnac was already dead. He was alive however and, after a short meeting with the Abbot, the Benedictines' Infirmarer — an elderly monk called Tobias — had taken William to the hospital to see him.

The hospital was housed on the first floor in the south eastern corner of the Abbey, next to the monks' dormitory. It contained six wooden cots, each with a thin straw mattress and blanket. Montagnac was the only patient and he was lying on the cot farthest from the door by a window that looked out onto the vegetable garden. His only visible injury was a large bruise on his temple. For the first two days after his fall he had been more or less unconscious, thereafter he'd been slipping in and out of sleep for long periods. Awake, he was silent and seemingly unaware of his surroundings. His sleep, in contrast, was often disturbed and fitful.

Brother Tobias was small and thickset, with a round face and a twinkle in his eye. He had been disarmingly frank about his medical skills which, he confessed, were limited to the treatment of broken bones, fevers, sprains and stomach cramps. He had no experience of head injuries and although he had plied his patient with various herbal potions, in his opinion Montagnac would die unless God intervened. William sat down to keep vigil on the cot beside Montagnac's. He didn't know whether Montagnac could hear him or make sense of his words; nevertheless, during the times he was awake, William, speaking slowly and quietly, gave him a full report on the progress of his mission. It was late in the day when a monk came with a message that he should attend the Abbot and, after whispering a brief prayer for Montagnac's recovery, he had followed the monk to the Abbot's office.

The Abbott nodded in response to William's prognosis of Montagnac's condition. "I agree; it does seem unlikely that he will live."

He left his chair and went to look out of the room's window from where he could see the stream that flowed past the Abbey and the little bridge that took pilgrims over it and onto the path that led them back to the Camino. For a few moments he watched a group of pilgrims — barely visible in the gloom under the path's canopy of trees — who were approaching the Abbey, seeking shelter for the night.

"Your Master is a man of considerable physical and spiritual courage, Brother William. I'm sure nobody thought he would survive the injuries he suffered at Alarcos. Many died with far less serious wounds. But I think he believes that God created him for a particular purpose, which he has not yet fulfilled: men like that do not die easily." As he turned away from the window, the Abbey's bell began to toll for Vespers. "I believe you served in the Holy Land. You must sup with me and tell me something of your time there."

William attended Vespers and was on the point of sitting down to supper with the Abbot when Brother Tobias interrupted with news that Montagnac was calling for him. Both men left the table immediately and went to the hospital. Night had fallen and the hospital's only illumination came from a couple of small oil lamps, nevertheless there was sufficient light to see that Montagnac was awake and alert. William knelt by the cot and Montagnac raised his head off his pillow and stared at him.

"The Order is in great danger," he said, between laboured breaths. "Find out why Cardiaye was murdered and report back to me. We must find his killers, no matter what the cost. Swear you will do this!"

William searched Montagnac's face, trying to see whether his Master knew to whom he was speaking; it was difficult to tell in the dim light.

"I swear, Master," William said, quietly.

"You are witness to this!" Montagnac said to the Abbot before lying back on his pillow. His breathing eased and in a few moments he was asleep.

While the Abbot knelt and gave praise for his recovery, William was wondering about Montagnac's state of mind. Had he understood the words William had whispered in his ear throughout the long afternoon, and was he issuing new orders? Or was he merely repeating those he'd given at Ponferrada? William decided that it didn't matter: Montagnac had granted what he wanted most — authority to find out why Cardiaye had been murdered and who'd paid for it — and his order had been witnessed by the Abbot.

They returned to their supper and the moment they sat down the Abbot began to question William about Cardiaye's murder. He had known Cardiaye, albeit superficially, and he was full of praise for the man's abilities; 'Christendom's greatest unsung scholar' according to the Abbot although, he confided to William, Cardiaye was known too for his ambition and love of food. William felt that in the circumstances he had no choice but to give his host an account of Cardiaye's murder. He was nevertheless mindful of Montagnac's initial instruction about keeping details of the investigation inside the Order: he said little about the events at Sahagun and he omitted to mention the way the Moor died, or of his duel with the 'fisherman'.

"I wonder whether you would do me a kindness, my lord?" he said to the Abbot at the end of his tale. "I found some pages written in Latin, I'm sure they have nothing to do with the murder but I would like to know what they say. I know the Abbey has a great library and many scholars among its brethren and I wondered whether someone could translate them for me."

The Abbot picked up a small bell and rang for the table to be cleared.

"We have one of the greatest libraries in Spain and a number of excellent scholars. But I'm sorry, I can't take any of them away from their duties just to translate a few pages of Latin — they're engaged on important work. I take it, from what you've said, that you've already caught the wretch that killed poor Rolfe. I would have thought that was the end of the matter. You say yourself that these pages have no bearing on the murder. Your Order has a literate chaplain or two, surely?"

"I am sorry to have troubled you." William said a quick prayer of thanks to God for his supper, rose from the table and bowed. "Thank you for your company Abbot and for an excellent supper."

"Wait a minute though," said the Abbot, as William reached the door. "There is someone here who might help you and I daresay he is bored. He will have no difficulty in translating Latin; he was — is — a learned man, a scholar at the University of Palencia. Strictly speaking, he is also heir to the old Count of Soria, although he renounced the title in favour of his niece. I will have someone take you to see him tomorrow, immediately after Prime. Don't leave your pages with him by the way; I've denied him pen and paper."

"Thank you, Abbot, I'm most grateful for your kindness."

"Don't thank me yet. You're a Templar and given his views he may refuse even to speak to you. Indeed, I wonder whether I should expose you to such as he."

"My lord?"

"He is in error. He was one of the finest scholars in Spain. He was destined to become the University's next master and I understand from my cousin — his Bishop — that he had been invited to lecture at the University in Paris: an honour for Palencia, if only the old fool could have seen it."

The Abbot muttered a brief prayer for his supper and stood up from the table. But William was intrigued to know more.

"Should I be careful of this man, my lord?"

The Abbot sniffed. "A soldier like yourself may think the War is about investing castles and conquering land. It's not. The War is about Truth. And the Truth lies in the words spoken by Jesus Christ. His words alone shall have dominion over mankind. All other ideas are false and those who believe in them are damned. This is why we are fighting the Infidels in Spain and the Holy Land. This man has spoken against the War. He believes we should respect the teaching of Mahomet, make peace with the Infidel and seek to convert him to the True Faith. This is blasphemy and an attack on

Mother Church, not to mention the harm it's done to Palencia. You are sworn to kill the Infidel: that's why he may refuse to speak to you. But if he should decide to make your translation, beware of things he might say."

"Are you asking me to report what he says to you, my lord?"

The Abbot waved his hand dismissively. "Of course not! I need no spy. He does not deny his views; indeed, he trumpets them to anyone who will listen. No, Brother William, I'm concerned that you guard yourself against listening to ideas that might harm your immortal soul."

"I will be careful my lord. What is the man's name?"

"Diego Delmirez del Soria."

23

In recognition of his rank William was provided with one of the Abbey's small guestrooms rather than a cot in the monks' dormitory and his seclusion enabled him to catch up on badly needed sleep. He slept through Matins and *Lauds* and woke shortly before the first hour of the day. After donning his knight's robe he made his way to the chapel to attend Prime. At its conclusion he was approached by a young monk who escorted him through the cloister until they came to a heavy door, which the monk opened with a large key that hung from his belt. William followed him along a short passage and up a flight of narrow stone steps that led directly into a large, white washed room.

Its three north facing windows made the room seem light and airy, although they offered a view of only the sky. Even on a summer morning it was uncomfortably cool and William guessed that as the room had no fireplace, it would be damned cold in winter. The sparse furnishings — a narrow cot with one thin blanket, small table and stool, a crucifix hanging on a wall, two earthen pitchers and a piss bowl — seemed to further emphasise the bleakness of the room. It was certainly better appointed than a dungeon; but it still had the feel of a prison.

"You're early, Brother Gabriel," said the man, who was sitting at the table, with his back towards the stairs. "Has the Abbot planned something special for me today?"

"You have a visitor," the young monk replied.

The man pushed his stool away from the table and stood up slowly, showing the stiffness that affects old bones and turned around to face them. He was stooped and thin with a long white beard that made him look old and frail. Nevertheless, there was an air of self-confident authority in his demeanour. He glared at William's robe.

"What do you want with me, Templar?"

William bowed. "William Stanley. An honour, sir." He brandished Cardiaye's saddle pouch. "I have a puzzle that you might be interested to solve."

"And what makes you think I will help *you*, Templar?"

"Because the Abbot said you wouldn't."

"Ha!" Delmirez slapped the table with the palm of his hand. "I see you have some wit. And what will I get in return?"

"The answer to the puzzle."

"I shall want more than that." Delmirez turned towards Brother Gabriel. "You can go, this gentleman will ring the bell when he wants to leave. And don't forget to lock the door behind you. I may overpower this brave knight and escape," he called, as the young monk descended the stairs. "He's a blockhead," he muttered, as the door slammed shut. "But a kind one all the same."

He turned to face William and bowed. "Don Diego Delmirez del Soria, as I expect you know. Well, Templar? What is this puzzle you want me to solve?"

William placed Cardiaye's journal on the bare table. "This belonged to a monk called Rolfe Cardiaye. I think it was his journal. He was Deputy Prior of —"

"He's dead?" Delmirez interrupted. "I know Rolfe Cardiaye. When did he die?"

"Eleven days ago. He was murdered on the Camino, at Foncebadon."

"Murdered! Dear God, what are we coming to? Poor Rolfe. He was a decent man, a scholar of integrity — which is probably why he never got the recognition he deserved. Who killed him?"

William tapped Cardiaye's journal with his forefinger. "I think the answer to that is in here."

Delmirez licked his lips and looked at William with eyes that were bright with curiosity. "Come on." He snatched up the journal, dragged his stool over to the cot, and beckoned William to sit on it. "Tell me," he said, once they had both sat down.

William had already decided he would have to take Delmirez into his confidence. He summarised the situation and concluded with brief comments on his own preliminary conclusions.

 "Why do you think Rolfe's manuscript might contain a clue to the identity of the man who hired his killer?" asked Delmirez. "You say yourself you can't read Latin?"

"I can read enough to be fairly sure that Cardiaye was keeping a journal about his pilgrimage. I know only that he was Deputy Prior of Cluny, but I am sure that nothing he did in his life there could account for his murder here, in Leon. He was killed by an assassin, not by some pilgrim in a taberna brawl; a villain from the tierras del mal who must have stalked him along the trail until he saw the right opportunity. The Moor was good at his job too: he killed Cardiaye and slipped away without any fuss. I found him only because he was greedy. I daresay his orders were to slaughter Cardiaye's palfrey, but he sold it instead. I can't prove it, but I'm sure it wasn't the first time he'd killed for the man who hired him. It all points to the murder being conceived and planned in Spain. Cardiaye was able and educated. People like him stick together: he'd have met others like himself along the trail. They'd have shared lodgings, sat together at table; he might even have stayed with some of them, as a guest in their houses. Who knows?" He pointed at Cardiaye's manuscript. "But I hope we'll find some of the names in there."

Delmirez tugged at his beard gently. "This man you call the 'fisherman': are you sure that's what the poor girl said? It seems a strange nickname for someone who roams the deserts of Leon and Castile."

"It's what I thought I heard her say."

"What about the Papal commission?"

"It was a personal commission signed by Innocent himself."

Delmirez nodded his head slowly while appraising William with shrewd eyes.

"Alright, William Stanley, I'll read through Rolfe's manuscript and tell you what it says. Come back in the hour before noon. But before you go tell me something about yourself. For example, why did you become a Templar?"

It was an hour later and William was walking back to his room when he realised that under a barrage of friendly but probing questions he'd given Delmirez an almost complete account of his life.

24

When William returned, Delmirez was lying on his cot with the pages of the manuscript spread in disorder around him.

"Come and sit on the stool next to me," he said, pushing himself up the cot so that he could rest his back against the wall behind it. "You're right about one thing at least: there is a puzzle here. As you had already discerned, Rolfe was keeping a journal of his pilgrimage to Santiago. It starts from when he left Cluny and the last entry was made at Rabanal. He kept a record of every day in a simple form of shorthand. I imagine he was keeping his comments brief so that they would be sufficient to jog his memory whilst ensuring he didn't waste paper. I can find nothing remarkable in his jottings, he's recorded the places and hospices where he stopped, where rivers can be crossed, shrines he'd visited and so on and so forth. Several people are mentioned too. I can list the names for you. But here's the puzzle, when he reached Carrion de los Condes the record stops for a space of four days. And he didn't write anything again until he was at Sahagun."

"It's about eight leagues from Carrion to Sahagun — a day's ride. Mind you there are quite a few shrines both on and off the Camino around there. If he'd visited them all it would have probably taken four days."

"It would, but every time he visited a shrine he made a note, irrespective of whether it was on or off the Camino. But he's set down nothing for that period, and it's not until he arrived at Sahagun that he began to keep a full record again. It seems that he just went missing for four whole days. Odd."

"And there's absolutely nothing to suggest where he was for those four days?"

"No, not as such. The only entry in the journal between Carrion and Sahagun is — I don't know how to describe it exactly — some kind of formula, possibly. Here, you look at it." He passed a page of the journal to William and pointed at a strange figure with his forefinger.

"What does it say?"

"It doesn't say anything, at least not in the way you mean. I think it's a formula, a code if you like, something Rolfe recorded in a form that only he could understand. It reads like this: 'MUP v RC—DP. IwillP'."

"Do you know what it means?"

"You understand the Latin word 'versus', do you?"

William nodded. "It means 'against'."

"That's right and as far as I can tell it seems to be one question or proposition versus another."

"What about the 'IwillP'?"

"Perhaps it represents the consequences of a victory of 'MUP' over 'RC—DP', or vice versa." Delmirez shrugged. "I've really no idea William, but it's certainly a puzzle. Still, I've got plenty of time on my hands, but it's a pity I don't have pen and paper."

William passed Cardiaye's leather pouch to Delmirez. "You'll find them in there. Ink too."

Delmirez snatched it from him and rifled through its contents.

"The Abbot's denied these to me. Did you know?"

"I'm not responsible to the Abbot and in my view solving Cardiaye's murder is more important than some argument between you and the Bishop of Palencia."

"Do you know the nature of the argument?"

"As I understand the Abbot, you believe we should stop the War, negotiate a peace and try to convert the Infidels to Christianity."

"And what do you say to that — as someone who fought in Richard Lionheart's crusade? Were our gains worth the bloodshed?"

"A few days ago someone was telling me we'd never hold onto the Holy Land because the Christendom's kings are too busy fighting among themselves. It made me angry at the time, but there's a lot of truth in it. The Franks in Outreamer are too busy arguing amongst themselves to work together and even if they did, they don't have enough men to hold out against someone who can bring the Saracens together. Neither the Hospitallers nor we can do it by ourselves: the only way is for Europe's kings to keep a large standing army out there."

"That's the military side to it. But what about the idea — is it right for us to go on fighting the Saracen, or the Moor, here in Spain?"

Although William took no heed of disputes between churchmen he had been immediately hostile to Delmirez's views. But he needed the old man's help and an argument could put it in jeopardy.

"How should I know Don Diego?" He shrugged. "I'm a Templar, sworn to obey orders, others do the thinking."

"If you believe that you deceive only yourself William. It seems to me that you have a sharp mind and I suggest you use it to think more about the things that occur in the world."

William bowed his head briefly. "Yes Don Diego, I will. Tell me though, when you first agreed to help you said you would want more than the answer to the puzzle. What would that be?"

"I want you to escort my niece along the Camino to Leon. The way can be dangerous as you know and I want to be sure she comes to no harm."

"Doesn't the house of Soria have sufficient men-at-arms of its own?"

"We do, but they're quartered in our castle at Soria. My niece stays temporarily at Villafranca del Bierzo."

"What you are asking isn't easy Don Diego; I'm a Templar, a soldier under orders, I can't just come and go as I please. If your niece can't use Soria men, why can't she hire mercenaries?"

"Mercenaries! Thieves, rapists and tavern rats every damned one of them! Do you really think I should give over the safety of my niece to that sort of scum? I've misjudged you, William Stanley. I thought you were a knight, sworn to protect a lady from harm. I can see now I was wrong. You're just a Templar aren't you? Unable to do anything but close your mind and follow orders. In that case, Templar, you'll have to find someone else to decipher Rolfe's code."

"I am a knight, God damn it!"

"Then prove it!" Delmirez scrabbled together the pages of Cardiaye's journal and thrust them at William. "Or get out of here and take this with you!"

William led his horse across the Burbia bridge and into Villafranca del Bierzo through a gaggle of pilgrims who were setting out on the long climb to Cebreiro. Once inside the town's boundary he turned right onto a wide, well-trodden thoroughfare that the townspeople called *Calle Agua*. It was part of the Camino and William was hailed by a number of pilgrims who were passing by. Its name — 'Water Street' — came from the floods it suffered whenever the Burbia and Valcarce burst their banks. It was parched dry now — in summer — but in winter it was often a quagmire. Nevertheless, the advantages of living next to a source of clean water in a town were so highly prized that its houses belonged only to the nobility. Those in the streets behind, which climbed steeply up to the Villafranca's plaza mayor, were much sought after too and families who had grown rich by supplying goods and services to pilgrims owned many.

Small patches of common land for grazing goats and sheep separated the dwellings on the street's riverside, whereas the houses on the town side were crammed closely together. But all bore the same mossy watermark on their walls at roughly the height of a man's knee — evidence of the annual floods. The houses on the riverside were built in a variety of architectural tastes. In contrast, every house on the town side was constructed in Moresque style: three floors high with white daubed walls, no windows that overlooked the street and a single entrance protected by strong gates on which were carved their owners' coats of arms.

William found the house he was seeking on the town side of the Calle, bearing the arms of the Counts of Lemos on its gate, some two hundred paces from the bridge. Lemos — a Galician noble family with blood ties to the Sorias — had been a powerful and influential voice in the region for over a hundred years and he was not surprised to find that their house was one of largest in the street. A large bell handle protruded from the wall by its gate, but he hesitated to grasp it because now that he stood outside the place where Dona Delmirez was staying his doubts had returned.

He had known from the moment he agreed to escort her that he was putting himself in danger and, on the journey from Samos, he had considered how he might defend himself if he were called before a court martial. In his favour, he was carrying out his Master's direct order to find Cardiaye's killers and, with the Moor dead, the only way forward was to decipher the formula. It was a task that required a scholar. The Abbot had refused his help and Delmirez was the only person available. If his price was escorting his niece to Leon, so be it. William wasn't making a special journey: Montagnac had always intended to report Cardiaye's death to the Provincial

Commander — he was going in his Master's stead. The Abbot had witnessed Montagnac's order and it overruled those of his acting deputy, consequently William was not required to obey Bescanson's command to report back to Ponferrada. He was a simple knight following his Master's orders. It was therefore unjust that he be punished.

He knew however that the issue was far more complicated than he would like to pretend. Delmirez might yet be charged with heresy and Spain's bishops had long since decreed that those who gave succour to heretics would be judged complicit in their crime. As a Templar he would be judged especially harshly; the bishops might even try to hold the Order accountable for his deeds. He also knew that whatever he might claim for the strictness of Montagnac's order, it was his duty to stop off at Ponferrada to give Bescanson news of the Master's situation. Indeed, to ride straight by was a serious breach of discipline. He would do it because he wanted to avoid meeting Bescanson, who might refuse to let him deliver Dona Delmirez to Leon. There were other charges too. He had been given no specific order to report to Leon. He had been less than honest with the Abbot about what he wanted translated and he had flouted his instruction and given Delmirez pen and paper. He couldn't expect the Abbot's support if these facts became known. And if Montagnac should die, what then? Young Bescanson would be the one who would hold him to immediate account. He was a fair man, but he was hard too and his justice would be most severe.

William stared uncertainly at the iron handle of the house's bell. The safest course of action was to get on his horse and ride on to Ponferrada. Once there, he would brief Bescanson on Montagnac's condition, his progress to date on Cardiaye's case and Montagnac's order to continue the investigation. If Bescanson countermanded it and handed the whole affair over to Leon it would be he who would answer to Montagnac, if Montagnac lived. But it would have been taken out of his hands and he could resume his normal duties. Leon would probably decide, for the sake of political expediency, that the Moor had acted alone and that his death had brought the case to a satisfactory conclusion. The truth about Cardiaye's murder would never be known. But did that matter? After all, he wasn't the first pilgrim to be killed on the trail and his death counted for little among the thousands who filled the cemeteries on the Way to Santiago.

If William had considered the question when he set out first from Ponferrada he would have said that finding the man who'd killed Cardiaye was the aim of his mission. But a lot had happened since then. Until now his time in Spain had been spent on long monotonous patrols, prayers and psalm singing. Montagnac had set him free from that and for a few brief days he'd been his own man again, able to act on his own initiative and make decisions. He had overcome difficult situations and felt an intoxication he'd not known since campaigning with the Lionheart. When he'd been dubbed a knight, at seventeen, he had prayed for a life of travel and adventure followed by marriage to a rich and beautiful lady. Dreams such as those had ended at Bruges. On joining the Templars he'd sworn two of his three oaths without demur — to be obedient to his Masters and to live a life of poverty. It was the prospect of chastity that brought fear. However, it was the penalty he knew he must suffer for killing Balleranche and he'd resigned himself to the fact that he would never make love to a woman again. In return God had been merciful and granted him part of his young knight's prayer: for, as a Templar he had travelled to the Holy Land and adventured.

He had given much thought to Philipe's comment that life was slipping by: he'd seen the truth of it and now that he'd shaken off the lethargy that had crept over him in Spain he didn't want to go back to patrolling the Camino. There was no immediate prospect that Spain's Christians would take up the *Reconquista*: they and the Moors had settled for an armed truce since Alarcos and Castile wouldn't be able to resume the fight for at least another five years. Outreamer was the place where battle would be joined. He reckoned he had the best part of ten years' fighting left in him and, if he wanted to get back into the fray, he had to find a way to get himself posted there. Death in battle held no fear; it was certainly preferable to dying, old and infirm, at Ponferrada.

To escape Ponferrada and Spain he would have to do something extraordinary, something that would attract the attention of the Provincial Commander at Leon. Finding those responsible for Cardiaye's murder was probably his only opportunity and he was damned if he was going to throw it away. Every time during these last days when he'd prayed for the Virgin's help She had answered his call. He was sure She approved him seeking out the truth and that She would continue to smile on him. He would chance his fate — the prospect of a court martial and dishonour against a posting to the Holy Land. He seized the bell pull and its clanging echoed throughout the great house. It woke the slumbering gate porter, servants stopped in their tasks, armed retainers reached for their swords and Dona Delmirez looked up from a text on 'The Lives of the Saints', which she had been studying. Fortuna heard the sound too and, caught in an idle moment, she turned her face towards William.

26

When William announced himself to the gate porter he had expected to be admitted immediately, but it was some time before the gates were opened and he was invited to enter. He led his stallion into a wide, cobbled corridor that ran along the complete length of the house front. Its low ceiling made it seem dark and it reeked of horses. A flat-bottomed wagon and a small four-seater coach were parked in the corridor to his left. The area to the right had a dozen or more horse stalls and the porter took the reins of his steed and led it into the nearest one. An internal gate made of heavy wrought iron was set into the wall opposite the street entrance; offering visitors a tantalising glimpse of the house's patio through its bars. A member of the house guard in Lemos livery opened it, requested William's sword, and beckoned him through. Entering the patio he was greeted by another liveried servant who led him to its far side and up four flights of wide stone steps. As William followed him along the colonnade with the sounds of water trickling in the patio's fountain and bees humming around the tall pots of flowers in each of its corners he thought, for a moment, how sweet his life might have been, if he hadn't killed Balleranche.

On reaching the second floor they walked along another open colonnade, passing doors and windows carved in an intricate Moresque style, until they arrived at a large door bearing the arms of Lemos. The servant banged it once with the hilt of his dagger before pushing it open and ushering William inside. It was a long room, measuring over forty paces and its air was cool. The walls were decorated with blue, green and white mosaics set in geometric patterns and its high wooden ceiling was similarly carved. The only furniture was a single large chair, set against the wall at the far end of the room, on which a woman was sitting, unattended.

"You may advance," she commanded, in a melodious voice.
William marched down the room, his feet, encased in chain mail, chinking on the white marble floor. As he advanced he noticed that the room's light came through cunningly concealed apertures, high up in its walls, which cast spots of diffused sunlight across the floor.
"Stand where you are," the women said, as William stepped into a pool of sunlight some ten paces from her chair. "I am Dona Cristina Leonor Delmirez del Soria. I can see that you are a Templar and I'm told you speak Castilian. Why do you seek an audience?"
William bowed deeply. "My name is William Stanley, my lady. I have —"
"William Stanley?" she interrupted. "What sort of a name is that? Are you a German knight?"
"No, English. I have ridden from Samos, lady. Your uncle, Don Diego Delmirez has asked me to escort you to Leon."

Ignoring courtesy he straightened up and looked directly at her, straining to see her face and form, but she was in shadow.

"If you come from Samos you will know that my uncle is accused by his Bishop and held prisoner. The Templars always stand with the Church and you are sworn to obey the orders of your superiors. I don't believe someone such as you would help my uncle. Who has ordered you here to deceive me?"

"No one, my lady. I have a bargain with your uncle. He has agreed to help me solve a problem, in return for his favour I have promised to see you safely to Leon."

Cristina Delmirez sat in silence, wary in case she might say something that could harm her uncle. They had been in secret communications from the time he had been taken to the Abbey and she was staying in Villafranca to make their dialogue easier. When they had agreed that she should petition the next Congregation of Bishops for his release she had wanted to set out for Leon immediately. But he had urged caution: his ideas challenged not only the Church but those secular interests who wanted the War for the land and booty that could be won. It was widely known that she supported him and it made her a target for fanatics. Once outside the safety of Soria's castle she was vulnerable to assassination and her uncle had insisted she have an escort to Leon; a knight ideally, who could not be bought. Neither of them knew such a man, but her uncle was sure that God would provide. But a Templar? Templars had but one purpose — to do battle with the Infidel wherever they found him. Why should this English Templar help her uncle; a man who spoke out against the War?

"Have you proof of this bargain?" she asked, at last.

William took a small scroll from his belt and held it up for her to see. "I bring a letter from Don Diego that confirms what I say. May I approach and give it to you?"

"No! Do you take me for a fool? My uncle is forbidden quill and paper. Who sent you here! And don't talk to me of bargains. Your purpose is to see I never get to Leon."

"I speak the truth, lady," said William, quietly. "I gave Don Diego pen and paper and I also gave him my word to see you safely to Leon. And I swear to you on my honour that I shall not break it."

"I presume your Master is Robert Montagnac. Does he know of your bargain with my uncle?"

"Robert Montagnac is my Master, but he knows nothing of my bargain. I happen to be going to Leon on the Order's business and I agreed to escort you on my own authority — it's a private arrangement between your uncle and me."

"On your own authority! I don't believe it! You do only what you're told!"

She stood up abruptly, strode over to William, snatched the scroll out of his hand and read it. Then she circled him a couple of times, looking him up and down as if she was appraising the qualities of a horse. The scroll's few words of Latin were in her uncle's hand and she knew from his message — 'God has given us a knight for our task' — that he had written it without duress.

Lucky for you you're not a man, thought William, as she walked back to her chair; I'd clap your ears.

"I hope you know what you're doing, uncle," she breathed to herself, as she resumed her seat.

Everything she knew about the English she had learned from her uncle: as a people they were a backward, ill mannered and always spoiling for a fight. If the latter were true this William Stanley would be formidable. She was a daughter of the warrior caste and had learned to judge a fighting man's mettle. The Englishman was no longer young, probably two or three years past thirty, but his physical qualities ranked with some of the best that she had seen. There was another, less definable quality about him too; a sense of vigour, confidence and self-possession which her father had called 'presence.' He had good looks, although he gave no sign of being sharp witted. As to his manners, well, if he would see her safely to Leon she would live with his belches and farts. The knight would do.

"What's the puzzle my uncle has promised to solve?"

"I am trying to find out why a monk was killed on the Camino. I believe the answer might be found in his journal, your uncle is translating it."

"You can't read?"

She hadn't meant her question to offend, but it sounded like an accusation to William.

"It's a little more complicated than that," he said, thinly. "When will you be ready to leave?"

"Won't you be punished if your Master discovers that you've escorted me to Leon?"

William nodded.

"Then why are you doing it?"

Although William returned Cristina Delmirez's appraising stare, the abruptness of her question had caught him off guard. This was the first occasion he'd been alone with a woman since leaving the Holy Land and apart from saying a few words to female pilgrims from time to time he hadn't spoken to one at length since he'd arrived in Spain. His mother had argued frequently with his father behind closed doors, but apart from Elizabeth and the Frankish ladies all the other women he'd known — his sisters, ladies he'd courted, even the whores — had respected male authority. Dona Delmirez acted like a man. He had expected her to distrust him, but she had interrupted him, held his stare and inspected him. Had the standards of women's behaviour changed that much in ten years, or was this one an exception? He could have excused her perhaps if she'd been fat and ugly but Cristina Delmirez was tall and slender, with large brown eyes, an attractive face, pale golden skin without blemish and tresses of jet-black hair. She was past the blush of youth — he guessed she was about five and twenty — but time had used her kindly and she was still most fair.

"I *am* a Templar, but I am a knight too, sworn to protect a lady from harm and defend her honour," he said and regretted it instantly; he hadn't spoken to a lady in troubadour fashion since leaving Outreamer and he'd sounded pompous rather than gallant.

"Oh sir knight, I can see I shall be safe with you," she simpered, sarcastically. William blushed. It was insufferable to be spoken to thus, but he was a guest in the house and she was of noble blood; more to the point he needed the help of her uncle. He held his tongue.

"All right, I'll accept your offer of protection," she said, briskly. "I can't just up and go of course, there are things I have to do. Once we've sorted out some details, perhaps I can offer you food."

27

William was grateful for Dona Delmirez's offer of refreshment and as soon as his audience was over he sought out her cook. He had eaten nothing since his noon meal in the refectory at Samos on the previous day and he wolfed a large bowl of mutton and bean stew. Then, ignoring the Rule's stricture on gluttony, he asked for a second helping. After washing it down with water and wine he went to the patio and selected the shadiest corner where he spread his bedroll and took off his hauberk and chausses. It was over twelve leagues from Samos to Villafranca, yet despite the difficult terrain he had covered the distance in less than fourteen hours, slogging his way over the Perdrafiti and Cebreiro passes by the light of the stars. He had arrived at Villafranca in the third hour of the day and he'd promised himself the luxury of a long snooze.

Dona Delmirez had said at the end of his audience that she would pack for the journey once she had bathed and dealt with some matters of administration. Her maid, Pilar, would accompany her and they'd travel together in the small coach. The only other person would be her coachman, a man of mature years who she could trust. She would take an additional horse, saddled, so that she could ride when she wished. Her baggage would consist of two chests that fitted easily into the coach's rear trunk plus a small stock of dried food and a dozen wineskins. All would be packed and loaded by noon. William had listened politely while she was telling him this, but he hadn't believed it. She was a woman and, whatever she might say, he was sure she would take her complete wardrobe and all the other things that ladies regarded as indispensable. She would be packing all day, he would tell her his travel plans in the evening and they would leave early on the morrow.

He was very tired and once he had settled himself down he was soon under the patio's spell. Lulled by the sounds of droning honey bees and the fountain's gentle lapping his eyes closed. And he was in a deep sleep when he was awakened by the clatter of servants, hustling and bustling to Dona Delmirez's commands. Feeling out of sorts he roused himself and once he'd rubbed sleep from his eyes he struggled to his feet. He could tell from the sun that it was not yet noon and he was astonished to see the house gates open and the small coach standing outside in the Calle Agua. It had been loaded, its horses harnessed and the driver was already aboard. A woman, around thirty, who he presumed was Dona Delmirez's maid, was sitting inside, talking to a groom who was standing next to the coach holding the reins of his stallion and a grey palfrey, which had been saddled for a lady.

Feeling cheated of sleep and bleary eyed; he dusted himself down and struggled into his chausses and hauberk. Properly attired, he was standing by the wrought iron gate when Dona Delmirez, dressed in a pale green riding habit, appeared at the bottom of the stairs in the far corner of the patio. After a brief farewell to the house steward she strode down the colonnade, across the patio and as she swept past him — acknowledging his brief bow — she thrust a bundle into his hands and continued on to the coach without breaking her stride. On reaching it she spoke to the groom and placing her foot into his cupped hands she stepped up and seated herself expertly onto the grey palfrey.

"Are you coming?" she called to William.

As he walked to his horse, William shook out the bundle — a knight's surcoat — that she had given to him. In the course of his audience they had discussed a number of practicalities, including how he could reduce the chances of being spotted by a Templar patrol. The obvious solution, in her view, was disguise. He was sure the Rule forbade it. But what if it did? A charge of being improperly dressed would be the least of his worries if he were caught and, before mounting his horse, he donned her surcoat, which proclaimed him liege knight, sworn to fight for the Counts of Soria. Riding along the Calle Agua beside Dona Delmirez he could not but respect the brisk and efficient way she had organised her leaving. He knew too that he no longer felt indifferent towards her. He disliked her and, now that he knew the reason for it, he couldn't understand why he hadn't realised it before. She was another Elizabeth Clermont. Not in looks — Elizabeth was shorter in stature and fair — but in her attitude: her haughty manner and condescending speech.

He growled to himself in anger as he recalled the way she'd said: "You can't read?"

It was the same tone that Elizabeth used when she'd chided him for his lack of courtly manners.

They continued down the Calle Agua, with William in the lead trying to blot out a tableau that was investing his mind. But the scene was too vivid, even after all this time, and he could not escape the images of a brief moment in his life that he thought he had forgotten: his last meeting with Elizabeth, when she had rejected him. It had been on the eve of the Bruges tourney when she had put away her patrician airs and graces and told him bluntly that while she might accept the love of a knight who lacked the requisite courtly charms she would never give herself to an impoverished one. She had always regarded his courtship as nothing more that a silly, harmless flirtation. Her intention, from the outset, was to marry the first born son of the Count of Flanders, Edmund Balleranche.

Once they had climbed the hill out of Villafranca he became preoccupied with thoughts of danger and, after passing by the little church of Santiago at the southern most limit of town, he set a cracking pace. If he were spotted it could spell disaster; Ponferrada was the most likely place and he could reduce the chance of being seen by going past it when the garrison was in chapel. The Rule prescribed seven services a day and three of these were held after noon: Noones began at the third hour and it was by far the longest, Vespers was held at dusk and after nightfall, Compline. His plan, devised during the journey from Samos, had called for a dawn start on the morning after he'd arrived at Villafranca with the aim of getting to Ponferrada — a distance of four leagues — before Sext, at noon. Four leagues in six hours was an easy journey. They would have arrived at the west bank of the River Sil well before mid-day, where they would have waited and, once they'd heard the castle bell calling the brothers to prayer, they would have known it was safe to sneak by. But Dona Delmirez had scuppered him. Although he had urged haste he'd never considered even the possibility that they would leave before the morrow. He could have insisted they keep to his plan of course and start the next day. Unfortunately however, as he had not told her of it, to do so then, when the coach was loaded and she was seated on her horse would have made him look a damn fool. She had left him no choice but to get on his own horse and go. She had been true to her word and it was clear to him that she'd thrown down the gauntlet: "I've kept my word to be ready by noon, now let's see what you can do!"

Four leagues in three hours. Sweet Jesus! It called for a Hell of a pace, but he was determined they would do it. Noones lasted for well over an hour. They would cross Ponferrada's iron bridge, skirt around the castle wall and be through the town before it had finished. Arriving too late wouldn't be a disaster necessarily because they could sit by the Sil until Vespers. Getting through Ponferrada would be easier at dusk, but that had to be set against the dangers of travelling after dark with two women in tow and if that happened he was sure Dona Delmirez would be ready and willing to take him to task.

Once they had sneaked through Ponferrada they could turn either north and follow a route that would take them to Astorga through the passes at San Roman de Bembibre and Manzanal, or they could continue on the Camino. The Camino was the better choice. It would be tough going at first because they would have to climb Monte Irago, but it was relatively easy thereafter and it was a much better road for the coach. It was safer too: the country to the north was virtually unpopulated whereas there were half a dozen little pueblos on the Camino between Ponferrada and Astorga.

The first of these was Molinseca, which lay in a valley about a league to the east of Ponferrada. Its pilgrims' hostal was rough and ready but it was clean, its fare was wholesome and if Dona Delmirez turned up her nose at it she would have to eat her own food and sleep in the coach. Starting at dawn from Molinseca, they would be over the top of Monte Irago and down to Foncebadon by late morning. After a short rest they could rattle down the mountain and nip through Rabanal at noon when its small contingent of Templars was saying Sext. Another couple of hours would see them clear of the Montes de Leon and onto the plain to the south of Astorga. They would stop close by a little Maragato village to give the horses and women a breather — the spot he had in mind was next to a stream with plenty of shade — then they would push on and by dusk they would be safely inside the walls of Astorga. The next night would see them in Leon.

They slipped through Ponferrada by the skin of their teeth. Once it was behind them and out of sight William called a halt to rest the coach's horses and while they were cooling down he and Dona Delmirez led theirs a short distance away from the coach and he explained his plan for the journey. She agreed to it, but with one small variation: instead of going to Molinseca they would leave the trail and head due south into the Valle del Silencio to visit a small community, which her uncle had founded.

"Why didn't you speak of this before?" snapped William.

"Why didn't you tell me your plan for the journey 'til now?" she snapped back.

"Because I didn't think you —"

"Needed to know?" she interrupted. "Well now you know why *I* didn't tell *you*."

William's temper quickened. He'd been duped; she wasn't going to the Valle del Silencio on a whim, she and Delmirez must have planned it long since. That's why she could pack so quickly. They must be communicating in secret. Christ strike me! he thought, they've used me as a go-between. And why was she going to this settlement? And what was inside those boxes? Was she even going to Leon? And why did they want him tagging along? He glanced down at his surcoat. Wearing a disguise had seemed a sensible precaution when she'd suggested it. But was that the real reason she'd proposed he don a Soria surcoat?

Holding back his temper, he dismounted and checked the saddle girths on their horses; he needed time to think. He blamed himself for the mess he was in; he had acted out of pride and God was punishing him for his sin. If ever it were known that he had accompanied her to this settlement there could be no excuses. He would be accused of being a disciple of Delmirez and judged accordingly. Christ damn it! He'd been the victim of a woman's guile once before. Elizabeth had ruined his life and he'd be damned if he were going to be deceived by another highborn lady. He had a choice: leave her and ride back to Ponferrada or keep his promise and see her to Leon. But to leave her alone on the trail without good cause would be a blemish on his honour: he had to test her first, to see whether she was false or true.

"My failure was a fault of omission, lady," he said, once he had remounted. "Yours was deceit. And before we go any further I want to know the truth. What is this settlement? Why are you going there? And, if you really are going on to Leon what is the reason for your journey?"

"How dare you question me!" she blazed.

"But I do dare lady and if I think you're lying I'll leave you here and go back to Ponferrada."

"I thought you gave your word to take me to Leon. You certainly seemed to put great store by it when first we spoke. But I see now that honour is a scarce commodity among English knights."

"If you were a man I'd kill you for saying that," he said quietly.

He was fuming with rage, he'd spoken instinctively without weighing his words and he didn't care. He fixed her with a freezing stare.

"Now you listen to me and listen carefully," he continued quietly. "I don't like the way you speak to me, I don't like your lardydary ways and I don't like you! Answer my questions or I'll not only go back to Ponferrada, I'll take you with me, under arrest and strapped over your horse. I'm sure there are lots of people who'd like to know about this place in the Valle del Silencio."

For the first time in years Dona Delmirez was lost for words. If the knight had yelled out his anger she would have shouted back until he was overcome. But the Englishman had spoken softly in a calm, cold anger and she'd retreated before it because she could see in his eyes that when his temper was roused he was capable of anything. She wasn't frightened of him — she wasn't frightened of anyone — but from now on she would be wary of him and treat him with respect.

"I was going to tell you as we came down the trail from Villafranca, but we were moving so quickly there wasn't any opportunity," she said, sincerely. "I'm sorry if you think I deceived you."

It was the first time she had said sorry to anyone since losing her father and brothers. Hearing the sincerity in her voice William nodded his acceptance of her explanation; if there had been time he would have told her of his plan on the way to Ponferrada too.

"And what about this settlement?"

"It's about half a league inside the valley, a little way off the track, before it starts to climb up to Penalbra. We call it *Nueva Vida*. We have over fifty people there — Christians and Musulmen. It's led by a priest and an imam."

"An imam?"

"Yes. People from the two religions live and work and worship together. We've built a church and mosque side by side, under the same roof, Christians pray in one half, Musulmen in the other. My uncle says it was once like that in Cordoba. They're self sufficient, but they sometimes need medicines and potions for the children and wine of course, for Communion. That's why I am going there, and to bring them news about what's happened to my uncle."

God Almighty, thought William, no wonder they called the place 'New Life'. He pointed towards the coach. "So those two chests are full of medicines?"

"One has medicines, the other has my clothes and things I shall need in Leon. Do you want them opened?"

"No lady. I'll take your word."

"I'm going to Leon to petition the Congregation of Bishops for my uncle's release."

"I see. Do you have any other plans I should know about?"

"No, after Nueva Vida I am going directly to Leon. I swear it, on my honour," she said, looking him straight in the eye.

Quickness of temper was an unfortunate characteristic of males in the Stanley family. But they were just as quick to calm and where they had given unwarranted offence they were ready to apologise without reservation. A treaty was generally agreed with their offender and the cause of their passion forgiven and forgotten. William regretted the violence of his words within moments of speaking them and, now that his temper had cooled, he was ashamed of himself. Abusing a woman was the act of a scoundrel. To threaten a lady with physical harm was unconscionable. He knew, even as he spoke, that the unbridled anger which had spewed from his mouth had come, not from the present, but from the past; an echo of what he wished he had said to Elizabeth on the night she'd rejected him. But instead of saying what was in his mind he'd stayed on his knees at her feet like a ninny, struck dumb by the revelation that she'd used him as bait to trap a far better prize. Later, when he had returned from her father's house to his quarters in a poor tavern, he had lain on his bed and relived every moment of the scene. It had been easy then to articulate the clever, courtly words that he should have said. But the time to say them had passed and as he lay in the dark with his wounded pride he'd begun to muse on how he might repay her.

Dona Delmirez returned his steady stare and he saw in her eyes that she spoke the truth. His anger died and for the first time since their meeting he saw her, not as an apparition from his past, but as a person of flesh and blood to be judged on her own merits. He recognised at once that she was a woman of sterling qualities. She might be proud and sharp-tongued, but she was also independent, serious minded, loyal to her uncle and, if he was any judge, truthful and honourable too. She was very different from the likes of Elizabeth Clermont. He had given his word to protect her and he would see the task through.

"I take you on your honour, lady. And since we are travelling together I ask that you forgive my words and we agree a truce. I was wrong to speak to you thus and I ask sincerely for your pardon."

Dona Delmirez hesitated, then she set aside her pride; she did not seek a quarrel with the Templar. She nodded her agreement and held out her right hand for him to grasp. William was taken aback momentarily, surprised that she'd reacted like a man, then he reached out and shook her hand. Turning in his saddle he looked a little way off towards the coach, where its driver and her maid were waiting patiently.

"We're turning off the trail at the next crossroad," he called to the coachman, "into the Valle del Silencio."

29

'Silent Valley' had always been a holy place: hermits had chosen to live there since Roman times and some said that the mountain above the tiny hamlet of Penalbra had once been sacred to pagan tribes. William had visited the valley twice before. Once, when he had escorted a senior cleric to the ancient monastery of San Pedro del Monte, which was high in the hills on the valley's western side. The second time, he had led a mid-winter patrol to the village of Penalbra at the very top of the valley. They had arrived in the midst of a snowstorm, but next morning the skies were clear and after visiting its tiny Mozarab church he had gone for a walk in the woods behind the village. Standing on the mountainside overlooking Penalbra he thought it must be the most beautiful and peaceful place on earth.

Very few people travelled the track that led into the valley: he had to search for it and by the time they turned off the Camino it was getting late in the afternoon. Initially, the trail passed through undulating meadowland and they made good progress, but as they entered the valley and the trees closed around them their pace slowed to a crawl. The track ran beside a river that snaked down the mountain and it was criss-crossed with exposed tree roots, which caused the coach's wheels to jolt and slide. It was ideal terrain for ambush and William was looking constantly to right and left for any movement in the deepening shadows. And it was only when Dona Delmirez said they were nearly there that he began to relax.

A little further on they came to old bridge across the river that led to a ruined farmhouse. It was narrow, its timbers looked rotten and William was chary of crossing it. However, Dona Delmirez insisted it would hold and she instructed Eduardo, the coachman, to get down from his seat and lead the horses while William stayed at the rear to watch the coach's wheels. There was no sign of a track on the other side and it seemed they had come to a dead end. Then William noticed a path — little more than a stretch of trampled grass — some distance beyond the ruin. It could not be seen from the other side of the river and after parking the coach out of sight, behind the ruined house, they followed it into the trees. They had not gone far when he noticed that the wood on both sides of the path was getting denser. About three hundred paces from the bridge they emerged suddenly into a clearing, containing a collection of huts. Eduardo helped Dona Delmirez to dismount, but William stayed on his horse, looking around uneasily.

There were fourteen huts in all, with walls made of interlaced sticks and twigs plastered with mud — in England they called it *wattle and daub* — and roofs thatched with thin branches. A more substantial building stood in the centre of the village and William was a little affronted when he saw the

Muslim half moon and star and the Cross, side by side on its roof. He struggled for a word to describe the village's centrepiece before deciding on the term, 'church-mosque'. An oven and fireplace were nearby. A fire had been lit and its embers were red-hot. The refectory, a large, open sided hut containing roughly hewn wooden tables and benches, was within a few paces of it. Sheep and goats — he counted two dozen or more — were tethered at intervals in the clearing. But of people there was neither sight nor sound.

"Call them out Eduardo," said Dona Delmirez and the coachman gave three long trilling whistles.

Several moments passed before William saw faces staring at them from the trees. Then the people of Nueva Vida came forward, cautiously at first, until they saw Dona Delmirez and ran to greet her. Sitting astride his horse, William watched as they gathered around her, men bowing, women curtsying, all competing to kiss her outstretched hand. From out of the corner of his eye William caught a movement at the edge of the clearing and he turned to see two men coming out of the shadows. One had a tonsured head and the habit of a priest. The other was an imam wearing long hair and a shaggy beard and dressed in black. The crowd parted and the two priests came into their midst. They bowed to Dona Delmirez who bowed in return and William was intrigued that it was a greeting between equals. He, in contrast, was an object of suspicion.

"Who is this knight, Cristina?" asked the Christian priest, pointing at him.

Dona Delmirez looked up at William and he smiled briefly at the priest.

"This is William Stanley, father. He's sworn to protect me. Surely you recognise Soria's colours? William's an Englishman, although his Castilian is so good you'd hardly know it."

"Where will he sleep?" asked the imam. "In the men's hut?"

"No, with us, in our hut," said the priest. "Our guest is a *caballero* and we should treat him as such. Welcome to Nueva Vida William Stanley, may God and Allah bless you."

It took a little time for the villagers to disperse and once they had gone back to their tasks Dona Delmirez and the two priests went into one of the wattle and daub huts. William dismounted and after giving the reins of his stallion to Eduardo he set about exploring Nueva Vida. He was accosted almost immediately by one of the boys who had been watching over the goats and sheep. He was about nine or ten, his name was Abdul and his bold manners reminded William of Pero. William said he wanted to look around and after some haggling it was agreed that Abdul would act as his guide if William would let Abdul hold his sword.

Their first stop was the ditch that had been dug to divert water from the river to allow the community a constant supply. William paced its distance — five hundred and twenty paces — and was impressed by the village's industry. After the ditch they visited the plot that had been cleared to grow vegetables and corn and William asked Abdul what it was like to live in Nueva Vida. He was not surprised to find Christians and Muslims living side by side — it was common in towns both in the Holy Land and Spain. What surprised him was that they had ordered their lives to accommodate their respective religions. They worshipped separately and Christians had adopted the Muslim practice of praying five times a day. They celebrated each other's great festivals and eating pork was forbidden. From its outset the village had instituted a council that met monthly and it seemed to work in a similar way to the Order's chapters. Women — even the Muslim women — could speak and vote in council meetings and, more surprisingly, they could even be elected 'village headman', although William got the impression the time for that had yet to come.

The way the community had agreed to share out the wattle and daub huts he also found surprising. The priest and the imam shared one, another was kept vacant and ready in case of a visit by either Delmirez or his niece and the community shared the rest. There were eight families in all; four Christian and four Muslim, and each family had a hut of its own where they might live together. However, in order to cope with the strains of family life — inevitable where, in one instance, there were ten in a family — four huts had been set aside; one for men, another for women, and two for the children, one for boys, the other for girls. Abdul said that the arrangement worked very well. But William was shocked by the thought of so much liberty until he remembered that they had not lived under the Rule for seventeen years and that he was judging their lives from the standpoint of a prisoner.

When the time came for William to honour his side of the bargain, Abdul put his finger to his lips for silence and led him to a little clearing. Surrounded by dense undergrowth it was virtually invisible from the path and the only way in was by crawling under the bushes on hands and knees. Once they were inside, Abdul explained that it was a secret place, which the children sometimes used in their games. William could see that it was an excellent place to hide. But why had Abdul brought him here? Abdul explained that the village council had banned war games: boys could make neither toy swords nor spears, bows and arrows too were forbidden. The rule was strictly enforced and any child caught making or playing with a weapon was thrashed soundly. He could play with William's sword in the hideout without being seen.

Returning from the secret place William found that the villagers had just concluded a council meeting. It was now very late in the afternoon and almost dark under the trees. Nevertheless, there was still sufficient light for William to see the anxiety in their faces.

"What's to do, lady?" he asked Dona Delmirez, nodding towards a small group who were standing in a huddle and speaking in low voices.

"I've told them what's happened to uncle Diego. They've been talking about what to do."

"Have they decided?"

"Yes. They're going to stay here and finish what we've started. It's a courageous decision. They're brave people."

William nodded in agreement. If her uncle was judged a heretic the prospects for Nueva Vida and its people were bleak.

"How many people know about this place?"

"Eduardo and Pilar, my uncle, me and now you."

"Aren't you afraid I'll report it?"

"You must have spoken at some length with my uncle. Can I ask what you talked about?"

"About my time in the Holy Land and how I came to be a Templar. I did most of the talking, he hardly said a word."

"Yes, that sounds like uncle Diego. He has a knack of getting people to talk about themselves without realising it. You must have impressed him — perhaps he saw that underneath your Templar's skin you are a kind and gentle knight. So will you betray us, William?"

William shook his head emphatically. "No, lady, I give you my word."

"Thank you. And please stop calling me 'lady'. Everyone's equal here, call me Cristina."

"Thank you, it will be my pleasure. Have you told them who I really am, by the way?"

"Of course not and please don't mention it. One sight of a Templar and everyone would scatter to the four winds."

"That's just as well because this place would be impossible to defend."

"What creatures you men are. Everyone here is committed to a life of peace. We would never fight."

"Would that everyone was. The world would be a better place."

"That's a strange idea for a knight," she said, looking at him quizzically. "It's time for prayer," she added, glancing towards the church-mosque where the villagers were filing in through its single door. "Will you join us in the church?"

"No, but thank you for the invitation. I'll say my Paternosters out here. I have a lot to catch up on, I've fallen out of practice these past few days."

30

Once prayers were over the women cooked a vegetable stew, candles were placed on the refectory tables and everyone sat to supper. William was invited to sup with the two priests and Cristina. They were sitting at a small table set a little apart from the rest and within a few moments of joining them he realised they were discussing Delmirez's ideas. Most of what they were saying was lost on him however and he was soon preoccupied with his own thoughts and wondering, as he watched the villagers talking and laughing over supper, whether they really understood the danger they were in. He wondered too how far the scholarly debate at his table was concerned with the real world, in which the village could be torched and its people killed. Listening to the two priests and Cristina talking he thought of another debate that he'd once witnessed.

That had been at the city of Acre, when two Patriarchs of the Church had argued the justice of killing Saracen prisoners that Saladin had agreed to ransom. Neither had addressed the rightness of Richard Lionheart's proposal to kill Acre's Muslim citizens, only the timing of their death. Richard brought their argument to an end finally by issuing orders for the executions and William wondered why the clerics did not stop it and chastise Richard for his sin. If he'd been a secular knight and not a Templar he would have protested vehemently to Richard against a barbarity that could bring only dishonour on the King's crusade. However, he had lived under the Rule for the best part of three years by then. Its insistence on silent obedience had always to be observed and he could only watch in silent horror while Richard's English soldiers butchered several thousand people. But, at the last, when they'd begun to slit open and search through the guts of the dead in case they had swallowed their jewels he'd found the courage to speak out.

He'd got to his feet and in front of the army, Patriarchs and Robert de Sable he'd crossed the gory field to where Richard was supervising his soldiers and seizing him by the arm he'd called on the King to stop. Richard, eyes wide with blood lust, had stared at him in disbelief, but he'd stood his ground and shouted that his King was disgracing himself before God. As Richard raised his sword in fury he'd knelt down before him and offered the King his neck. He'd been ready to die, but Richard's anger had relented: he'd set aside his sword, and seizing William's arm he'd pulled him to his feet and clasped him tight. He was forgiven and Richard had never spoken of it again, but Robert de Sable, Master of Jerusalem and supreme head of the Order of the Temple had not been so inclined.

As his companions' debate came to an end William's thoughts returned to the present and a few moments later the two priests took their leave.

"You didn't say anything William," said Cristina Delmirez, once they had gone.

"I don't know enough about your uncle's ideas to have an opinion."

"Would you like to know more?" And before William could demur she began to speak. "My uncle has always been a scholar; before he joined Palencia University he studied for years in Paris. He can read Latin, Arabic, Hebrew and Greek and ever since he went to Palencia he has been studying texts that have been written by the Moors. They have many scholars, you know. Have you heard of their philosopher, Averroes?" William shook his head. "No matter, I'll start with Saint Augustine."

"I've heard of him," he interrupted.

"Then it's a good place to start. According to Saint Augustine, Christians should fight only wars that are 'just' and he defined a 'just war' in three ways. One, they must be attacked first. Two, only someone with the proper authority — a king, prince or pope — can declare war. And three, those who fight must be pure of heart; they must fight for the war's cause, not to gain power or riches and they must use only necessary force. Do you understand, or shall I go through it again?"

William shook his head. It seemed simple enough. "So how did your uncle get himself into trouble with the Church? Did he say Saint Augustine was wrong?"

"No, he said the Church was wrong: the crusades to the Holy Land aren't 'just wars'."

"How so? We didn't start the War. The Saracens attacked us and took away the land that was rightfully ours. We're just trying to get it back. I think Saint Augustine would have approved."

"It's true that all Popes since Urban have claimed that. But if you examine the facts, you'll see that what they're saying can't be true. The Holy Land never belonged to 'us'. It belonged to the Jews. It was promised to Moses and given to them by God."

"And it was conquered by the Romans, they became Christians and we inherited it when Rome fell."

"I'm sorry, but it's more complicated than that. The Popes can't substantiate our right to make such a claim for two reasons. First," Cristina held up an index finger, "the Holy Land was given to the Jews by God. The Romans conquered it against God's Will, which makes their conquest uniquely unlawful." She held up another finger, "Second, at the time of the conquest the Romans were pagan, not Christian. So you see, we can't rightfully claim land that was taken against God's Wishes by pagans. Logically, if we want to fight for the Holy Land our aim should be to give it back to the Jews."

"The Jews! They killed Christ!" William spluttered. "And what about our Holy Places? Do we let the Saracens have them? Or does your uncle think we should give those back to the Jews too?"

"We don't need to fight for them. All Christians actually want is to be able to visit our Holy Places in safety and we can achieve that by negotiation. Your King Richard agreed a treaty with Saladin that gave us the right to go to Jerusalem. We could agree permanent rights of access with the Saracens. Don't you see? We don't need to fight for the Holy Land. The only reason we need to send soldiers over there is to protect our pilgrims against brigands and if the Saracens have a problem with that we could use their troops and pay them for it. The Saracens have never stopped us practising our religion; according to my uncle their Holy Book says they mustn't persecute Christians, or Jews. If we can be as tolerant of their religion as they are of ours all of these issues can be resolved and we could settle our differences peacefully."

It was a ridiculous argument and he'd been eager and ready to contest every point, although her mention of Richard's treaty with Saladin had prompted a moment's reflection: it was the first thing she'd said that touched on his experience. As one of Richard's personal bodyguard he'd been an observer at some of the discussions between the Christian leaders that had led to the treaty. The army was in sight of Jerusalem's walls when the argument about what to do had broken out in the Lionheart's council. One view, favoured by Richard and voiced by many who had come from overseas, argued for the city to be besieged. The leaders of Outreamer's Christians contested it however. In the Franks' view nothing would be gained because even if the siege were successful they could never hold it with their slender resources and, once Richard's army had sailed home, the Saracens would retake it. Their advice, which was supported by the Masters of both Templars and Hospitallers, was to withdraw to the coast. The debates had been heated, but Richard had seen finally the sense of their argument: the army had withdrawn and a treaty, giving pilgrims right of access to Jerusalem, had been agreed.

Although William was exasperated by the forthright way she expressed herself he accepted her point about the value of negotiation, but on grounds of military common sense, not because of her uncle's half-baked ideas. It was obvious to everyone that the Holy Land could be cleansed of Saracens only by the sword.

"What does your uncle say about Augustine's second justification?"

"Oh that's not an issue: a Pope can declare war. But the third justification can't possibly be met. I know some crusaders believe they're fighting for Christ; fanatics, like you Knight Templars and the other military orders, but the majority fight for spoil. My uncle shows that quite clearly. And none of the Christian armies pay much heed for the lives of ordinary people, whatever their religion. The sack of Jerusalem in the first crusade showed that. And the last crusade was an affront to God."

For the first time in their discussion his anger was kindled: she had no right to speak that way about Richard's crusade. He had been there, in the thick of it, from beginning to end. Acre's citizens had been killed, that was true and he'd protested against it, but he knew, strictly speaking, that Richard's order to kill them was within the provisions of war. Saladin had delayed paying the ransom as a way of buying time and putting pressure on the Christian armies — if it had been paid promptly the people of Acre would have been spared. For the rest of the time both sides had fought with honour. At Jaffa, for instance, Saladin had sent two horses through the lines to Richard to replace the one that had been killed under him.

"What does your uncle say about the Reconquista? God didn't give Spain to the Jews; it was Christian long before the Moors invaded. Does he think we shouldn't fight to get it back?"

"He thinks we should negotiate with them. There's no reason why we can't live together in peace. The lines between us haven't always been as tightly drawn as they are now; in his time El Cid fought for both Alfonso of Castile and the Emir of Zaragoza and my uncle says there are lots of examples like that."

"Good God! I can see why he's got himself into trouble. The Spanish kingdoms do fight among themselves from time to time, that's true, but I've never met a Spanish knight who wasn't totally committed to the Reconquista, and we will throw out the Moors in the end, no matter how long it takes. I speak as one of your uncle's 'fanatical Knights Templars' of course," he added, sarcastically.

"Actually, I don't think you are a fanatic. You wouldn't be here if you were. Why did you join the Templars, by the way?"

It was an unexpected question and he wasn't sure how to respond. The Order instructed brothers not to speak about the Temple's business to anyone on the outside, especially a woman. But to say nothing would be rude: it could bring their discussion to a premature end and he wanted to know more about her uncle.

"I was sentenced to serve in the Order," he said, at last. And to avoid any more questions he gave a brief account of his life as a Templar, omitting any reference to either the Order's internal affairs, or to the fighting in Outreamer. However, when she probed the circumstances that led to his sentence he lied.

"I didn't know they used the military orders as a sort of prison."

"There's not many of us. I was lucky to be sent to do holy war, they were minded to hang me before the news came about Hattin."

"Ah yes, that's the other thing. A 'holy war' is not the same as a 'just war'."

"I suppose your uncle has a view about that too, does he?"

"A 'holy war' aims to achieve God's wishes on earth," she continued, ignoring his sarcasm, "to ensure that all men know His name and worship Him or, if they refuse, to kill those who deny Him. Fighting and killing Saracens and Moors because they're non-believers can never be justified. It's a direct breech of Jesus' second commandment — 'to love thy neighbour as thyself'. In saying that, and in admonishing Peter for cutting off the ear of a Roman soldier, Jesus was showing us that all men are brothers. And only an idiot would condemn people for not being Christian when they haven't any knowledge of the Scriptures. It's true that God wants us to convert infidels and pagans, but He wants us to do it by teaching and persuasion, not at the point of a sword: that's sinful and to kill them for not being Christian is murder. Don't you agree?"

He both did and didn't agree. To kill people for denying Christ when they had never heard of Him did seem idiotic. But he knew from personal experience that it wasn't as simple as that: the Saracens also converted by coercion, Saladin had beheaded Templars summarily, without mercy and if Christians were guilty of murder, Muslims were too. There was no sense in arguing with her however: she was a woman with a woman's view of the world and an argument could lead easily into a quarrelsome disharmony that might last all the way to Leon. But he would not let her remark about the Lionheart's crusade go unchallenged.

"I don't disagree with one or two of the things you've said, but I'm not prepared to sit hear and listen to you criticise King Richard's crusade. You weren't there, you don't know anything about it and to say it 'affronted God' is outrageous."

"I never said that!"

"Yes you did! You said the last crusade was an affront to God."

"I wasn't talking about *your* crusade, William. I was talking about the *last* crusade, the one that Innocent declared on his accession." She realised suddenly that he didn't know what she was talking about. "You didn't know about it?"

He shook his head.

"They don't tell you much in the Order, do they? Innocent called for a crusade in '98. It set out from Venice three years later, but instead of going to the Holy Land its leaders chose to sack Constantinople instead. That's what I meant when I said it was an affront to God."

"Why would they attack Constantinople? It's the capital of the Greek Christians, for Heaven's sake. When did it happen?"

"In April 1204."

"You can't be serious?"

"Oh for God's sake, William, don't be so naïve! It's what I've been saying; it's Augustine's third justification. Only a few go on crusade purely for the love of God. Most go for booty. That's why they sacked Constantinople — to steal its treasures and get rich. So," she paused, "what do you think of my uncle's ideas?"

In the light of this new information, he didn't know what to think. What else was going on in the world that he knew nothing about? Perhaps he should have paid more heed to what Philipe had been saying. How should he answer? He decided to hold his tongue. Against her superior knowledge he was in the same position as the men he'd seen making foolish comments in King Richard's council: better to stay silent and appear wise.
"As I said to your uncle, I'm a soldier, I don't think, I do as I'm told. "
"But you don't always do what you're told, do you? You're not supposed to be here, are you? But you are."
"I'm here as part of a bigger duty; to find a murderer." He decided that the best way to escape her inquisition was to go onto the attack. "Why are you here?"

"What do you mean?" she asked sharply.
He shrugged. "It's a simple enough question. Why are you here? Why aren't you married with lots of children like every other lady?"
"Don't be impertinent. It's none of your business."
"My apologies, I hadn't understood that the game was only to question me. I'm sorry if I upset you, please excuse me."
He made to rise but she reached out and touched his forearm; she had been stung by his remark, nevertheless it had been fair comment about her behaviour.
"I can tell it quite simply. My father was heir to the title. He had four sons; I was his last child and only daughter and my mother died just after I was born. When my brothers were sent to become knights I was left to my own devices, until my uncle Diego encouraged my father to find me a tutor. I learned to read and write in Latin as well as Castilian. I was betrothed at fifteen and my wedding was planned for the following spring, but the Battle of Alarcos intervened and my husband to be, my father and all of my brothers were killed."

"I'm sorry for your loss, lady, and for my insolence in asking."
"It was ten years ago; I'm over the worst of it now. I still think about my father and brothers, but my betrothal was by proxy: I'd never met the man I was going to marry. When my grandfather heard news of Alarcos he shut himself away in the castle; since then he's been a recluse."
"Your uncle renounced the title in your favour I understand?"

"Yes, uncle Diego was never interested in anything except his studies; he's been a cleric for over thirty years. He'd moved from Paris to Palencia a month or two before the Battle. When he heard the news he came to stay at Soria, but only for a little while, once he saw I was all right and that I could run our family's affairs he went back to his studies." She smiled to herself. "When I think of it now it frightens me, I was only sixteen. Well, there you are William," she added abruptly, "now you know something of me."

William bowed his head briefly to acknowledge her compliment in sharing a confidence with him.

"Do you really think the Church will release your uncle? And what will he do if they let him go? He'll have to recant before he can go back to his studies at Palencia, or to any other university presumably and I'd say, from what little I've seen, that he's not the sort of man to do that."

"He's not just any old priest, William. Our family is connected to some of the greatest Houses in Spain. We have friends in the Church too and I don't believe it wants to try him for heresy. It would be too public. Look what they've done so far: five years ago he was due to become the new master of Palencia University; then he published his treatise; his Bishop asked him to withdraw it and he refused. The Bishop said he would be examined, but it was another three years before they established a special court. It met for six months and it was another six months before it reached a decision. They gave him months to re-consider and recant his ideas. Then suddenly he's arrested by the Bishop and packed off to Samos. It's all about delay. I know the way they work you see, they don't want to make a decision. It's easier to keep him locked up in Samos until he dies. Well, I'm going to fight them. I'm not going to let him die there and I won't let them snuff out his ideas. I know which bishops can be bribed and once I get to Leon I shall be talking to them. I'll stuff their mouths with gold and the Congregation will release him, I'm sure of it. Once he's free and back at Soria, I shall ask the King of Castile to support us and in return I'll ask him to choose a husband for me. I know the Bishop won't let uncle return to Palencia, but he doesn't need to, he can come to Soria and continue his studies there."

"Your new husband might have something to say about that."

She glared at him. "Don't you worry William Stanley, I shall be mistress of Soria for as long as I live. I'm not one of those empty-headed ninnies you see at Court, swooning over every silly man they fancy. My uncle taught me to use my wit and I've managed my own affairs for far too long to be ordered about by a husband."

William smiled briefly. "I don't doubt it. And what of Nueva Vida, and its people?"

"I shall continue to support them of course. They're a living embodiment of my uncle's ideas and I'm not going to desert them. Only cowards cut and run."

William's first thought was to argue: that the Church would order the village's destruction if it were so minded; the community should escape south into the wilderness, or it should search for a site that could be defended. He decided, on second thoughts, that it was better to say none of these things.

He sighed. "I admire your courage," he said, simply.

He meant it. Now that he saw Cristina in her own right he'd begun to admire her. He didn't agree with her uncle's views but he was impressed by her loyalty to him. He smiled to himself as he remembered one of his innocent amours in Outreamer with Gertrude de Bouillon, widow to Conrad of Haifa, who, when her husband lay dying, had donned armour and marched his soldiers into battle. She was ten years older than he was, but still handsome and although they'd met infrequently he'd always looked forward to talking with her. Cristina had a similar nature and he guessed that in adversity she too would be formidable.

31

They left Nueva Vida at dawn after saying their prayers and eating a breakfast of thin porridge. On rejoining the Camino they continued east towards Monte Irago, resting only briefly before beginning its ascent. The path to the top was rutted, stony and steep. It was slow going and when they reached halfway William called a halt and roped his stallion to the coach's team. With Cristina on her palfrey, Eduardo urging on his enlarged team and William, by turns, walking and jogging alongside, they made more rapid progress. After cresting the summit they stopped for a short while at Foncebadon to drink and eat a little. Their energies renewed they continued down the mountain, passing through Rabanal at midday and reaching the place where William had planned to stop for a rest in mid afternoon.

The spot he had chosen was in sight of the Camino, by a river under a small stand of trees about four hundred paces downstream from a ford. A little Maragato village was close by, its houses shimmering in the afternoon heat. There was neither sight nor sound of its people and, if he did not know better, a traveller might think it deserted. Eduardo spread a large blanket on the ground and Pilar laid out food and drink that they had brought from Nueva Vida. Cristina and her maid sat on the blanket to take their refreshment while Eduardo and William sat on the ground with their backs resting against the coach wheels.

It was less than four leagues to Astorga and it seemed churlish to deny Cristina's request for a siesta; both the women and horses needed a brief rest and while she and her maid were dozing he could wash in the river. They were a little way off the trail; it was safe to leave them for a short while. Since joining the Camino that morning they had met over two score pilgrims, walking in small groups. Their numbers had dwindled as the day progressed and they had met none since Rabanal. They all looked harmless, but he was mindful of the advice in the Codex about those who travelled to commit sin. He would not have left his party unguarded earlier, but it was mid afternoon now. A group of pilgrims were coming down the trail from Astorga. However, they were still a long way off and he guessed that if they had made so little progress by this time of the day they must be old or infirm. He checked one last time that nobody was about and, telling Eduardo to keep watch, he set off for the river, leaving Cristina and Pilar asleep on the blanket.

It was shallow, little more than a stream, and he followed its course until he found a deeper part, a hundred or so paces from their bivouac. It was safely out of sight and once he'd removed his sword and dagger, hauberk and chausses he stripped off his linen shirt and breeches and waded in, naked.

After washing his linens he laid them out on the bank where they would dry quickly in the hot sun. Then he returned to wash himself in the cold water; it acted like a tonic and he was still splashing and wallowing when he heard a woman scream.

32

After talking together for a few minutes Cristina and Pilar settled back on the blanket for a siesta. They had made good progress since leaving Nueva Vida, but it had been hard going and they both felt the need for a rest. After a brief sleep Cristina opened her eyes to see a pair of eagles circling high above and she wished, for a moment, that she could soar above the earth and leave her cares behind. It was impossible of course: she had been born a Delmirez and she would do her duty. In one more day she would be in Leon and as soon as she'd secured uncle Diego's freedom she would go to Burgos, where she would ask the King to choose her a husband. Alfonso would seize her offer happily, but whom would he elect to be the next Count of Soria? Would he act out of greed and pick one of his kin, or use her as a pawn in some political game? And what of the man who would take her as his bride? Would he be young or old, handsome or ugly, a clever man with guile, or an oaf? She told herself that she didn't care as long as he was kind. She wondered — if she was free — whom she would choose for herself. No one came to mind and she realised suddenly that in spending most of her time with her grandfather she too had become a recluse. If the King offered her a choice she would certainly take heed of her uncle's advice. He had chosen well in William Stanley who, despite her initial dislike, had shown himself to be a courteous and gentle knight. He had intelligence too, although his Order forbade him to use it.

"My lady, we have visitors." Eduardo's voice, tinged with alarm, interrupted her thoughts. "Some men have left the trail and they're coming over to us."
She sat up. There were six of them, on foot. She guessed the one to the fore was their leader and as they came on she noted his cocky swagger. None were dressed in pilgrim garb and she caught her breath when she saw they were armed. She got to her feet quickly.
"Pilar, wake up!" She nudged her maid with her foot. " Stand up!" she hissed and, as Pilar awoke, she seized her arm and pulled her onto her feet.
She glanced round, looking for William, but he was nowhere in sight. Where had he gone? Had the men killed him? Should she call out? But it was too late: they had entered the camp.

Their leader looked at Pilar and Eduardo and then spoke directly to Cristina. "Good day to you lady," he said, in a peasant's dialect. "Or should I say *ladies*," he added, bowing low to Pilar with mock gallantry and glancing, briefly, over his shoulder at his companions who laughed at his wit.
He was short, stocky and coarse featured, his soldier's leather jerkin, breeches and boots were filthy and it was plain from his demeanour that life had misused him. His companions came from the same brood: swarthy, hard faced brutes who, born into a life of nothing, had endured a childhood of

poverty, beatings and pain. She wasn't sure whether they were ruffians on the loose or bandidos. If they were ruffians she might see them off, as long as she kept her nerve.

"Good day to you sir," she said, looking the leader straight in the eye as if she had no fear. "Please don't think us rude, but we are just on the point of leaving." She glanced at Eduardo and spoke to him firmly. "Make ready to go."

"Stay!" the man commanded Eduardo. "A moment lady, if you please," he added, softly. He turned aside to one of his companions — a taller man with a scarred face and a patch over one eye. "Recognise the crest?" he said, pointing to Soria's arms that were etched on the door of the coach. The man shook his head.

"They're the arms of the Counts of Soria," said Cristina, hoping that mere mention of her family's name might frighten them away.

"The arms of the Counts of Soria," the man mimicked. "And do we have the pleasure of addressing the Countess of Soria."

"I shall be Countess, yes," Cristina replied, stiffly.

"Do you 'ear that lads, we're talking to a real Countess." He bowed low. "An 'onour to meet you, me lady," he said, with exaggerated politeness. "Well this is a surprise. Tell me, and I 'ope you won't think me too bold, what is a 'ighborn and beautiful —" He paused and his companions 'oooed'. "What is a lady such as yerself doing out 'ere without an escort? You might be safe in Soria, but it's not wise to travel without guards around 'ere. In fact it was the first thing we noticed. Wasn't it boys? And as soon as I saw you from the road I said to myself here's someone who needs my 'elp." He glanced around furtively, as if he feared that he might be overheard. "You won't know this, me lady 'cos Soria's a long way off, but me and me boys 'ave devoted our lives to 'elping pilgrims. You might say we're sort of road sweepers: we look after the stragglers who're finding it difficult to make their way. Makes no odds to us whether they're rich or poor, we're always ready to offer a friendly 'and. Aren't we lads?" The rest of his gang grunted in affirmation. "So what do you say, my lady? Would you like a bit of protecting?"

"Eduardo, we're leaving!"

The gang leader grabbed at her. She aimed a punch at his head but he brushed it aside, hit her in the stomach and seizing her shoulders he put his heel behind her ankle and shoved her down. She fell backwards onto the blanket with him astride her, his knees pinning her arms. She heard Pilar scream as she too was wrestled to the ground. Fighting for breath, she twisted and turned trying to free her arms, hitting his back with her knees, trying anything to unseat him. But he was too strong. He tried to kiss her, but she twisted her head, recoiling from his pox-scarred face and foetid breath. He tried again and she spat in his face. He sat back on his haunches and chuckled grimly.

"Don't you worry, me lady, I'll have a kiss off yer once we've finished," he growled, wiping her spit off his cheek. "Now, let's see what yer got."

He ripped her bodice apart exposing her from neck to crotch.

"Jesus, you're a beauty!" he gloated, as his filthy hands closed around her breasts.

She redoubled her struggles: twisting, turning, grunting and pitching, arching her back and kicking up her feet. But he squeezed hold of her breasts and steadying his balance he stayed astride, glorying in his mastery over her. He slapped her face hard to quieten her down, then slapped it again to knock the fight out of her and then once more to half stun her.

"I always like to know where I'm going," he crowed, gleefully, sliding his hands down her belly and into her crotch. "What do yer say, lady, shall we have a feel of yer cunny?" She felt his fingers probing. "We'll need to widen it first, my sweet maid."

He pushed two of his fingers deep inside her. She screamed with pain and closed her eyes tight to blot out his face. Sweet Jesus, she thought, has my life come to this? She felt cold suddenly and detached, a spectator, not a player in this horror. His nails scratched her flesh, his muscles tightened, he shuddered, coughed gobbets of spittle onto her face, and then fell across her.

She opened her eyes to find he was dead and it was his blood, not spittle that had spewed on her face. With her cheeks hot and stinging from the power of his blows she struggled to release her arms and hands. Then she was pushing and shoving in a panic to escape the dead weight of his corpse. Free of him at last and pawing in disgust at the blood on her face, she sat for a moment appraising the scene. Beside her on the blanket Pilar was lying silent and still, legs splayed wide and skirts over her head. A man was across her, his back oozing blood and she knew he was dead. A dozen or so paces beyond the blanket the other four men were fighting with William. He was naked, but for his breeches and they were circling him, eyeing him warily, cursing and taunting, looking for opportunities to dash at him with lunges and swings of their swords. And he was swivelling and side-stepping, moving always, backwards and forwards, parrying to right and left with sword and dagger, fighting off their blows. One thought only exploded inside her head: they were too many for him!

Looking round for a weapon she snatched the dagger out of her attacker's belt, got to her feet, hitched up her skirt and ran at the nearest man. He caught sight of her movement and half-turned towards her, but she sprang on his back and he was staggering under her, twisting and turning, ducking and wheeling, flailing his arms backwards, trying to hit her. But she stuck to her bronco: legs gripping his sides, ankles crossed around his waist, arms strangling his neck, hugging him tightly with every last bit of her strength. She felt and heard him gasping. He was tiring! His efforts to unseat her slackened for a moment, this was her chance and she seized it. Grabbing his hair, she yanked back his head and stabbed at his face with her dagger. She stabbed in frenzy, blood spouting; piercing flesh, jarring bone and teeth until, at last, the point went in his eye and she rammed her dagger home with a shout of triumph. It slid inside his head, she gave one last push and it grated to a stop, wedged within his socket by its hilt.

He staggered several steps with her still on his back and then fell with a crash, tossing her forwards and over his head. She hit the earth with a thump that knocked the breath out of her. Lying lay face down in the dust, sucking in air she heard steel against steel, ringing and ringing. There was a bellow and a scream. Brushing hair from her eyes with bloody hands she looked to see a man, his entrails spilt, and another, dead, by his side. A third man was close by, crawling slowly on his belly.
"Mercy," she heard him croak, before William killed him.

The blood rush that had fuelled her began slowly to subside leaving her feeling exhausted and desolate, vile with filth and dirty, *dirty*.
"Oh, Sweet Mary, save us." It was the Templar who was kneeling beside her and pleading: "God in Heaven, lady. Please, forgive me."
She struggled to stand up and he reached out to help, but she shoved him away: she wanted no man near her. Avoiding his eyes, she turned away and walked slowly towards the stream.
"My lady?" he called, coming after her.
"Go away!" she screamed.
She walked into the stream and, sinking to her knees, she plunged her head into its cold water, letting it swirl around her mouth and face. Sitting up on her haunches she began to wash: first her hands and arms, then her face and hair, dousing, scrubbing and wringing until she'd cleansed herself of blood. Then she attacked her breasts and crotch with water by the handful, splashing, kneading and rubbing until her flesh was raw, trying to purge the feel of his hands and redeem her person.

Time slipped by, but she wasn't aware until, despite after noon's heat, she shivered. She was still in the stream, her hair was wet and her clothes were sodden. She couldn't stay there. She crawled to the bank on hands and knees and rolled over on her back and stared up at the sky.
"Its over," she said to herself as she closed her eyes. "My life is over."
How could she carry on? How could she face her grandfather and uncle once they knew of her fate? Christ Jesus! Even the servants would know! Pilar wouldn't gossip because she'd been similarly treated. But Eduardo would

talk to anyone who'd listen and once they knew of it they'd be gabbling and sniggering behind her back, or giving her condescending looks of sympathy. And what of her plans? Sweet Mary Our Mother, she whispered, as the tears that she'd resisted began at last to flow. Once word got out she'd have no respect. She'd be pitied of course, for her person and rank, but behind the pitying eyes they would think of her with contempt. The King perhaps, the Church certainly and especially her uncle's enemies would condemn her, either in whispers behind their hands or publicly. All were men and she was a 'fallen woman' and most would say: "she must have deserved her fate."

"My lady?" It was her maid who speaking softly to her.
She opened her eyes and saw that Pilar was kneeling beside her.
"Are you hurt badly my lady? May I help you?" Pilar's voice was high pitched with anxiety.
Clamping her teeth together, Cristina wiped her eyes and swallowed on her tears. She knew what Pilar wanted to know, but dare not ask and if she showed how she felt she'd confirm the maid's suspicions. That would be a disaster. She must hold onto herself, she must control her feelings and act in her normal way: the way that Pilar and Eduardo had always perceived her. She must get on her feet, stare the world in the face and speak with a voice that was clear and steady. But most of all, if she wanted to convince them that she hadn't been raped, she must take charge. She sat up and stared into Pilar's eyes.

"How are you my dear?" she said, reaching out and holding her maid to her. It was an uncharacteristic gesture and Pilar was surprised and touched to receive sympathy for her own situation.
Cristina hugged Pilar gently. "Did he — ?" she said, softly in Pilar's ear. She had intended to say 'violate' but she found suddenly that she didn't want to articulate the word.
"No my lady. Bless the Virgin, our knight saved me. Were you — ?" Pilar suspected her mistress had been defiled, but it was not her place to ask such a thing and at the very last moment she dared not to complete her impertinent question.
"No," Cristina said, firmly. "He came in time, luckily."
"Oh thank God for him," Pilar whispered, wondering whether her lady was speaking the truth.
"Thank God for him? God damn his eyes you mean. He gave his word to protect us! If I'd been born a man I'd take a sword and kill him! As soon as we get to Leon I shall send for his Commander and report him!"
"Yes my lady," said Pilar, quietly.
Hearing her mistress speaking her displeasure so forthrightly she began to doubt her suspicions: no woman could suffer rape and not be changed. She'd been lucky too, like her mistress: she'd held off the man who'd thrown her to

the ground and she hadn't been penetrated, although her emotions were still in a parlous state.

"Please, my lady, the village close by is Maragatos, they may come out and hurt us, can we get away from here, please."

"I doubt they will harm us, they're God fearing people, but don't worry we'll soon be on our way again," said Cristina, getting to her feet, "First we'll have to see how Eduardo is."

Holding her tattered bodice together she put her arm through Pilar's and together they returned to the coach. She noted as they reached it that the Templar had a shown her at least the respect of dragging away the dead.

Determined to show that she'd not been breached and her spirit was undaunted she insisted that Pilar climb into the coach and, once she was inside, Cristina reached for the cloak that was kept under the coachman's seat and slipped it on. She was tying its collar thongs when she heard, behind her, the sound of someone approaching. The Templar cleared his throat softly to indicate his presence. There and then she resolved not to turn and face him.

"I'm sorry, my lady," said William, dropping onto one knee and bowing his head. He would have said more, but he could find no words to describe his sense of dereliction and shame.

"Where were you?" she accused him bitterly, not deigning to turn and look at him.

"I was washing in the river. My lady, I —" He hesitated, he should never have left them unguarded and nothing he could say could excuse it. He thought not to ask his question, but the need to know whether he'd kept at least a shred of honour was overwhelming. "My lady?" he said hesitantly. "Are you all right? Did he — ? Were you — ?"

She swung round to face him. "Don't you dare ask! You —" She bit back the words she was about to scream in his face. They would have told the whole world of her dishonour. Besides, she wouldn't bandy words with a common knight. She wasn't a damned kitchen girl — she was daughter to a Count. "Don't ever speak of it again!" she commanded, in a quieter voice. She turned away. "I damn near came to harm through you. Now get out of my sight, you bloody man!" she said, showing her back to him.

Hearing him retreat she turned around and fixed her eyes on Eduardo. Struggling to show composure she went over to where he was sitting, determined to allay any suspicions he might be harbouring about her person. "How are you old fellow? Can you drive us?" she asked, patting his shoulder.

His forehead had been slashed and an eye was bruised badly, otherwise he seemed unharmed.

"I'll mend, my lady," he said looking up at her, "and I can drive as soon as you're ready, if it please you."

"Thank you, but you need tending first."

She turned to look at the Templar, who was standing a little way off, looking forlorn and helpless. He'd put on his chausses, she noticed, but left off his hauberk and the chest of his linen undershirt was covered in blood.

"Why don't you do something useful!" she snapped at him. "Go to the stream and get me some water."

While he was getting water she left Eduardo and went to the back of the coach and, after untying the thongs on its boot flap, she grabbed the handle of the box containing her clothes and heaved it onto the ground. Making sure she was out of the men's sight she stripped off the cloak and her tunic and put on a gown.

"Put it next to Eduardo," she commanded Stanley when he returned from the stream with coach's horse bucket. She pointed at his bloody chest. "And take off your shirt so I can have a look at you."

"I shall be fine my lady."

"Damn you sir! Do as you're told!"

She tore up the remains of her bodice and knelt down by Eduardo.

"Thank God for our knight," he said, as she washed the cut on his forehead. He pointed towards William. "Appeared out of nowhere. It was like seeing the Archangel Michael. I've watched your father and brothers training with sword many a time, but their skill couldn't begin to compare with —" He realised, suddenly, that his words might be taken as a slight on her menfolks' memory. "I'm sorry my lady, I meant no disrespect."

"I know Eduardo. We're all undone and out of sorts."

His wound was quickly washed and bound and she called the Templar to attend her. He came quickly and meekly.

"Lie on your back!" she instructed.

She'd often bandaged her brothers' cuts and bruises and she was used to male nakedness, above the belt at least. The cut ran across the width of his chest. It was bone deep too and she saw immediately that it needed to be stitched. Telling him to lie still she went to the coach for her needles and thread. Kneeling once more by his side she threaded a needle.

"Don't worry I know what to do," she said.

"I can do it myself, lady."

She looked at him squarely for the first time since the attack. She saw the shame on his face, but seeing the question in his eyes that he dare not ask hatred for him boiled up inside her. He'd betrayed her! She'd been defiled because this damned Templar had gone to the stream to wash! Damn you to Hell! she thought. Damn you! Damn you! Damn you!

They entered Astorga by its south gate. It was the last hour of the day and the city's streets were crowded with pilgrims. Once they arrived in the plaza mayor William set out to search for a suitable hostal. He found one eventually, as it was getting dark — an expensive little place down a side street not far from the west wall. Its high prices kept out the rabble and Cristina was able to command a room of sufficient size for herself and Pilar. She would sleep in its bed, Pilar on a blanket on the floor. Eduardo was left to his own devices and he chose to sleep in the hostal's stable so that he could be near the horses. William's emotions were in turmoil and he did not care where he laid his head.

His years inside the Order had spawned a sense of isolation and indifference to the affairs of other men. Indeed, the Temple meant it to be so and its Rule, which ordered almost every aspect of his life, reinforced his separation from the world. It was a Templar principle that knights were not required to think for themselves and it had been emphasised to William in the Holy Land by Robert de Sable, when he'd addressed his knights following his election as Master of Jerusalem. A Templar's first duty was to obey the orders of his superiors. Responsibility for the consequences of any order was borne by the Master and his senior officers: an ordinary knight who followed orders, without question, had God's blessing and was absolved from all guilt. Up until the time that he'd witnessed the massacre of Acre's Muslims, William had believed the Master of Jerusalem's words were an immutable rule. Thereafter he'd made himself a promise that while he would follow commands obediently, he would not be a slave to them. In particular, he would not murder innocents unless God Himself ordered it.

As things turned out, during the remainder of his service in Outreamer he was never in a position where he needed to protest orders, although he'd interpreted them occasionally in ways his superiors had not intended. His duties in Spain were tedious rather than exacting and, under Ponferrada's previous Master, William and his fellow knights had enjoyed a little discretion. He observed his vow of obedience and Robert de Sable's words still gave him a feeling of righteousness about everything he did. But he saw them as guidance, not a commandment that was always to be observed without question. He'd struck a compromise between conscience and obedience that had given him a sense of inner peace. But that had vanished the moment he had failed to keep Cristina from harm. Now he was in despair: his self-righteousness, values, everything that gave his life meaning had gone.

In pursuing his mission he had set aside his compromise: he'd directly disobeyed orders and he'd acted entirely on his own authority. He knew Montagnac would have forbidden him to make a bargain with Delmirez. He knew too, as he was kneeling by his bed in the hospital at Samos that Montagnac was only repeating his original order. He'd deceived the Abbot and flouted his rules and he'd ignored his duty to Bescanson. He'd sailed close to the wind in the past, but that had been out of conscience; this had sprung from pride and vanity. The Devil was always in wait for those who thought to commit sin. Satan had snared him with his new-found sense of freedom and independence, and the horror of Cristina's rape showed the devious workings of His mind. Her suffering was to show him that in usurping the authority of his superiors he had also usurped their responsibility to God. It was *he* who had committed the fault, not his superiors: it was *he* who had given *his* word to protect her; it was *he* who had failed; it was *he* who was responsible ultimately for her rape and God would hold *him* accountable.

He was responsible for Cristina's fate and he could not set it aright. She had been defiled and she'd know the touch and smell of it until they laid her in her grave. He lashed himself with recriminations. He had promised to protect her. He should have stayed by her side. Instead he had left her to frolic in a stream. Sweet Mary! How could he have been so foolish, so neglectful of his duty? Damn it! He had seen there were people coming down the trail. He should have stayed at the coach — that was the proper thing to do. Then she would have been safe: the bandidos would have left them alone and gone in search of easier pickings. He had sworn to her on his honour: his only possession. He cherished it, it was the essence of his being and he'd cast it aside. Not in pursuit of some great cause, but to wash in a river. Jesus Christ! He was beneath contempt.

As they continued across the plain and the hill, with Astorga atop it, came into view he'd relived every moment of the catastrophe that had befallen her. His first reaction on hearing the scream had been a mixture of fear and panic. A moment later, when he'd dashed from the stream and scrambled up the bank to see the melee around the coach his anger surged. When he reached it, sword and dagger in hand, and seen everything in detail — Cristina fighting to free herself, bodice ripped, her breasts exposed — lust to kill, without mercy, sparing nobody had consumed him. Even at Jaffa, when he had jumped off the prow of a galley, into the water, alongside Richard and hacked a path through the Saracen infantry he had kept a spark of sanity. But when he saw the man astride Cristina his rage had taken him beyond reason.

His father had taught him that rape was as heinous a crime as murder. Common soldiers might regard it as rightful booty, but he had never countenanced it and in the Holy Land, whenever he'd seen them attacking a woman he'd driven them off. He'd never dwelled on it however and once he'd seen the woman safely on her way he had returned to his duties. In contrast the rape of Cristina had truly appalled him and images of her struggling with the bandido were still burning his brain. He was responsible for it. But it was not his own fall from grace that was crucifying him; it was the knowledge that Cristina's life would never be the same. She was a lady, soon to be a Countess, honour was precious and she could not live her life without it.

He had seen the change in her already: from the moment she'd told Eduardo she would ride in the coach. Refusing his help she had climbed inside and they'd continued the journey in deathly silence. He had ridden to and fro and each time he'd passed the coach he had glanced inside. Her posture and attitude were always the same; sitting upright, her back stiff, head held high, staring straight ahead and silent, showing no cognisance of the world outside. Could she find a way to suppress her memories and survive, he wondered, or would she turn inward and retreat from life? He could not believe that someone with Cristina's courage and tenacity would chose to retreat from the world. He marvelled still at the way she had attacked and killed the bandido. He had no doubts now that she and Gertrude de Bouillon were a pair. But Gertrude had turned her back on the world: tired out by the deceit and struggle of political life she had entered a nunnery to find peace. Surely Cristina would not choose that.

Why was her welfare so important to him? he wondered. He crushed his answer before it could blossom. He could not believe that he cared for her: he'd only known her for two days. Dear God! Before they'd spoken together at Nueva Vida he'd actually disliked her. He would not believe it. He was indifferent to women. He had conquered his wayward nature — no one could enter his heart. He'd felt love's sting and he knew the pain of wanting someone who was out of reach. To lie down each night at Ponferrada and struggle with love was a terror he could not face.

34

Once Cristina and Pilar were safely inside the hostal he went to its stable to tend his horse. He found to his annoyance that the stallion had already been fed and watered by Eduardo, who was now in the process of rubbing it down. At any other time he would have thanked the coachman, but tonight he had wanted to do these tasks himself because they would have distracted him and their familiarity would have brought some comfort. He couldn't tend to his horse so he would have to find other ways to pass the time. He certainly wasn't going to stay in the stable all night, listening to Eduardo's prattle: the man was only a common driver. Worse, he'd been witness to his humiliation and shame. Sitting on a straw bale he struggled out of his hauberk and chausses. Then, taking a firebrand from its bracket on the wall he began a hunt for his saddlebags. On finding them he shook out his plain linen cloak and old leather boots and put them on. After giving his sword and armour to Eduardo for safekeeping he told the old man that he was going to find something to eat. He wasn't hungry: it was only a means to excuse his absence. He didn't think Cristina would want to see sight of him that night. He certainly lacked the courage to face her and he dreaded the thought of their meeting in the morning.

For the next hour or so he walked aimlessly, in the anonymity of his plain cloak, through the jostle of people in Astorga's ill lit streets, hearing snatches of pilgrims' conversations and vendors bawling their wares of food, water, and saints' relics. The hour before midnight found him standing outside a noisy and dimly lit taberna in a dark, narrow side street near the city's north gate. He was thirsty. It looked inviting and he still had some of the money that Montagnac had issued him. His conscience said that he should observe the Rule's insistence on sobriety and walk away. He ignored it.

"Wine!" he shouted to the barkeeper over the hubbub. "A pitcher!" he added, as the man reached for a small jar.
He tossed a coin on the bar, snatched up the pitcher of foaming red wine and went in search of an empty table. He found one at the back of the taberna, next to a door with a roughly drawn sign. One glance confirmed his suspicions — the door led to the rooms for the taberna's harlots. He looked around immediately for another table; he wasn't in the mood to be bothered by any of them. All of the other tables were occupied however and, setting aside his distaste, he sat down with his back towards the door and downed a long draught from the pitcher.

"I say, you're thirsty," said a young woman's voice.

He turned around. He could tell immediately that she was a whore and he guessed she'd just got rid of a customer. Ignoring her, he drank the rest of his wine and put down the pitcher.

"Arturo! Bring two pitchers of wine here," she called to a passing waiter, before sitting on the stool opposite him.

"Hello sweetheart," she said, looking directly at him. "What's a good looking man like your 'onour doing in 'ere?"

He returned her stare. Sixteen or seventeen, with a slender frame, largish breasts and long curly hair and he could see, even in the dim light, that she was pretty and not yet ravaged by the demands of her profession. He was on the point of telling her to go and park her arse elsewhere when the waiter put her order for wine on the table.

"There yer are," she said, sliding one of the pitchers towards him. "I'm Luisa. What do they call you?"

"William."

"You look tired William. 'ad a 'ard day?"

He grunted to himself and swigged more wine.

She poured wine from her pitcher into his. "Want to talk about it?"

He shook his head. He'd had eaten very little, the wine was strong and it was blunting his memory of the day's events.

"Well, what would yer like to do?"

William looked up from his wine and gave her a hard stare. Her words had sounded innocent but they both knew what she meant.

"We can talk about something else, if yer like," she added quickly, frightened a little by the way he'd looked at her.

William stared down morosely at the table and she took the opportunity to have a better look at the man she'd picked as her last *mark* for the night. He was getting on, probably old enough to be her father, not that she cared — her preference was for one of the other girls. But there was something about the way he'd stared that had frightened her. In the two years since she'd taken up whoring, only once had she been seriously knocked about: by a half demented soldier, when she'd try to steal his purse. It was a mistake that she'd never repeated: she didn't steal off her marks now and, if she could afford to be choosy, she wouldn't go with anyone she thought was *loco.* Her instincts told her that this one was dangerous and she wasn't sure whether to take a chance with him. There had been a couple of likely looking marks at the bar when she'd sat down, but they'd been claimed a moment ago by two of the other girls. The rest of the customers were just the regular drinkers. Come on girl! she thought, you're putting too much time into this bastard, get off your arse and go, and if he wants it, charge him double.

"I'm sorry yer 'onour, I thought yer wanted company. Thanks for the drink."

She started to rise, but he put his hand on her arm. He'd taken a large dose of self-pity with his wine and it had overcome him. He had nothing that he could call his own, not a soul in the world cared whether he lived or died, he'd tried to kill the only real friend he'd ever had and now he'd brought dishonour on himself. He had squandered his life and Philipe's besides. He hadn't even got a place to lay his head. He was afraid suddenly: of leaving the noisy taberna and spending the night with his thoughts in the stable. But most of all, he was afraid of being alone.

"No, don't go, stay and talk to me," he said. "Don't worry," he added, as heard her disgruntled sigh, "I'll pay for your time. What's the usual price?"

"It depends whether it's just a quick one or yer want me for the night."

He reached under his cloak and slipped a coin out of his purse and slid it across the table. "Will that be enough? I only want to talk."

She stared at the coin in disbelief. She had readied herself to ask double, thinking he'd turn her down flat, but what he was offering was as much as she'd earn over several nights. She'd be loco if she walked away from money like that. She hadn't marked him as one of the types who wanted to talk before they had her — the shy ones, or those that wanted to save her for Jesus — but she was sure, with the money he was paying, that he wanted her for the night.

"What do yer want to talk about?" she asked, although she knew from experience that men wanted to talk only about themselves.

"Tell me about yourself. Tell me all the reasons why you're working here tonight. And get Arturo to bring more wine."

He didn't know whether her story was true, or not. She had been orphaned when she was eight years old and an old woman — her grandmother she thought — had given her to the nuns, who had beaten her and used her as a drudge. Escaping from their clutches when she was fifteen she had been seen on the street by the taberna's owner and offered a job as a bar wench. She'd soon found out that bar wenches had to rely on customers tipping and most customers expected to get their hand up her skirts if they were tipping. After several months of being groped she'd decided that if the customers wanted to get their hands on her they'd have to pay the going rate, so she became a whore.

While she talked she watched him drinking, assessing whether he was getting to a state where he'd be incapable. She'd seen from the first that he was tired and she was sure she'd have a quiet time with him, if she could keep him swilling. He'd spend his seed, and then she'd leave him snoring while she spent the night with Camilla. She kept on talking, spinning it out, encouraging him to keep drinking and, when at last she finished her story, she thought she'd drawn most of his sting. He'd got spark enough for 'quick one', but once he'd shot his bolt he'd spend the rest of the night sleeping.

"Come on sweetheart," she said. "Let's 'ave yer up on yer feet."

He struggled to stand, but the combination of wine, weariness and melancholy had sapped him and he was willing to accept her help to get up from the table.

"I'll get us a room." She turned towards the bar and nodded at Arturo who acknowledged her gesture by raising his finger.

"No, I've got to go, I'm leaving for Leon at dawn," said William.

It sounded half hearted and she ignored it. She'd had trouble before with marks who'd said 'no', but then turned nasty when she'd walked away and she knew that whatever they said, once they'd paid their money, they wouldn't be thwarted. Putting her arm around his waist, and his over her shoulder, she guided him through the door with its sign for the taberna's whores and down a dark corridor. After a dozen or so paces they came into a small room, whose only light was the flame from a reeking taper.

"Please, I have to get back to the stable," he muttered, "I've got to be up by dawn."

"Don't worry, sweetheart." She chuckled, briefly. "You'll be up, and down again well before then."

35

The sky in the east was bright pink when William, wincing every time its hinges squeaked, eased open the door of the hostal's stable. He slipped through and, after closing it gently behind him, he tiptoed across to an empty stall and lay down on the straw. Lying on his back, listening to Eduardo's steady snoring, he asked himself what he should do. When he'd left the stable less than ten hours earlier he was already twice damned in the eyes of God: he'd broken his vow of obedience, worse still, he had broken his oath to protect Cristina. Now, he was unchaste. He smiled to himself grimly; the only vow he hadn't broken was his commitment to poverty. In the course of just one day his world had disintegrated — he'd lost his honour, his self-respect and destroyed the life of a lady he admired and respected. How had he come to this? What, in Christ's name, had possessed him? He knew the answer; it was pride. It had puffed him up and then it had betrayed him: even with the whore he had been guilty of it.

She had woken him with a beaker of water laced with wine as dawn was breaking and, as he drank it, he'd surveyed the mean little room where he had spent the night. It smelled of stale sweat and urine and it was filthy. He felt squalid and, although he couldn't remember the way of it, he knew from the stains on his linens that he'd spent his seed. He'd thought to ask whether he'd entered her, or if she'd merely stimulated him. But he'd been with whores aplenty in his youth and he knew, however much he pleaded, that she'd merely praise his prowess and tell him what all her marks wanted to hear. He realised too that he was only intent on splitting hairs. To argue the manner of his sin before God and the Temple was of scant consequence. In the eyes of both there was only one truth, simple and inescapable — he had lain down with a woman. Why hadn't he listened to his conscience as he'd stood outside the taberna? Pride; that was why. He'd thought he knew better and the Devil had led him into drunkenness and fornication to compound his sin.

What should he do? He could turn away from virtue and say nothing in the confessional, but that would mean denying the oath he'd sworn as a knight. He would have to confess to lying with a whore and Ponferrada's chaplain would have no option but to report it. However, the burden of his remorse came not from breaking his vows to the Temple — although he knew they would serve up hard punishment — but from his feelings for Cristina. He might try to deny it, but he knew in his heart that he cared for her and that his guilt over the harlot sprang, not from his love of the Templars, but because he felt he'd been unfaithful to Cristina.

"Good morning, your honours!" the stableman's voice boomed, making William jump and jolting Eduardo out of his sleep. He strode across the stable and flung open its doors so that they banged loudly. Then he looked up at the sky and sniffed. "It's going to be a hot one today and no mistake," he said to himself. "Come on now gentleman, rise and shine!"

William stood up and went over to the horse trough. Ordinarily he wouldn't have exposed himself, but it would be blisteringly hot on the trail and he didn't want Cristina or Pilar scenting the smell of a woman about him. To Eduardo's and the stableman's astonishment, he stripped off his clothes and lay full length in its stagnant water.

"You'll catch your death, for Christ's sake!" the stableman roared, as William swirled water vigorously around his crotch.

"Give me something to dry myself," he said, to Eduardo, once he was thoroughly doused.

The coachman threw him a horse blanket and he was standing in the trough, rubbing himself down when, without warning, Pilar and the hostal's maid — a girl of about sixteen — entered from the street.

"Holy Mother!" breathed Pilar, the moment she saw him.

"How do you fancy a bit of that?" whispered the maid, to no one in particular.

He wrapped the blanket around his middle quickly, but not quickly enough to hide himself and he cringed inside. Jesus Christ! he thought. Is there no end to my humiliation?

The maid was carrying a tray with his and Eduardo's breakfast. Leaving Pilar standing in the doorway, she came over and balanced it on the edge of the trough. After giving him a smile and a wink of her eye, she dropped a brief curtsey and left.

"My lady wishes to leave as soon as possible your honour," said Pilar, who had regained her composure.

He saw her reddened eyes and the dark blotches on her cheeks and felt shame anew at his failure to protect her and Cristina.

"Please tell Dona Delmirez that we shall leave as soon as the horses are harnessed," said William, wanting to say something to show how badly he felt for deserting her at the coach. But he decided it was best not to speak of it in front of Eduardo and the stableman. "Does the lady intend to ride today?"

Pilar shook her head. "No, your honour, my lady will ride in the coach."

She curtseyed quickly and had turned to go when William called softly after her: "Pilar, can I speak to you for a moment?"

To ask after the state of her mistress was improper he knew; he would do so nevertheless and, clutching the blanket he stepped out of the trough, and with one hand holding on to it tightly, he guided Pilar a little way down the street.

"How are you this morning?" he asked, quietly, once they were out of Eduardo's and the stableman's hearing.

Pilar had witnessed every word that had passed between the knight and her mistress at the coach and she'd wanted to shout and rail at him too. But she'd thought about it a lot since then. It had been terrible, there was no denying it, but the men were dead and neither she nor her mistress had been violated. Eduardo had told her about their knight's prowess, nevertheless she had her doubts: if he hadn't had surprise on his side she wondered whether he could have overcome all six of the swine in a straight fight. And if he'd been killed there was no telling what the bandidos would have done to her and Lady Cristina.

"Still a bit shaky sir. I find myself weeping every now and again, I try to stop it, but it just comes over me. I expect it'll pass though. Mind you, things could have been a lot worse. It was only when I was falling asleep last night I realised I hadn't thanked you for saving us."

Her honest words of gratitude pierced his guts like a dagger.

"I don't deserve any thanks. If I'd stayed with you at the coach it wouldn't have happened."

"You can't be sure of that your honour. From what I saw of the swines they'd have chanced their luck whether you were there or not. If you ask me it's probably lucky you weren't. There were six of them you know sir, and they were all armed to the teeth. It must have been a surprise when you came at them out of nowhere. Eduardo says —"

"And how is your mistress?" William interrupted.

Pilar shook her head slowly. "Although I shouldn't say it, your honour, she's an awful proud lady, and this has been a terrible shock for her. She cried a lot last night. Sobbing quietly, trying not to let me hear her. She was just the same when her father and brothers died: one face for the world, another in private —" Pilar sighed. "But I'm sure in a little while she'll get over it. I mean, neither of us was actually — well; you know what I mean sir. We weren't, you know— ?"

"I understand what you mean Pilar. And thank you for talking to me."

"You're welcome, your honour."

He was overwhelmed by a surge of relief: Cristina had not been raped. Thank you Mary, Mother of God, thank You, thank You, thank You, he whispered. He realised a moment later however that Pilar's news had chased only some of his woe away. He might be relieved that the Virgin had saved Cristina from a woman's worst fate, but nothing had changed for her. She had been dishonoured horribly, as far as she was concerned it was the same as rape. She would never forget it. He was responsible and nothing he could say or do would bring comfort to her.

Eduardo was finishing his breakfast when William returned to the stable.

"Are you wanting to eat some of this your honour?" he asked. "Or shall I give it to the stableman?"

William's first thought was to deny himself food as penitence. His head was aching, his mouth was rank, and he felt weary too. But the scent of fresh baked bread was tempting and if anything should happen on the trail that day he'd overcome it better with food in his belly. He would eat.

"Did you find a good place to sup last night, your honour?" asked Eduardo, watching William tuck into bread and blood sausage like a ravenous hound.

William filled his beaker with a mixture of water and wine and drank it straight off. "Yes, it was good."

"Hmm. I suppose they must have served up small portions then," Eduardo said, slyly, continuing to watch William cramming the remaining food in his mouth. "You missed a good meal here, your honour. Her Ladyship sent down a brace of roasted partridges and a big empanada. The pastry was just right and it was stuffed full with chicken and ham. That serving girl came with it just after you'd gone. I didn't think you'd be coming back with an empty belly so I had the lot. By the time I'd finished it was almost midnight. You didn't say where you were sleeping so I left the latch up on the stable door, just in case. I hope your honour got in all right?"

"Yes, thank you. Did Dona Delmirez send down to speak to me while I was away?"

Eduardo shook his head. "No your honour, not a word."

"Right! Let's get going. I'll get dressed and saddle the stallion while you harness the team. And be slippy about it, I don't want to keep your mistress waiting."

"Immediately, your honour," said Eduardo obsequiously, but once William's back was turned he smiled: he was a cunning old devil and he knew that he'd just scored a couple of points off the Templar. He wished he could have done a lot more: after what had happened on the trail he wished with all his heart that he could have set about the bastard and given him the thrashing he deserved. He couldn't of course, he wasn't a bloody knight, he had to touch his forelock and bow to his betters, but he prayed that God would punish the Templar. Look at the swine. he thought, watching the knight putting on his chausses. He couldn't swear to it, but he was almost certain the Englishman had spent the night in a brothel. So much for the Templar's vow of chastity, he thought, all that strut and swagger and the first chance he gets he's off with a whore.

It was nine leagues from Astorga to Leon and William estimated that it would take about nine hours. The plain that lay between the two cities had been forested once, but it was featureless now and dead. While the identity of those who had destroyed the forest was uncertain, everyone knew the Camino followed the road that the Romans had built to carry gold from their mines in Galicia to the city of Zaragoza. Its gullies had collapsed with the passing of time and its paving stones stolen for building elsewhere, but it had left an indelible mark on the landscape and from Astorga to Leon the trail ran as straight as an arrow.

They had set out at the beginning of the second hour when the air was still fresh and cool. As each hour passed it grew hotter and by the time the sun was nearing its zenith it seemed as if the land itself was pulsating. There was no shade and the only relief came from an occasional westerly breeze. William's linen shirt and breeches were sodden under his armour, his head was pouring sweat and he longed to strip off and wash, even though the Rule forbade it when he was on duty in the field. In both Spain and Outreamer he'd disobeyed when he'd thought it safe to do so, but after what had happened outside Astorga he would follow the Rule henceforth and endure. Orbigo was the first stopping place and they could only plod on, under the scorching sun, listening to the horses panting and the coach, banging and bumping over the old road's stones.

Orbigo, or to call it by its full name — Hospital de Orbigo — was a large hostal with facilities for sick pilgrims. It stood on the eastern side of a river some two hundred paces north of a bridge. The river was deep and wide and, as there was no ford within easy reach, traffic had to cross it at Orbigo's bridge. Rome's Legions had built it to carry their road and it had received scant maintenance since. Crumbling stone had been patched with mortar, its arches were shored with timbers and unless a patron could be found to rebuild it, the bridge was destined to fall.

An hour away from Orbigo they began to meet pilgrims who had left it that morning on their journey westwards to Santiago and, as William's little party continued east, they met more and more. Some were on horseback or riding in coaches. A few — of noble birth — rode with their armed retainers. Merchants and others with money enough had mercenaries in their company: old soldiers mostly, or bounty hunters — the type of scum that could be found in any of the low tabernas in the Camino towns. Most pilgrims were walking however and attired in traditional dress: a dun coloured cloak and long wooden staff, drinking gourd and food pouch hitched around their waist, a wide brimmed hat and sandals on their feet, except for the truly devout who went barefoot.

Arriving shortly after noon, they found Orbigo already crowded with pilgrims who had stopped there for a siesta. The noble and the rich had commandeered their customary spot on the north side of the bridge. The trees grew more densely here and the shade was better. More importantly, it was upstream from the hostal's open sewer that carried a constant flow of vile effluent into the river. Canopies and tents, brightly coloured in hues of red, yellow and blue, had been pitched by servants for their masters and mistresses who were lying on rugs and cushions, eating and drinking, talking and laughing, or simply taking their ease. It reminded William of a tourney field.

Not a scrap of shade had been left unclaimed and, once they had crossed the river, William led Eduardo off the trail and down the dusty track that ran along the top of the riverbank on the south side of the bridge. This was the preserve of common pilgrims. It was crowded too, but most had congregated within the immediate vicinity of the bridge. A few had stripped off and were disporting, naked, in the filthy river, jeering and catcalling their more modest brethren. The majority however was lying on the ground, snoozing, with the cowls of their dun cloaks pulled over their heads to block the sun.

By the time they had gone a hundred paces, the riverbank was almost free of them. In another fifty paces it was deserted and William turned off the track and dismounted in the shade of some trees. Eduardo pulled up his team; William pulled down the coach's step and offered his hand to help Cristina and Pilar to step down. Pilar dipped her head in thanks, but Cristina did not acknowledge even his presence. The food that Pilar had ordered from the hostal's kitchen was placed on a blanket and consumed in an icy silence, with Pilar and Eduardo choosing to sit some distance away from each other and further away still from their mistress. William ate little and his eyes were roving constantly: on guard against anyone who might think to enter the space that he had designated as theirs. He thought it unlikely that they would be accosted. He was taking no chances nevertheless, and when several French pilgrims came down the track from the bridge singing a rude song he stood up to face them with sword drawn. They were rowdy with too much midday wine, but the moment they saw his bared blade and the meaning in his silent stare they departed quickly.

An hour after leaving Orbigo the wind backed to the south and grew in strength as it sucked hot air from the *meseta*. As afternoon's heat increased so did the breeze and by the third hour clouds of yellow dust, borne on a howling wind were buffeting them. Hot fine grit pricked their eyes and blocked nostrils and ears; their hair and faces, slick with sweat, were soon caked with it; and it found ways to insinuate itself inside clothes and boots where it soon began to itch and chafe. Most of the pilgrims they passed had discarded temporarily their broad brimmed hats and were walking, eyes cast down, heads sunk deep inside the cowls of their cloaks, which were flapping and slapping against their ankles and calves.

The dust storm abated finally in the late afternoon and within an hour Leon came into view. Sensing they were nearing the end of the journey the horses quickened their pace and in no time at all William, who was riding a little way ahead, could see the detail of the bastions on the city's old Roman walls. He pulled up his stallion and waited for the coach to catch up.
"Where will you stay, my lady?" he asked, bending forward in the saddle to speak to Cristina.
"At the Guzman's Palace. Do you know it?" she replied without looking at him.
"Yes lady, I know it."

They followed the Camino into Leon, crossing the bridge over the river that flowed by the western side of the city. A little further on they passed the great Hospital of San Marcos, built by the Knights of Santiago as both a sanctuary for weary pilgrims and their Order's headquarters. At this time of day in high summer it was thronged with pilgrims, sitting together in groups, talking and laughing or engaged in serious discussion. Continuing on, they entered the city through the Puerto de Castilla and once inside they turned right into Plaza de Castillo. It was full of pilgrims and their babble was deafening and, as they pushed through the crush, William heard spoken French, both langue d'oc and langue d'oil, German and Italian as well as tongues unknown to him.

Once across the square they made better progress and they soon came to the Basilica that contained the sacred bones of Saint Isidoro. As they passed by its *Puerta del Pardon* — the first 'pardon door' on the Camino — William crossed himself, saluting its power to give absolution to those who were too sick or weak to reach the blessings of Santiago. Past the Basilica, he signalled Eduardo to head towards the widest thoroughfare on the south side of its plaza. It was a short street and it led directly into another square that was dominated by the Guzman's Palace. William rode up to announce the arrival of Dona Delmirez to the guards in Guzman livery who were standing outside and, after a brief glance of verification, they signalled for the gates to be opened and bid them enter.

They came immediately into a large enclosed courtyard with a cobbled floor and low ceiling that made the coach wheels' clatter seem very loud. Eduardo halted the horses beside a set of bronzed doors that led directly into the Palace's large patio. They were open and William could see the garden beyond. As he dismounted several servants emerged from a side door and walked quickly across the cobbles to the coach. They opened its door and bowed to Cristina as she stepped out. After giving instructions to Pilar and Eduardo she signalled to William to accompany her into the patio.

"This is far enough," she said, as they reached the fountain at its centre.
Turning to face him she reached inside her sleeve and took out a small scroll of paper. William recognised it immediately as the letter he had brought to her from Diego Delmirez.
"You will need to give this to my uncle when you return to Samos. It tells him I have arrived safely. He won't help you unless you give it to him, so don't lose it."
"My lady, I know there's nothing I can —"
"Don't interrupt me!" She took a deep breath. "When my uncle asks you how I am, I expect you to tell him I am well and that you delivered me safely. I don't want him to know what has happened. Do you understand?"
"Yes."
"Good! I also want to make it plain that I hold you to your honour never to breathe a word of it. Not even to your confessor. Is that clear?"
"You have my —" He was about to say 'word' but he saw her stiffen with anger. "Yes, my lady," he said, bowing his head in obedience.
"Good. That's all. You may go."
"Your surcoat, my lady?" he asked, hesitantly, as she turned away.
"Just go, damn you!"

37

It was the third hour of the day, the bells were tolling for *Terce* and William was in the Leon commandery, waiting to see Henri Pelet, knight of the Temple and its Provincial Commander for Leon and Castile. In ordinary circumstances he would have gone to the Order's house on the previous evening to report his presence in the city and he would have stayed there overnight. But the circumstances of the previous evening had been far from ordinary. After Cristina's dismissal he'd sat in the square outside the Guzman Palace for a long time, remembering every syllable and nuance in her last words to him. She hated him. He was a Judas and, like Iscariot, he had no hope of redemption. The prospect of reporting to the Order's house and resuming normal life was too dispiriting to contemplate and on the spur of the moment he had gone directly to *El Vellon de Oro*, one of Leon's better hostals, where he had taken a room for the night.

The 'Golden Fleece' was on the west side of the newly named Plaza de Catedral and, after giving his horse into the care of its stableman, he had taken his saddlebags up to his room. It was quite small: a big featherbed occupied most of it, a table with a water jug, wash bowl and towel were crammed into a corner and the piss pot was in the usual place, behind the door. The room was cool however and it looked out onto Cathedral Square and, once he'd opened the window's shutters, he could see men digging the foundations for Leon's Cathedral, which had been decreed by the King the previous year. After removing his armour he stretched out on the featherbed. It was soft and comfortable, its white linen cover smelled fresh and clean and he lay on his back for some time, watching the sky getting darker, reliving his last moments with Cristina Delmirez. He deserved her contempt. He had sworn to protect her; instead he had betrayed her and he would carry the shame of it forever. Closing his eyes he thought back to their first meeting and wondered in the light of the way he felt now, how he could have been indifferent to her.

It was near dusk when he awoke. Summoning up sufficient energy, he rolled off the bed, stripped and washed off the Camino's dust. He felt wretched. Nevertheless, he must drink down the gall he'd been served and take up life again as a Templar — there was no other choice. And he would start by going for a walk to the plaza mayor. He would have to be careful however: staying at the Golden Fleece rather than the commandery was a serious infraction of the Rule. The Order kept only a small complement of men in Leon and it was unlikely that he would be seen, even so he took the precaution of slipping Soria's surcoat over his shirt and breeches. Then, after buckling his sword, he went out to face the world.

Leaving the hostal he turned right and walked, in the pale glow of evening, across to the south side of Cathedral Square and into the narrow streets of the *Barrio Humedo*. The 'Humid Quarter' was the heart of the city and for hundreds of summers it had played host to those who travelled the Camino. Pilgrims were everywhere: queuing in unruly little groups outside shops, bargaining with street vendors and cramming into *bodegas* and tabernas. In some drinking places the press was so great that they had spilled outside and were drinking their wine in the street. He continued until he reached Leon's main square, which lay at the barrio's centre. That too was packed with people. Leon's citizens, dressed in bright fashion, were strolling in family groups to take the evening air, soldiers, in their colours, were lounging outside tabernas and servants, in vivid liveries, were hurrying by on errands, but the pilgrims' dun garb was the dominant colour.

Moving into the melee, he let himself be carried along by the crowd as it swirled around a labyrinth of market stalls. On the outer edge of the plaza they were selling hot food: chicken, pork ribs, goat's meat on skewers, slices of boar, partridges, quail and other wild birds and legs of baby lamb. An inner ring of stalls was selling cold cuts of mutton, pork, beef and ham, wines and cheeses. The smells and sounds of the market assaulted his senses: people shouting orders, squabbling over queuing; the sizzle and scent of meat cooking; pine wood smouldering and smoking, making eyes sting; the rush of heat when he passed an ox roasting. Swept along by the crowd he came finally to where the street players gathered. There were acrobats, dancers, jugglers, jesters, fire-eaters and a magician, all dressed in motley of red, green, yellow and blue, and people were laughing at their antics and crowding around them, jostling their neighbours and craning their necks to see. Others, on the fringes of the crowds, were on the lookout too: gamberros, tough and wise beyond their years, pickpockets, pimps and their whores, all scouting for a likely mark. The crush was suffocating. Standing in the plaza's centre, watching the street lighters fire it torches and intoxicated by the sights and cacophony of sounds, he almost forgot what had happened outside Astorga.

He felt hungry suddenly. He felt too that this was his last night of freedom and on the spur of the moment he decided to search out a bodega called *Racimo de Oro*. After some searching he found it in the southeast corner of the little Plaza San Martin. The owner of the 'Bunch of Gold' claimed it had been founded nearly fifty years earlier, in 1160; nobody knew if his claim was true but it was known throughout Leon for the excellence of its food. He ordered roast suckling pig and a pitcher of good wine. The pork was delicious — the best he'd tasted in years — and he ate with gusto. It was later, when he was sitting alone at a table and sipping the last of his wine that he decided it was time he cleared his slate with God.

He knew the proverb, 'pride goeth before a fall' and he saw now the truth of it. Pride was his god; he might speak of 'honour', but in reality he thought only of himself and how the world judged him. He had always blamed Elizabeth for Balleranche's murder, rather than himself. Her rejection had been a grievous wound to his pride and killing the object of her desire was the best way he knew to repay her. Now Fortuna was paying him back in kind. Cristina was everything he'd ever searched for in a woman: brave, beautiful, independent yet loyal, resourceful and wise. He cared for her deeply — no matter that he'd sworn to deny womankind — and he would live with love unrequited for the rest of his life. He could see the justice in Fortuna's judgement and the better part of him saluted her sentence, but before he began it he had to stand before God, open his heart and admit his crimes.

At dawn on the morrow, dressed in nothing save his breeches, he would walk barefoot to the church of San Marcos, where he would confess his sins. He would commence by telling the priest that he had never truly repented the murder of Edmund Balleranche and ask for forgiveness. Then he would confess his sins of pride and fornication. Afterwards, when he had completed his penance, he would kneel before the altar and talk to God about Cristina. He was the cause of her suffering; he would never forgive himself and he would not ask God to do so. He would pray instead for Him to bring her comfort. And he would swear to go to her aid if ever she needed it, whatever the cost to him. In his pride he had been quick to judge Philipe and he'd nearly killed him for speaking the truth. He would ask God's forgiveness for it. His friend had paid dearly for a crime that he, William, had committed and he would promise to tell Philipe the truth and seek his forgiveness when next they met. Finally, he would tell Him of his failures of duty over the past days — ignoring his superiors' orders, forgetting to say his Paternosters and being out of proper uniform — he would restate his vows and ask God to accept him back as a loyal knight of the Temple.

He paid for his meal and feeling a little happier for having made his resolution he began to walk back to the Golden Fleece. It was noisy still in the direction of the plaza mayor but the streets in the barrio were almost empty of pilgrims and those that were still abroad were scurrying back to their hostals, their minds preoccupied with next day's journey. William too was thinking about the morrow and rather than dawdle he took the quickest way back to the hostal, along a street that led, by twists and turns, from Saint Martin's to Cathedral Square. It was wider than many and lit with torches, although their guttering flames seemed only to deepen the shadows.

He stepped out and had almost reached Cathedral Square when he heard footsteps behind him, coming quickly along the street. It could have been pilgrims but his instincts told him he was in danger and, offering a quick prayer, he turned on his heels. Facing him were the two young Castilian knights that he'd seen earlier in the plaza mayor. Close up, in the torchlight, he could see that there were little more than boys.

"Are you walking my way, sirs?" he asked in a friendly way.

"I doubt it," said the taller of the two. "You're sworn to Soria: anyone going your way believes we should surrender to the Moor."

William glanced down at his surcoat and thought, for an instant, to tell them that they had made a mistake and that he was really a Templar. He discarded the idea immediately. It was too complicated to explain and they were too drunk to hear him out.

"Don't look down when I'm talking to you!" said the tall one. "Look me in the face and tell me we should be friends to those swine. Come on, I dare you! You wear Soria's colours. Speak up for your masters!"

Was God testing him to see if he could abide by the Rule? On the matter of duelling and the tourney, it was categorical: 'a Templar knight must not shed the blood of another Christian knight unless he be so ordered by his Master.'

"Calm down Cristobel, for Jesu's sake!" said his companion. "Can't you see he's an old man? Let him go home."

Cristobel turned on his friend. "Can my father or uncles go home? No, they can't!" He spun round on William. "And do you know why? Because they were killed at Alarcos by the vermin that Diego Delmirez wants us to be nice to. Were you at Alarcos, old man?"

William shook his head. "No."

"No, I bet you weren't. Too busy kissing the Moor's arse I expect. Well, just for that I'm going to teach you a lesson!"

He reached for his sword, but before it was clear of its scabbard William brought the heel of his hand up, under the young knight's jaw, with such force that it lifted him off his feet and backwards onto the ground. Clenching his fists William turned to strike the other knight, but he stepped back quickly, holding up his hands in a gesture of surrender.

"What's your name?" William asked him.

"Rodrigo," he said as he knelt to examine his friend.

"Is he bleeding?"

"No."

"Thank God for that. Where are you staying?"

"In the knights' dormitory at San Marcos. We've come to Leon to take our vows to become Knights of Santiago."

"I'm going your way then, come on I'll give you a hand as far as Cathedral Square."

Between them, they hauled Cristobel to his feet and helped him along until he was steady enough to walk unaided.

"By the way," said William as they arrived outside the Golden Fleece. "I think you should know that Diego Delmirez lost his brother and four nephews at Alarcos. And as for you my friend," he added, squeezing Cristobel's arm, "don't be so anxious to fight. You'll live longer. Goodnight and God go with you."

Back in his room, he undressed down to his shirt, blew out the taper and knelt by the bed. If his encounter had been a test he thought he had passed it. He would keep vigil until dawn as he had on the night before Philpe's father had dubbed him. Then, at first light, he would go to San Marcos to confess his sins and rededicate his life as a soldier of Christ.

Returning to the Golden Fleece from San Marcos the next morning, William had gone to his room where he had washed himself and put on his hauberk, chausses, Templar's surcoat and sword. Arriving at the Order's house, he had gone to the first floor and announced himself to the clerk, who had asked him to sit down and wait.

"Will the Commander be much longer?" William asked the clerk, after he'd been waiting for half an hour outside Pelet's office.

"I really can't say sir," said the clerk, without looking up from his work.

His words were polite; nevertheless, from the moment of his greeting his manner had betrayed a disregard for ordinary serving knights: particularly those bumpkins who were stationed in the wastes beyond Leon.

Bored, William gazed around the anteroom to Pelet's office for the umpteenth time. It had one small window and the room was so dim he wondered how the clerk could see to work, even though he had lit two acrid smelling tapers and stuck them in their holders on his desk. He was surprised too by the volume of paper in the room. He had never seen it in England when he was a boy. In Spain however it was almost abundant. He had heard the Moors had developed a cheap way of making it by pressing rags that had been saturated with water and he wondered whether they traded it, or whether Christians had learned the same technique. He counted several scores of scrolls. Some were big; others small, all secured with red ribbons and stored on shelves that ran across two of the anteroom's walls. What on earth did they record? And why was it necessary to write so much down? The sound of a small bell tinkling interrupted his thoughts. The clerk left his high desk, rapped his knuckle once on the door of Pelet's office and entered. William could hear voices talking, but their words were muted and indistinct. After a few moments the clerk reappeared.

"The Commander will see you now, sir," he said to William.

The Commander's room was bright and spacious. It looked out on the plaza mayor and sounds of people at the morning market were coming through its open windows. Two knights were sitting in ornately carved chairs on opposite sides of a table, which was set with a pitcher of wine, two gold cups and a bowl containing walnuts and dried fruit. Both were dressed in Templar uniform — a white robe with a single red cross — and the first thing William noticed was that their's were made of far richer cloth than the standard issue. One knight was old, probably over sixty, completely bald, with watery eyes and a long, bushy white beard. The other, who was nearer to Montagnac's age, was overweight from lack of exercise and his face bore the scars of a childhood pox.

Neither spoke to William as he entered, nor did they rise to greet him. Indeed, the only recognition of his presence came when the older one pointed to a low stool by the office door and nodded that he should sit on it.

"Our clerk says your name is William Stanley and that you're based at Ponferrada. Is that correct?" asked the younger one in Castilian flavoured with the nasal twang of langue d'oil.

"That's correct," said William, as he sat down. He glanced at each in turn. "And you are?"

"Wait a minute, you're not *the* William Stanley, are you? The one who was in Richard Lionheart's bodyguard?" asked the older knight, speaking in langue d'oil.

"Yes. Were you there?" William looked at the old man trying to remember if he'd seen him in the Holy Land.

"No. Never been to Outreamer unfortunately. Wanted to mind you, but the powers that be always found work for me elsewhere. I know a lot who were though." He turned to his colleague. "This is the knight I told you about, the one commended for valour by England's King, Richard." He stood up and held out his hand to William. "I'm sorry, I'm Henri Pelet, Provincial Commander. This is my deputy."

"Roland Meaux, pleased to meet you," said the young one. "Is it true you killed more Saracens at Jaffa than the Lionheart himself?"

William smiled, briefly. "I don't know, I wasn't counting."

"What are you doing here?" asked Pelet.

"I've been sent by Robert Montagnac to report a murder —"

"No, what are you doing *here*, in Spain?"

"I was posted here after Alarcos."

"Christ's Blood! I would have thought they could have found someone other than you — you're one of the best we've got — you should be in Outreamer, not here. Who was the fool who thought that up?"

William shrugged.

"And do you mean to say you've been stuck at Ponferrada since — when was that damned battle?"

"1195. I arrived here in '97. I'd like to get back to Outreamer, if I could sir."

"You see Roland?" said Pelet. "This is just what I've been talking about. Sweet Mary! How many more of our best men have been sent off to rat holes like Ponferrada, I wonder? God in Heaven, we're governed by idiots!"

Meaux sighed. "You were telling us about a murder?"

"Yes. Ten days ago a monk called Rolfe du Cardiaye was murdered on the Camino at Foncebadon. He was Deputy Prior of Cluny and he was on Papal commission."

"What was the purpose of the commission?" asked Meaux.

"We don't know. His authority was stained with blood, it was impossible to read it."

"Why did Montagnac send you here to tell us this? And why has it taken so long?" Meaux asked again.

"He wanted to carry out a preliminary investigation, before everything went cold. He believes, and I do too, that there's a lot more to this than meets the eye."

"And what does he believe?"

"A conspiracy of some kind. When I found the murderer —"

"You've found the murderer?" interrupted Meaux. "Who was it, someone important?"

"A Moor, a horse thief, but when I found him he was already dead; killed by the man who'd hired him."

"And is he important?"

"I don't know, but I think so. I found Cardiaye's journal and I'm sure it will tell us why he was killed and who did it."

"Have you brought the journal with you?"

"Yes."

William took the journal out of Cardiaye's leather pouch and passed it across the table to Meaux, who scanned the pages quickly.

"It reads like a record of a journey to me," he said. "Where does it say who's going to kill him?"

"It doesn't exactly, but if you look at the last page you can see he's written down some kind of formula."

"This you mean?" asked Meaux, holding up the page and pointing to the formula. "What does it say?"

"I don't know. It's in code, but I've got someone deciphering it."

Meaux passed the page to Pelet, who studied it for several moments before handing it back. Meaux put it on top of the other pages, secured them with their binding ribbon and passed the journal back to William who returned it to the pouch.

"Let me see if I've got this right, William," said Pelet, briskly. "Montagnac's sent you to tell us that a monk's been killed on the Camino. You say he was Deputy Prior of Cluny. Well, that may be so, and a hundred or even fifty years ago that would have been news, but Cluny is nowhere near as important as it used to be, but never mind. Now, you say this monk was on a commission for the Pope, but you don't know what it is. A horse thief killed him, but when you found the thief he was already dead, killed, you think, by the man who hired the thief. This man might be important, but you don't know who he is and you can't prove that he hired the thief. But we'll know what all this means once that — what did you call it, a formula? Once that's been decoded. Is that about the strength of it?"

Meaux smiled at William. "A monk has been murdered, a horse thief did it and now he's dead. What does Montagnac think we should do with this vital piece of intelligence? Report it to the King? Tell it to the Legate so that he can

Stuart J Dimmock

write to the Pope? Or perhaps he thinks we should send news to the Master of Jerusalem?"

"I'm sorry William, but you can see what Meaux's saying," said Pelet. He shook his head. "It's not your fault; we're not blaming you. But this is typical of Montagnac. He sees conspiracies everywhere. He was exactly the same when he was working at the Court of Aragon. I know he's your Master and I shouldn't be saying this but, between you and me, this was the reason I sent him to Ponferrada, where he couldn't do any harm."

"But I think he's right this time sir," protested William.

"Listen William," said Meaux. "You're a fine soldier, and I mean no disrespect, but you have to realise and make your Master understand that there are a lot more important things happening than a monk being murdered by a horse thief. Right now, for instance, we have reports from our spies in Seville that the Caliph is trying to buy mercenary troops in Africa. Now, it might be because the Moors are about to have one of their periodic falling outs over which favourite bastard son is going to inherit which *taifa*, on the other hand they might be going to attack us. Do you see what I'm saying? We will inform the Legate of your news, as a matter of courtesy, of course, although I doubt whether the Pope will be interested. He's pretty busy at the moment with this Cathar situation in southern France. Some say he might even call for a crusade. That will have huge implications for Aragon, it may even affect the Reconquista."

"So you can see why we're not very enthusiastic about your report," said Pelet. "But it was good to meet you and the next time you're in Leon you must come and see us so you can tell us about your time in Outreamer. All right?"

"I would like to —"

"If there's nothing else you may go," said Meaux, cutting across William's attempt to request a posting to Outreamer. "We'll need to keep a record for our files though, so you better give a few details to the clerk, but keep it brief, no suppositions or theories, just the facts."

"You've found the thief who murdered Cardiaye. Tell Montagnac the case is closed," said Pelet, as William rose from the stool.

Facing Pelet, he came to attention. "Sir, I would like to request a posting to Outreamer."

"Don't you know the rules? I can't deal with a request like that, but if you put it through the proper channels I'll see what I can do."

William had spent the next quarter of an hour in the anteroom retelling his report so that the clerk could prune it back to a half a dozen lines.

"What will you do with it?" asked William once the clerk had set it down in his spidery Latin script.

"All the miscellaneous stuff goes in there." He pointed at a wooden chest in the darkest corner of the room; even in the dim light it was plain to see that it was covered in thick dust. "I call it the 'just in case' file. Will you be staying here overnight? I'll need to tell the cook if you are."

"No, I'm leaving Leon directly for Ponferrada. My mission's over. I just have to collect my horse."

William rose from his stool and walked to the door.

"Have a safe journey sir. We wouldn't want you being attacked like the Bishop's man."

William came back into the room. "What did you say?"

"When?"

"Just now, about 'the Bishop's man'."

"I only heard about it the other day. Nicolo Clarini, he's secretary to the Bishop of Palencia. Well, not exactly secretary, a sort of jack of all trades really. Mind you, they say the Bishop holds him in high regard. That's why they call him 'the Bishop's man' I suppose. He was attacked by bandidos on the road from Toledo. God knows why he'd chosen to travel without an escort. Stupid if you ask me. It couldn't have been all that long ago. Let's see." He glanced through his note of William's report. "Yes, I thought so, it was around the time you were hunting this Moor. In fact you couldn't have been very far away when it happened."

"What became of him — 'the Bishop's man'?"

"He got back to Palencia I understand. Lost an eye though. He'd have given as good as he got mind you. They say he's a brilliant swordsman."

Holy Mother of God! No wonder he and Delmirez had been baffled: the Moor's girl hadn't said 'fisherman', what she'd said was 'Bishop's man'.

For a moment he thought to go back into the Pelet's office and tell him this new piece of information. He didn't, because he was certain that Meaux would dismiss it out of hand and treat him to another patronising lecture. He would discover the truth without their help. He snatched Cardiaye's journal and saddle pouch off the clerk's desk.

"Heavens, I nearly left without it," he said.

Indeed, after hearing Pelet's decision he had intended to leave it behind, but it was vital now to keep it.

"I'm sorry sir, you'll have to leave the journal with me. It has to be filed with my notes."

"Can't do that I'm afraid," William said brusquely. "You know the King's law: the effects of those who die on the Camino must be returned to their next of kin by the proper authorities. Ponferrada reported the death: it's our responsibility to see that these are returned to the Abbey of Cluny. Good day to you."

39

Leaving the commandery, William walked, almost literally, into Philipe de Tankerville who was coming across the crowded plaza mayor. They stood a few paces apart, oblivious of the people around them with Philipe eyeing William warily. William had already determined, at the altar of San Marcos, what he must do when next they met.

"I owe you an apology Philipe," he said, holding out his hand. "I shouldn't have hit you. I'm sorry, I've always loved you like a brother."

"By the Blood! I never thought to hear you say sorry," said Philipe, who'd expected that William would want to continue their fight. He looked him up and down and was surprised to see how gaunt and tired his friend looked. At the Maragatos taberna he'd been a picture of rude health, now he looked ill. "What's happened to you Will? You look awful."

"I've been taught a lesson."

"Who did that?"

"God, and the Devil."

"What did they teach you?"

"That I was too proud."

"That must have been hard for *you*."

"Philipe —" William glanced up at the sky momentarily, as if seeking guidance. "You were right about Balleranche, it wasn't an accident, I planned to kill him and I ruined your life in the process." Guilt welled up inside and he tried to hide his tears. "I wanted to say I was sorry, even at Bruges, but I lacked the courage to admit murder, even to you. I won't ask you to forgive me, not after all this time, but I want you to know that I am truly sorry."

Philipe was dumbfounded by William's sudden repentance. He knew his friend well enough to see it was genuine and he was unsure what to do. He'd thought a great deal about their meeting in the Maragateria. At first he'd been angry. He'd been humiliated publicly and in front of men he did business with and he'd wanted revenge. Once he'd sobered up he'd even thought to duel with William, although he knew he wouldn't win. He'd always been the wiser head however and on further reflection he'd realised that he'd been the architect of his own humiliation. He'd become a hardened drinker since his posting to Paris, although he'd taken care never to be intoxicated in front of other Templars. But seeing William in the taberna he'd set out to get drunk because he hadn't the pluck to accuse his friend of murder when sober. They had never exchanged blows in anger throughout all the time they'd been together, nevertheless he was well acquainted with William's temper and to get to the truth he'd goaded him into violence. He should have known better and appealed to William's honour. He was still unsure, even after William had hit him, whether Balleranche's death had been happenstance or murder. It could have been an accident. Injury and death were hazards of any tourney and several knights had spoken in William's favour at his trial. Indeed, some whispered that had Balleranche been a no-account, penniless knight it would have never come to a trial. Now William had told him the truth.

He'd always wanted an apology; he believed it was his right. William had just given him one and tears of heartfelt contrition. So, what should he do? Although he'd nursed his grievance for many years he'd always recognised that William had acted honourably towards him in the Bishop's Court. He had refused to plead murder, but he'd sworn repeatedly that his friend was innocent of any charge and argued violently when the Bishop refused to believe it. They'd had very little contact after their sentence: they'd been kept in different cells in the Bishop's gaol, they'd sailed to Outreamer separately and once there they'd served in different units. The only opportunity they'd had to talk was when William visited him in the infirmary at Acre, but it was not long after the amputation and he'd been far too ill to talk. Perhaps, if circumstances had been different, William and he would have spoken about it long before. William had a quick temper, but if he saw he was in the wrong he had always given the other man his due. Over the years Philipe had raged against his fate and thought of a host of ways he might get revenge on William. Now, this morning, facing his old friend in Leon's plaza mayor, he realised that he had two choices. He could act like a knight with honour, accept William's apology and forgive him, or he could spit in William's eye and walk away and spend the rest of his life whining about his fate like some damn clerk.

He reached out and grasped William's hand. "God in Heaven Will! Two sorrys in a single morning. It must have been one Hell of a lesson."

"It was." William clasped Philipe to him and sobbed. "I'm sorry old friend for what I did to you."

"Come on now Will, dry your eyes." He patted William's shoulder. "This isn't like you."

William wiped away his tears and they kissed each other on both cheeks.

"Tell me," said Philipe, as they broke their embrace, "who did you see at the commandery — Pelet or Meaux?"

"Both of them." He sniffed and wiped the last of his tears off his cheeks with the back of his hand.

"And what do you think of our Commander and Deputy? Have you met them before?"

"No." William paused. "I think they're very well suited to the tasks the Order has given them."

"That's very diplomatic of you Will, you don't usually beat about the bush. You're right though; they're a pair of popinjays. Clever, mind you, I wouldn't deny that and I hear they do an excellent job for us with the King.

But they've never seen a bloodied sword in their lives and Meaux would probably faint like a girl if he did. Still, I suppose we need men with brains as well as brawn."

"I wonder Philipe, could we go somewhere quiet? I want to talk to you about something."

"Of course, I know several places where we won't be disturbed."

They walked together across the plaza to a taberna with the sign of an eagle above its door. It's low ceiling and walls were stained with the smoke of many winters' fires and it seemed gloomy after the brilliant sunlight. Philipe asked for the keeper and when he appeared they agreed a small charge for the use of the patio and his promise that they would not be disturbed. Philipe gave the keeper a coin and he led them through the bar room, with its old wooden barrels that were used as tables, up a short flight of stairs and into a small, shady courtyard furnished with tables and stools. He offered them a free pitcher of cold wine, Philipe and William nodded their agreement and, after the bar wench had brought it, they settled down to talk.

"I haven't seen you in fifteen years," said William. "Then we meet twice in a couple of weeks. How is that?"

"When was the last time you were here, or in Burgos?"

"Here? Over a year ago and I haven't been to Burgos since God knows." He shrugged. "1203?"

"If you'd visited them more often I'm sure we would have met." Philipe smiled slyly at William. "Still, I expect you're too busy enjoying yourself riding up and down the Camino, huh? What do you like best — boredom or the dust? Still, I suppose Ponferrada's not a bad place to see out your sentence. A damn sight easier than being in Outreamer."

"I hate being at Ponferrada, it's just the same thing day after day, there's hardly any action. I want to get back to Outreamer. I told Pelet so."

"And what did he say?"

"He ignored it."

"Are you surprised — after what you did at Acre? God dammit Will, you challenged a King! And you did it in front of Robert de Sable."

"And he punished me for it."

"How?"

"A week or so later, before we marched south to Caesarea, I was ordered to attend him in Acre's citadel. The knight who brought the message said it was a minor matter and I didn't give it much thought. When I got there I found de Sable with a couple of his senior lieutenants and about a dozen knights in tow. I guessed what I was in for the moment I saw that they represented all of our different units. De Sable called on everyone to witness the punishment, then he read out the charge, I was stripped and he laid about me with a whip."

"How many lashes did you get?"

"Ten. I don't think de Sable wanted to beat me so that I wasn't fit enough to fight. It was about humiliation; to teach me about the importance of obedience and to make sure the message got back to everyone."

"But we heard in the infirmary that Richard had forgiven you in front of everybody."

"He did."

"So, do you think he asked de Sable to punish you, behind your back? De Sable would have done it, certainly. I mean, Richard virtually appointed him to his post as Grand Master. I know it was all done according to the Rule, but de Sable had hardly finished saying his joining vows when the Jerusalem chapter voted him."

"If Richard had wanted to punish me he'd have done it himself, in front of everyone, he wouldn't have sneaked off to de Sable. He wasn't that kind of man."

"Did he find out about it?"

"No. Why should he? It was Templar business, de Sable wouldn't have told him and I didn't."

"What happened after?"

"I was ordered not to report to the Infirmarer so I went and found a physician. Some of the scars from the Bishop's scourging had opened up again. He rubbed salt on my back and bound me. It hurt like Hell for a time and I had to wear an extra shirt under my hauberk. De Sable was in Richard's council so we were always bumping into each other, but he didn't speak of it and neither did I." He shrugged. "Why should we? I'd had my lesson; the business was over and done with."

"You really think so? Have you never thought to ask yourself why you were transferred to Spain?"

"Yes, but that was in '97, Gilbert Erail was Master of Jerusalem by then, de Sable had gone long since."

Philipe smiled and shook his head. "It wouldn't have mattered if Christ Himself had been Master. Do you know that people were still talking about it when I arrived at the Paris Temple? You're a marked man, Will, a troublemaker, that's why you were transferred out here, so that you couldn't cause any more upsets. I bet you didn't help yourself either, did you? Not even after the whipping. I know you Will — if you think you're in the right there's no stopping you. I bet you still stuck to your principles, even after the beating."

"All right, sometimes I didn't follow my orders to the letter. But I never disobeyed them directly; I just found ways to interpret them slightly differently. Anyway, I'm a knight, not a murderer."

Then he remembered his confession to Philipe — he was a murderer.

"As long as a knight of the Temple carries out the orders of his Master he is absolved of all guilt," Philipe intoned, imitating Robert de Sable's sepulchral tones.

"You don't believe that, do you?"

"Of course not! But most do and Pelet is one of them. I daresay too that he knows about your reputation — good and bad. He might deny it to your face, but I don't think anything you do will persuade him to post you back to Outreamer. He's not the sort to stick his neck out."

Philipe's words were a revelation and William was still trying to come to terms with them. He'd thought to argue, but Philipe was far worldlier wise than he was and, after a few moments' reflection, he'd seen that it was true. He realised too that his pride had always blinded him to it. All that heart searching he'd done outside the Lemos house in Villafranca, he thought, risking all for a transfer to Outreamer. Pelet would never send him back there, despite the kind words about his record. That's why he'd told him to go through the proper channels — it could take years to get a decision. What a stupid, preening fool he'd been. He wouldn't get back to the Holy Land, even if he walked on water.

Philipe leaned across the table and patted William's arm — the man's disappointment was plain to see. However, he was sure that he'd been right to tell his friend, because he'd never have come to the truth on his own. What man is there who does see the truth about himself? And getting a transfer back to Outreamer wasn't completely impossible. It wasn't God who sealed the orders — it was men of flesh and blood and there were other officers, senior to Pelet and better men, who might see things differently. Keeping a soldier like William locked up at Ponferrada *was* a sin. Notwithstanding his cynicism, Philipe believed still that the War in Outreamer had to be won and men like William were needed to do it.

"I don't want to raise your hopes, Will, but it can be done. I've come to know quite a few officers — senior to Pelet — since I was posted to Paris. It might not be easy, but memories fade and it all happened a long time ago. Philipe de Plessiez is Grand Master now and Outreamer's desperate for good men. I suppose you heard about the last crusade? Set out for Egypt, finished up in Constantinople." He sighed deeply. "It may take a little time, but I'll see what I can do."

"Thank you Philipe, although after what I did to you I really don't deserve it."

Philipe refilled their beakers and leaned back on his stool. "In the plaza, you said you wanted to talk to me about something. What was it?"

40

The investigation into Cardiaye's murder took time to tell and in the course of it they ordered another pitcher of cold wine and bread with goat's cheese. Philipe listened without interruption as William gave a comprehensive briefing of all that had happened, from seeing Cardiaye's corpse at Ponferrada to leaving the Leon commandery. However, his journey with Cristina Delmirez was never mentioned.

"You've been very busy since last I saw you," said Philipe when William had finished. "And you say that Pelet dismissed it out of hand? I'm not surprised, mind you, he and Meaux are so puffed up with their own importance I'm surprised they agreed even to see an ordinary knight."

"I was partly to blame. I didn't give a good report, I knew it sounded trivial even as I was speaking. I can understand why they didn't give it any credence: to an outsider it does look like a simple case of a monk being robbed and killed; it's only from the inside that you can see there's a lot more to it."

"And you believe this Nicolo Clarini is your man?"

"Yes I do."

"What are you planning to do about it?"

"I'd go back and tell Pelet about the 'Bishop's man' if I thought that he'd listen." William hesitated. Philipe was a cynic: he had to speak his thoughts coherently. "I told you when we first met this morning that I'd been taught a lesson about my pride; I won't bore you with the details. But the fact is that when I walked out of Pelet's office I thought I'd been taught another lesson and I had every intention of telling Montagnac that the Order's official policy is that Cardiaye was killed by a horse thief. I was even going to leave his journal behind. But now — after what the clerk said — now I think I've been given a sign."

"By God or the Devil? It could be simple coincidence."

"I don't believe that and I don't think you do either. It was meant to happen; I was meant to be in that office and the clerk was meant to say what he did. And if I don't do something about it, who will? The clerk will file my report and that'll be the end of it. This Clarini has killed two people; he damn near killed the boy and he tried to kill me. And I am sure this wasn't the first time he's killed. I think I've been called on to stop him. The clerk said he worked as a jack of all trades for Palencia's Bishop and from what I hear of the Bishop that covers a multitude of sins. I can't believe this Clarini would ride out from Palencia into the tierras del mal to pay a man to kill the Deputy Prior of Cluny on his own account. He must have done it on the orders of his Bishop. I'm going after him and if that means going after the Bishop too, so be it."

"By the Cross, Will! You're getting yourself into very deep water with this. Now you listen to me before you go charging off like some knight in a troubadour's tale. Don't underestimate Clarini. I haven't met him; he stays in the background, in fact I'm surprised the clerk has heard of him, but there are stories and they're all bad. He's good with a sword, ruthless and clever. And don't even think of getting involved with the Bishop. You say you've heard stories about him, so have I; he might be a pious man of God on the surface, but underneath he's a man of hard politics. He knows what he wants and he'll stop at nothing to get it. And what are you going to do when you get to Palencia — ride up to his palace with your warrant as acting captain of Knights Templars and say you want to ask him some questions? He has absolute power over his city — ecclesiastical and civil. Believe me, if you start sniffing around Palencia you could finish up inside a sack in the Carrion River. And who's going to support you if things go wrong — Montagnac? I think Pelet's criticism of him was right on target. I wouldn't deny his bravery at Alarcos, not for a moment. But he was a damned menace at Paris and from what I hear he was no better at Aragon. It wouldn't be so bad if he was clever. But he's not: he's just ambitious, and stupid. He's certainly not the type to stay at Ponferrada, believing it's God's will. If I know Montagnac he didn't want to go there in the first place. You say yourself you don't trust him and that he's a careerist. He's going to find a way out if he can and he'll use you to do it. And he won't give a pile of dung about what happens to you in the process. Of course there's also the possibility that he's dead. Have you thought of that? He wouldn't be the first to die after falling off his horse. And his successor isn't going to do anything, he'll follow Pelet's orders."

"What are you saying Philipe?"
"I'm saying, as your friend, that whatever it is you're thinking of doing, don't. Forget about this damned monk and go back to your duties. Keep your nose clean and stick it out at Ponferrada and give me time to try and get you back to Outreamer."
"And I'm very grateful Philipe. I really am and I love you for it. But I can't turn my back on this and just walk away. Don't you see? You might think I'm mad, but I know somehow that I'm being tested, I don't know whether it's by God or the Devil, I just know that if I turn away now I'll regret it for the rest of my life. I've got to do this."
"God almighty Will! Can't you see you're playing with Fate?"
"On the contrary, after what happened this morning I think Fortuna's playing with me. How else can you explain it? I'd never heard of Clarini until the clerk mentioned him. The Infidels believe that their god writes a man's fate from the moment he's born; perhaps they're right, I don't know. But I do believe that going after Clarini is my fate."

"It won't matter a whore's fart whether you're playing with Fortuna or she's playing with you, if you end up dead!"

"You think it's just pride that make's me want to do this?"
"Pride? No! You're just stubborn and pigheaded, you always were. Look, let's say you have been given a sign to go after Clarini, what are you going to do once you've got him?"
"Bring him to justice."
"Now come on Will! You've got more sense than that! You can't have lived in Richard Lionheart's company for as long as you did without seeing how the world works. You may be right, maybe the Bishop is involved, but he's not going to let you bring Clarini to justice, as you call it. His man kills the Deputy Prior of Cluny? He wouldn't survive the scandal. He'll kill both of you to keep it dark. And what's Montagnac going to do when you tell him the Bishop of Palencia's involved in murder? Or Pelet come to that?"
William smiled. "Pack me off to Outremer?"
"Oh you can laugh, but you know what I'm saying is true. You can't win against people like the Bishop."

"Tell me Philipe, do you remember what your father said to us the day we won our spurs? 'Courage, virtue and honour are the only measures of a knight'. Do you remember? I don't think I could stand in front of him now and swear that I'd lived by them."
"It was a long time ago Will. We were boys, now we're men and we've travelled and seen things my father never did. The world's a sinful place, men are greedy and vicious and few care for anything, except themselves. I know my father believed in the knight's code, but he was an honest man."
"So was my father. That's why he sent me to your's to be trained. And I betrayed them both when I killed Balleranche."
Philipe shook his head sadly and gave a long, world-weary sigh. "You know that Elizabeth died?"
"No! When?"
"In the spring of '93. I heard about it in Paris. She married Balleranche's younger brother as soon as she decently could apparently. She died giving birth to her first child."
"Sweet Jesus," William whispered. Would things have been different if she'd married Balleranche, he wondered, or was that always to be her fate? He closed his eyes for a moment and wished her God's mercy.
Philipe reached out and squeezed his arm. "All for nothing Will, all that pain and heartache, all for nothing." He sighed. "Still, it can't be undone and if it means anything to God, I forgive you. After all, if you think about the way we were in those days and all the things we got up to it was only a matter of time before we got ourselves into serious trouble."

"Thank you Philipe. I doubt that God will forgive me though; I might have confessed my sin but I never regretted killing Balleranche, until now. Perhaps I can redress the balance by doing something about Clarini."

"We were sentenced to twenty years in the Order for your crime; twenty years of penance. A few more and it'll be over; we'll be released and you'll be a free man. What are you going to do then? Assuming you don't finish up in the Carrion."

"Stay in the Order I suppose. Fighting is the only thing I know." He shrugged. "Pray you can get me back to Outreamer and hope that a Saracen kills me before I get too old to take the field. What about you? What will you do?"

He laughed. "What else? Retire to a palace and count my gold."

Philipe rose from his stool and walked once around the small patio before sitting down again.

"Well, if you insist on going ahead you better tell me what I can do to help," he said. "You'd better have some money for a start. You can't ride all over the country without anything in your purse." He reached inside his surcoat and brought out a fat leather purse and spilled a small portion of its contents onto the table and gave five gold *Ferdinands* and some smaller coins to William. "That should be more than enough. And don't worry about paying me back; the Paris Treasurer makes sure the Temple's debtors pay for our expenses. Now, when you get to Palencia go to the Jewish quarter — it's on the south side of the church of San Miguel — and ask for the house of Solomon Ben Gurion. Tell him I sent you. He knows just about everything that goes on in the city and he should be able to help, he'll be able to point you in the right direction at least. But don't tell him too much. I don't want him finishing up inside a sack in the Carrion River. He's far too valuable."

"Who is he — apart from being a Jew?"

"He's a merchant and a moneylender. We do business from time to time."

"The Order does business with Jew money lenders?"

Philipe sighed. "Please, William, start living in the real world. I told you before, the Order looks after money for most of Christendom's kings. Of course we do business with the Jews. People want to borrow money; the Jews lend it and we act as honest brokers. The Order's the only body that both Jews and Christians trust. Now, if you need me I shall be here in Leon for the next four days. Then I'm going to Burgos to see a Count who wants to arrange a loan for his daughter's dowry. That will take at least a week, then I'm returning to Paris and I'll be back in Burgos with the Count's gold in the second week of November. When I'm in Burgos, I always stay at a hostal called *El Campeador*. Ask anyone where it is. As soon as I get back to Paris I'll start working on getting you posted to Outreamer."

They hugged each other and kissed on both cheeks. "I'll pray for Our Lady to protect you, Will. You better pray for Her protection too, because by God you're going to need it."

They parted in the plaza mayor, Philipe to make his courtesy call on Pelet, William to return to the Golden Fleece to pay the bill and pick up his horse and saddlebags. While he was waiting for its stableman to saddle his stallion, he reckoned up the distance between Leon and Palencia. If he followed the Camino east to Carrion de los Condes and then turned south onto the road that followed the course of the Carrion River it was about thirty leagues. Riding south east directly to it would be a league or so less but the road was poor and it went through a lot of wild, empty country without much water. The distance saved was insufficient to offset the dangers of riding alone in hostile territory: he would take the Camino. It was not yet midday. If he could cover a league an hour, with a night's stopover somewhere between Sahagun and Carrion, he would be in Palencia by early afternoon on the morrow.

41

William arrived at the *Puentecillas*, the old Roman bridge that crosses the Carrion River on the south side of Palencia, in the third hour after noon. Up until then his journey had been without incident. However, as he was about to cross the bridge he saw a man with a young woman on a donkey coming towards him. She was carrying a baby in her arms and the man was pulling and tugging at the donkey's reins in a desperate effort to outrun half a dozen jeering youths that were chasing them. He saw in a moment from the man's long beard and side locks that he was a Jew and he turned his stallion so as to block their way off the bridge.

"Please lord, I beg you, let me through," said the Jew, clasping his hands beseechingly.

"Why are they chasing you?"

The Jew glanced fearfully over his shoulder at the youths approaching from the city side of the bridge. "For sport my lord."

As he spoke a stone missed the woman's head by a whisker.

"Stay here!" ordered William.

Urging his horse forwards onto the bridge he stopped a little way past the Jews to protect them from any more stones and to bar the youths' path.

"Stand to!" he shouted as they came running up.

The gang stopped dead in its tracks and stared at him, uncertain about what he might do.

"You!" he said to the burliest of them, who looked as if he was their leader. "What have these people done to you?"

"They're Jews."

"Have they robbed you? Or abused you?" They looked at each other, baffled by his questions. "Then why are you throwing stones?"

"You're supposed to protect us Templar, not the Jews!" said someone in the gang.

William didn't see who had spoken and he ignored it.

"Take your friends and go back to the city," he said to the burly one.

"Jew lover!" taunted the same voice and this time he identified its owner — a dirty little villain with the beginnings of a man's beard.

"I shan't tell you again," he said, talking still to their leader. "Now get off this bridge!"

The youth looked at William and drew breath as if to speak, then turned away. "Come on, let's do as he says," he said grudgingly, pushing his way through his friends and starting back across the bridge.

William waited until they had gone half way, then he spurred his horse forwards and seizing the belt of the one who had been calling out he hoisted him across his saddle and slapped him several times, hard on the arse.

"That's to teach you some respect!" he said, before shoving him off.

He watched him limp away and once he and his friends had cleared the bridge he walked his horse back to the Jews.

"Thank you my lord," said the man, while the woman smiled shyly.

"Are you going far?"

"Only to the village of Banos de Cerrato, my lord."

"What's your name?"

"Joseph, my lord."

William looked askance at him. A Jew called Joseph, with a woman and babe on a donkey — was this another sign?

"And your wife's name and the child?"

"Ruth and Simeon."

"God go with you Joseph," he said, turning his horse in the direction of the city.

"And with you lord. We will thank Him for you in our prayers," the Jew called after him.

Entering Palencia through Sancho the Great's Gate he dismounted and walked with his horse through the streets to the Barrio Judio — which lay between the church of San Miguel and the south east corner of the city wall. It was easy to find and at the end of siesta when the shops in the Jewish quarter opened he asked directions to Solomon Ben Gurion's house. Leading his horse, its shoes clopping on the cobbles, he set out to search for the house in the barrio's maze of anonymous lanes. Every one he went down looked almost exactly the same: narrow and dark, with whitewashed, featureless walls and heavy doors marked with the Star of David. He found what he was looking for eventually at the far end of a blind alley. The plaster on both sides of the alley's walls was pocked and dirty, its cobbles sprouted weeds and the only clue to the house's existence was an old wooden door. On closer inspection however he saw that it was made of stout oak. A small iron grill was set into it above a tiny Star of David and after hobbling his horse with a thong he went and banged on it with his fist. The grill was pulled back and a man, whose face was hidden from view, said, "Yes?"

William gave his name and Philipe's. The grill slammed shut and he'd waited for quite a time before he heard the sound of the door's bolts being drawn.

"Come in, please, your honour," said a bearded, young man as he opened the door.

The house's vestibule was small, its walls and floor were tiled in blue and green and it was blissfully cool.

"Would you like to sit down your honour?" The young man pointed towards a cheap, low table and a couple of old stools, which were drawn up under an ancient, iron oil lamp that hung by a chain from the ceiling — the only source of light in the dim little room. "Solomon Ben Gurion will be with you soon."

"I tied up my horse outside. Will it be all right?"

"Don't worry, I'll have someone watch it for you."

He left and returned a few moments later with a boy.

"Don't get too close to him son," said William, "he's a stallion and he doesn't like strangers."

The man translated William's Castilian into Hebrew and the lad left through the front door.

Not long after, William heard an internal door somewhere nearby being opened and closed. A moment later there was a rap on the vestibule's inner door. The young man opened it with a key and a man in a black robe entered. He was tall and thin with stooping shoulders an abundant grey beard and sidelocks.

He bowed to William. "Good afternoon your honour, I am Solomon Ben Gurion."

William bowed in return. "William Stanley, your honour, knight of the Order of the Temple."

"You say that Philipe de Tankerville sent you?"

"Philipe de Tankerville is my friend, your honour. He thought you might be able to help me."

"I mean no disrespect your honour, but could you tell me the name of your friend's mother and the special name she called him?"

William was knocked off his stride for several moments. Why hadn't Philipe warned him he would be asked these questions and told him the answers, in case he had forgotten? He closed his eyes in concentration.

"Beatrice," he said, eventually. "And she called him — Plodkin."

"A friend of Philipe's is my friend also. Welcome to my house. Please," He gestured William to follow him. "It is more comfortable inside."

They left the vestibule and entered a long dim corridor with a heavy door at one end, which, William noted, had no handle. Ben Gurion rapped on it twice and another bearded young man who William took to be another son, opened it. Stepping out of the dim corridor into the bright daylight he was astonished. The dirty little alley and mean vestibule was a disguise: in fact Ben Gurion lived in a spacious Moresque house. Seeing its well kept colonnade, ornately carved doors and lavish patio with a central fountain, fig trees and brass fire crucibles he was a little jealous of the Jew.

"Perhaps your honour would like to take his ease," said Ben Gurion.

He led the way across the patio to a shady corner of the colonnade that contained a large brass topped, Moresque table and a low padded seat covered in rich blue cloth and strewn with brightly coloured cushions.

"You will take some refreshment?" asked Ben Gurion as they sat down. "Some cooled wine perhaps and sweetmeats?"

"Thank you."

After his meeting with Philipe he had resumed observance of the Rule; consequently he'd had nothing to eat since the previous night's supper. He didn't know whether it forbade eating with a Jew; if it did he thought, in the circumstances, that God would forgive him. Ben Gurion clapped his hands. A few moments later a serving girl, her face obscured by a veil, came and placed on the table a tray containing a silver wine jug, two goblets and a plate laden with sweetened dates and small cakes coated with honey.

"Please help yourself," said Ben Gurion. "With your pardon I will not share in it, except for one of these." He leaned forwards, picked up a date and popped it into his mouth. "I'm afraid I can't resist them," he said, as William filled a goblet with wine. "They say that a Templar saved a man and his wife from a gang of rascals on the Puentecillas earlier this afternoon. Was that you?"

"Yes. How did you know?"

"Word travels quickly among my people your honour. Thank you for protecting them."

"Were they relatives of yours?"

"No, just Jews. Now, how can I be of help?"

"I'm seeking help on a couple of matters. First, do you know a good surgeon? I've got some stitches in my chest and it's time they were taken out."

"Yes of course. I'm sure my physician can do that for you. And the second thing?"

There had been plenty of time on the journey for William to decide how to tell to Ben Gurion his story and what he said was to the point. He was investigating the murder of a pilgrim on the Camino; he wanted to know whether Nicolo Clarini worked for Palencia's Bishop, whether he had been wounded of late and if possible the nature of his wounds.

"Aren't you out of your territory?" asked Ben Gurion. "You say the murder took place in Leon. This is Castile."

"I'm not accountable to any king, only to the Pope through my superiors."

Ben Gurion looked at him, thoughtfully. "So be it. In answer to your first question, there is a Nicolo Clarini who works for the Bishop."

"What does he do for him?"

"That is not altogether certain."

"Well, is he a secretary? Does he work for the Bishop's Office? He must have some function."

"No. Nor does he celebrate mass, I believe, although you must understand as a Jew I cannot vouch for this personally."

"He's a priest!"

"I believe so. He has a — ?" Ben Gurion traced a circle on the top of his head with his forefinger.

"A tonsure. He has a tonsure?"

"Yes. Although his hair grows so thick one cannot usually see it. He is not often seen about the city: other priests, secretaries, those who work in the Office of the Bishop, the Bishop even, they are often seen going about their business, but he stays inside the Palace."

"Why is that do you think?"

"Please my friend, you are a Templar, he is a servant of the Bishop and I'm a Jew: I do what every sensible man does in this city — I say nothing about its government outside my home. Please understand; its bishops have governed Palencia since the time of Sancho the Great. Each has built on the power of his predecessor: our Bishop is our master and his rule is absolute. And while you are here I advise you to be careful of asking questions."

"The Bishop has spies in the city?"

"How else can he know what men say?"

"What's Clarini's part in this?"

Ben Gurion leaned forwards and picked another date off the plate. "It is said that he is in charge of them, amongst other things."

"And what might these 'other things' entail?"

There was a long moment's silence as Ben Gurion inspected his sweetmeat. "Last year, three of the city's *senori* petitioned the Bishop for a change in the way decisions were made in the Council. All three are now dead. One fell from the city wall while taking a night time stroll, although I'm told that he had never gone for an evening walk before. The second died in a fire at his place of business — that, too, was late at night. The third man went to visit his brother at Carrion de los Condes. Not a dangerous journey but he went with a two-man escort nevertheless — men who had served him for years. They never arrived and a search found no trace of him nor his escort or their horses. All three deaths have been explained officially of course. However, their petition has never been spoken of again. Does your honour understand what I'm saying?"

William nodded. "Yes, I understand."

"What was your other question?"

"I believe Clarini's been wounded recently, in the eye; I would like to know more about the nature of his wound, if that's possible."

Ben Gurion gave William another long thoughtful stare. "If your honour comes here to my house later on today I may be able to answer that question and deal with your other request at the same time. Shall we say the eleventh hour?" William nodded. "At your convenience, sir."

"That is good. Now, where are you staying?"

"I've only just arrived."

"In that case, I suggest you try *El Jabali*, it's on the north side of Plaza San Antolin. Philipe always stays there. If you mention his name I'm sure they will give you a good room. Prices are much cheaper here than Burgos or Leon. No pilgrims come to Palencia you see." He sighed wistfully. "If only they did, it would make us all rich and the Bishop would be able to realise his plans for the city. You will excuse me now your honour. I have other business to attend." He rose from the pile of cushions on which he'd been reclining and William followed suit, although he struggled momentarily under the weight of his hauberk to get off the low seat.

"If I may make a suggestion about this evening," said Ben Gurion as they walked together across the patio. "You will learn more if you leave the talking to me."

42

Retracing his steps to the church of San Miguel, William made a mental note of some of the barrio's features so that he could find his way back to Ben Gurion's house. On reaching the church, he walked across its square and took a street that led to San Antolin, Palencia's Cathedral. Built at the command of Sancho the Great, it stood in the centre of the city's largest square and he found the 'Wild Boar' hostal in its north east corner between a baker's shop and a taberna. He obtained a bed for the night without reference to Philipe and, once his horse was stabled, he went upstairs to inspect his room. It lacked some of the comforts of the Golden Fleece: the bed was smaller and harder, its cover smelled stale and there was a covering of dust over everything. But the window offered a commanding view of the square, there was water enough in the jug to wash off the journey's grime and it was a lot cheaper than the hostal at Leon.

Once he had towelled himself, he lay naked on the bed and let the breeze from the open window cool his skin. When it grew cooler and shadows in the square were beginning to lengthen, he dressed in his Templar's robe and, after saying his Paternosters, he went downstairs, taking his sword and armoured mittens. If the Bishop used spies he had to make sure he didn't compromise Ben Gurion's security and he went into the dining room determined to make a fuss and thereby draw attention.

After complaining loudly about what had been a reasonable supper of vegetable broth, bread and roast mutton, he went for a stroll. The sun was low in the sky and, unlike the cities on the Camino at this time of the day, Palencia's streets were almost clear of people. It was only the tenth hour and he spent some time walking around the Plaza San Antolin and taking wine in its noisiest taberna. He felt he was being followed soon after he had left the hostal and by the time he arrived outside the church of San Miguel he was sure of it. His shadow, which he had noticed first in the taberna, was not the sort of man who stood out in a crowd: of average height, neither fat nor thin, nondescript clothes and hat, his only distinctive mark was an iron-spiked stick that he carried under one arm. The next step was to get rid of him so that he could go to Ben Gurion's unobserved.

After sauntering slowly around the church he strolled away from the Barrio Judio to the north side of the square and entered a street with several twists and turns, where he increased his pace. He prayed to the Virgin for help and found what he was looking for around the next corner: a narrow, roofed passageway that ran between two houses. Hidden in its deep shadow, putting on his iron-encrusted mittens, he waited for the sound of his follower's footsteps and, as the man passed by, he stepped out of the passage behind him.

"Good evening," he said quietly.

The man turned in surprise and fell like a pole-axed pig when William punched him on the jaw with his mailed fist. Seizing the unconscious man's arms he dragged him into the passageway and after checking the street was clear he walked back to San Miguel and made for the Jewish quarter.

43

"Come in your honour," said Ben Gurion, rising from the low seat where they had sat earlier. "You can leave us," he added, to another of his sons who had accompanied William across the patio.

He had arrived on the strike of the eleventh hour and was surprised to see that fires had been lit already in the brass crucibles. "Please. Sit down, sit down — Now," Ben Gurion said, once William had settled himself on the cushions, "in a few moments we will be joined by my family's physician. He is a Moor of course — all the best doctors are — he loves to talk about medicine and he's also a bit of a gossip. The most important thing however is that he is physician to our Bishop. Ah, here he comes now."

A figure in a white *burnous* appeared in the opposite corner of the colonnade and came across the patio towards them.

"Let me do the talking!" Ben Gurion whispered. "Well, my friend," he said, rising to greet the tall dark faced physician, "do you bring me good news?"

"I do indeed, I have examined your new grandson and found him healthy. The midwife I sent you has given excellent service."

William rose from his cushions, pressed his palms together and offered the traditional Saracen greeting to the physician. "Ssalamu 'lekum."

"Ssalamu 'lekum," replied the physician with equal courtesy and an assured air that was free of the wariness that generally characterised first meetings between Moor and Christian.

"William Stanley, your honour, it's a pleasure to meet you," he said, reverting to Castilian.

"Musa Ibn Nusair, I am pleased also to meet your honour," the physician replied in perfect Castilian. "You are here on business with Solomon?"

William smiled. "Indeed."

Ben Gurion clapped his hands for a servant. "You will take your usual refreshment?" he asked Ibn Nusair, inviting the physician to sit down on the low padded seat.

The same girl that had served them in the afternoon came with a tray bearing mint tea and a large plate of roasted almonds.

The conversation between Ben Gurion and Ibn Nusair dwelt on customary niceties that are exchanged by patriarchs of families everywhere: events in their city — particularly the Bishop's plans for rebuilding the University and his dreams for other civic projects; inquiries about their respective sons and other members of their houses, business and health. Listening to them talking about their lives, William thought on his own existence and was envious. Nothing in his life was relevant to their everyday concerns: he had nothing to say that would be of interest to them and it was only when Ben

Gurion asked after the health of Ibn Nusair's brother that he was brought into the conversation.

"I almost forgot," said Ben Gurion to the physician. "Our friend here has some stitches in his chest. Could you take them out?"

Ibn Nusair smiled at William. "Of course, but I'll need more light."

Ben Gurion called to the servant who was tending the fire crucibles and he came, carrying two firebrands, and stood by the table. Ibn Nusair opened his leather bag and brought out scissors and a small dagger with a curved tip and gestured to William to take off his robe and shirt.

"By the way," Ben Gurion said to William, as Ibn Nusair inspected the stitches. "This is the man you need to talk to about your friend." He turned to speak to the physician. "William was telling me this afternoon that a friend of his has been wounded in the eye during sword practice. Where did you say it happened William — in Leon? Something like that must be impossible to treat, even for you my friend," he said to Ibn Nusair.

"Not necessarily Solomon," said Ibn Nusair, as he inspected William's stitches. "It depends on the wound. A straight thrust to the eye usually kills a man of course, but in other situations the eye's orbit can give good protection. I am treating a man at the moment who has received an injury to his eye from a sword."

"My friend's injury was caused by an upward thrust," said William, as the physician began to remove the stitches. "I had to leave before his treatment was completed, but I presume he'll lose his sight."

"My patient has lost his left eye; probably from a similar blow to the one your friend received." With his long forefinger he traced a line from the left side of his mouth, up over his cheek, past the eye and across his eyebrow. "When was your friend injured?"

"About two weeks ago."

"The cut to his face should be healing well by now, provided it was properly stitched. As for the eye itself." He shrugged his bony shoulders. "That depends on the skill of his physician. Personally I think it is best not to remove it, unless it's diseased. Whatever happens I wish your friend well."

"Thank you."

"Who are you treating?" asked Ben Gurion, innocently. "Anyone I know?"

"Now Solomon, you know I never talk about my patients. Particularly when they are as important as this one."

"So it's true what I hear then?" whispered Ben Gurion. "His man Clarini has been injured. Has he really lost an eye Musa?"

"Shush, I can say no more," whispered the physician, putting his finger to his lips. "That's the last one, put on your shirt," he said to William. "The stitching was good: my compliments to your doctor. Now Solomon, pour me another mint tea, then I will have to go."

As soon as Ibn Nusair had finished his drink he took his leave.

"You have the answer to your question," said Ben Gurion once the physician had left.

"Thank you Solomon. I don't know what I'd have done without you."

"It has been my pleasure to have been of service, my friend."

"I wonder whether you would grant me one more favour."

Ben Gurion gave William another of his thoughtful stares. "What is it?" he asked suspiciously.

"Can you recommend a scrivener? I want a letter written, in Latin."

"Of course, there are several in the city. The best one is the Mozarab, Yusif Salado. He has a stall outside the cathedral. He charges more but he works quickly and he's an accurate translator. But one of my sons can read and write Latin — for our business you understand. He can write your letter."

"Thank you for the offer, but it's better that neither you nor your family are involved any further."

"I see. Tell me your honour, have you brought danger to my house?"

"No, I took care not to be followed. Only your physician knows I was here and once I leave your house tonight you will never see me again." He noted the look of relief that sped across Ben Gurion's face.

"Does Philipe know why you came to Palencia?"

"Yes."

"In that case your honour I wish you good night and God speed."

He returned to El Jabali by a circuitous route through dark and empty streets. Everywhere was quiet, even in San Antolin Plaza, and the hostal's guests had retired to their beds. He asked the night porter to light the way to his room in case someone was waiting there to waylay him, but neither his room nor saddlebags had been disturbed. Nevertheless, before saying his prayers he took the precaution of placing the washbowl and jug against his door to warn of unwelcome visitors. Lying, naked, on the bed, enjoying the night breeze he felt pleased with his progress, but intrigued by the close friendship between Philipe and Ben Gurion. Some time later he fell asleep and dreamed of Cristina.

44

The Abbot of Samos had been on his way to chapel to lead the dawn service when the Infirmarer told him of Montagnac's recovery. Leaving instructions for his deputy to take Lauds, he hurried to the hospital to find Montagnac awake and conscious of his surroundings. His breathing was regular, his eyes were bright and clear and his speech coherent and the Abbot could see that by God's grace he had overcome his injury.

"Brother Tobias tells me you've been awake since before dawn," said the Abbot as he sat down on the edge of Montagnac's cot. "How do you feel, my son?"

"A little tired, Abbot, although Brother Tobias tells me I've been asleep for the best part of eleven days. And hungry too, I confess. But I'm recovered, thanks be to God."

"Thanks indeed: we thought you would die."

"What's been happening?"

"I think it's better you regain a little of your strength before we talk about anything like that. I will come again on the morrow, in the meantime I want you to eat and get plenty of rest."

He nodded to the Infirmarer on his way out and Tobias joined him in the corridor.

"What do you think?" he asked.

"He's very weak, Abbot. He needs feeding; lots of broth and bread in the first instance and then meat. And I think we should have him up and walking about a little."

"See to it then. I'll come again tomorrow, after noon."

****

By God's grace, Montagnac had both a body that was quick to heal and iron fortitude: he improved rapidly under Tobias's care and when the Abbot returned he was surprised at the improvement. He was bright, a little colour had returned to his cheeks and although the Abbot found him resting he had walked up and down the full length of the corridor thrice that morning with the Infirmarer's help. On the previous day the Abbot had decided not to speak about his knight's transgression but seeing Montagnac's progress he decided the time was right.

"Do you feel well enough to talk of other things?" he asked, after inquiring into Montagnac's health

"Indeed yes, I had little recollection at first but my memory has now returned: I know how I got here and I'm anxious to know what's been happening while I've been out of the fray."

The Abbot sat down on the empty cot next to Montagnac's. "Do you remember being visited by one of your knights?"

"You mean Hugh Bescanson? Yes, I made him my deputy."

"No, the other one, William Stanley."

Montagnac thought hard for several moments. "I remember dreaming that he was very close. And I kept seeing his face. Oh, wait a moment, I ordered Bescanson to send him here. Did he come?"

"Nine days ago. Tobias tells me that he sat with you for several hours in the after noon. You awoke later and told him to continue the search for Rolfe Cardiaye's murderers. Do you remember?"

"How do you know about Cardiaye?"

"I was here, in the hospital when you gave the order. He told me about Cardiaye afterwards."

"I can't remember any of it. What did he tell you?"

"That Cardiaye had been murdered on the Camino and that he'd found the murderer. Poor old Rolfe, I knew him you know, he was a good man, fine scholar."

"Stanley has found the murderer? Thank God for that. Who was it? Did he say?"

"Some horse thief. He buried the villain at Ponferrada. But I know now that there's more to it than that."

"What do you mean?"

"Do you know the name Diego Delmirez?"

Montagnac shook his head. "The only Delmirez I know are Counts of Soria. Their estates are on Castile's southern frontier."

"It's the same family. He's a guest here — prisoner really. He used to teach at the University of Palencia; in fact he was highly regarded. He lost his way I'm afraid; published criticisms of the Pope and the Church and says we should abandon the Holy Land and the Reconquista and make peace with the Infidels."

"Is he mad?"

"He's as sane as you or I. He was given a chance to recant by his Bishop and he refused. Instead he accused the Bishop of chicanery."

"Why hasn't his Bishop hanged him?"

"The Counts of Soria have blood ties with the King of Castile's family and most of its nobility. The last king wasn't so kind to Palencia, but Alfonso VIII has always had a strong regard for both the city and its bishops. Putting Delmirez in front of an ecclesiastical court might jeopardise that; the Bishop wants to avoid it if he can, so I agreed to lodge Delmirez here where he can't do any harm."

"I see. But what has this got to do with William Stanley?"

"I gave strict instructions that Delmirez was to be denied paper, pen and ink. I granted his request for them when he first came here, but then I found he was writing secretly to his niece and I took them away again. The point is I told your knight of this and he disregarded my order."

"William Stanley! Where would he get pen and ink? He's barely literate."

"He's literate enough to know the importance of Cardiaye's journal it seems. He found it apparently and asked Delmirez to translate it."

"But that can't be: there isn't a journal, Cardiaye was brought into Ponferrada without even his habit."

"I know nothing of that. All I know is that your knight disobeyed my orders and I think he deceived me deliberately. He told me he had a few pages of Latin he wanted translating — nothing important — and rather than bother my people I suggested he ask Delmirez — I felt sorry for him, you see, locked away with nothing to occupy his mind. The truth is that not only did your knight have Rolfe's journal he also had his writing materials. And he gave them to Delmirez."

"And I'll punish him for it Abbot! Damned harshly."

"I expect nothing less. But unfortunately it's not as simple as that; Rolfe appears to have recorded who his murderers were."

"But that's impossible, he couldn't have, I saw the body, he was stabbed in the heart, he must have died instantly

The Abbot sighed. "I'm sorry, I don't want to overtax you. I'll come back later when you've had a rest."

"No Abbot! Tell me now. I want to hear it. Just understand; this is all new to me."

"You're right, I'll take it slowly. Very simply then, your knight gave the journal to Delmirez — I don't know how or where he found it. Delmirez read it and told your knight what it contained. Cardiaye seems to have recorded something that happened to him on the Camino — a few days before he was killed — something that made him fear for his safety. He wrote it in code apparently but Delmirez has studied it and he says he knows what it means."

"What does it mean?"

"I don't know. Delmirez refuses to tell me. But what he will say — indeed he wants to shout it from the rooftops — is that it's a scandal that will rock the Church from top to bottom and I have the impression that it involves the Bishop of Palencia who, by the way, is my cousin. I don't know how much your knight knows, but he's out there somewhere doing God knows what on your orders."

"What orders? I didn't even know Cardiaye had a journal 'til you told me just now."

"That's what I was saying a few moments ago: I was here with him when you gave the order, you woke up for a short while and you told him to track down Cardiaye's killers, whatever the consequences. Mind you, I wondered at the time whether you knew what you were saying."

"Holy Mother of God! I can't be blamed! I can't be held responsible for something I said when I was out of my mind! Can't you do something? Can't you get the truth out of Delmirez?"

"I'm his gaoler, not his inquisitor."

"So what are you going to do?"

"In six day's time the bishops will hold their annual Congregation in Leon. I attend for the last few days generally and I'm taking Delmirez with me. He's in Palencia's jurisdiction not mine: my cousin will have to decide what's to be done with him."

"How are you travelling?"

"By coach of course, I'm too old to sit a horse for five or six days. And I don't want to put Delmirez on one; the damned old fool might try to run off."

"Can I ride with you?"

"Do you feel well enough?"

"I must get back to Ponferrada as soon as possible Abbot, well or not."

"Then you better get some rest, we will be leaving here at dawn tomorrow. I'm taking it in easy stages; I'm not galloping up Cebreiro. There's plenty of time; the Congregation lasts for two weeks."

Yusif Salado, the scrivener, was short and thin and his hands were stained irreparably with ink.

"Are you sure you don't want me to address the letter?" he asked William. "It's all in the price and it's considered bad manners not to address the receiver by his name and rank."

William shook his head. "Not on this occasion, thank you."

Salado shrugged. "Well, it's your letter. Now, let's see," he said, examining it once more to see if the ink was dry. "That's fine. Would you like me to read it back to you — I usually do. I like to be sure I've put down what the customer wants to say."

William glanced over his shoulder to see if there was anyone who might overhear.

"You must wonder sometimes at what people do say."

Salado smiled. "My dear sir, I write scores of letters, about business, love and who knows what else. If I spent my time wondering about every letter I wrote I'd go mad. Now do you want me to read it back to you or not?"

William thought now that it would have been better to have a clerk in Leon write the letter, except he had no real proof, in Leon, that Clarini was the man he wanted.

"Please do," he said, deciding not to do anything out of the ordinary that might excite Salado's interest.

Salado cleared his throat. "Are you ready? It says: 'Here is proof that we have the monk's journal. It says what you already know. We can send it to those who should know or we can trade. If you want to trade ring all your bells at the second hour of this night.' I've dated it of course," added Salado, "and I can arrange for it to be delivered, if you wish. The carrier I use is very reliable and he charges a fair price."

"No thank you, I'll make my own arrangements. Can you to seal it securely." William handed Salado a single sheet of tightly rolled paper. "And can you enclose this?"

Salado took it from him and rolled it up inside the letter, which he bound with a thin ribbon and sealed with a dab of hot wax.

"I hope you will come here again," he said, when William paid him.

Salado's small, brightly coloured stand was sited in the south west corner of San Antolin Plaza, only a short walk from the Bishop's Palace. It was the second hour of the day, the Palace was open for business and William thought it was a good time to deliver his letter. Apart from the Cathedral the Episcopal Palace was the largest and most impressive building in the city: testimony to the power and wealth of its bishops. A wall surrounded it, and its style borrowed from the Romans, with a broad flight of steps leading to its entrance, set under a portico supported by six columns. Armed guards, wearing the Bishop's colours, were stationed at its gate and they were questioning everyone seeking admittance. He watched them for several moments and it soon became obvious that while the poor were being treated rudely those in rich or respectable dress were admitted after only a cursory question or two. If he acted as though he had absolute right of entry he'd probably pass through without scrutiny.

Walking swiftly up to the gate he spoke to the guards with authority.
"You there!" he said to a man-at-arms who was standing amidst a group of peasants, who were waving petitions in the air. "I have an important message for the Bishop."
The soldier saw William's uniform and stiffened to attention.
"Yes sir! As you enter the Palace hall you'll see a desk on your left-hand side. Ask there and they'll direct you to the right office."

The entrance hall continued the exterior's Roman theme, but here the classical columns stood against walls that were decorated with paintings of Biblical scenes. The desk to which the guard had referred was the only furniture in this echoing space. It was large and imposing — big enough to seat two clerks — and surrounded by a small herd of common people with petitions for their Bishop. William barged through them and acted on the authority bestowed by his uniform.
"I have an important message that must be delivered to the Bishop immediately," he said, speaking over the din and interrupting discussions that were in progress between clerks and petitioners.
Both clerks looked up from their papers, affronted by his interruption, but neither wanted a public confrontation with a Templar.
"Up the stairs, third on the left," said one of them tersely before they resumed their work.

46

The Bishop had risen late and, after saying prayers in his private chapel, he was enjoying a late breakfast in his study. As usual there were many things on his mind. His chief preoccupation this morning was the business that would be conducted at the Congregation of Bishops when it met at Leon in three days time. It was an annual event, attended by every bishop in Spain and its purpose was to agree issues of principle that would shape the religious and secular policies of their episcopacies over the next year. The agenda was always very long and the whole business lasted two weeks. There were two items of general concern this year: revitalising the Reconquista, which required, in the minds of most, a direct intervention by Innocent; and ways to increase Church taxes. The latter was of particular interest to the Bishop because although his city's revenues were adequate to meet the costs of his administration and for one or two minor schemes, such as rehousing the University, they fell far short of what was needed to fund his ambitions.

His University's influence had declined of late, largely due to the blasphemies preached by that dangerous old fool, Delmirez. The Bishop was baffled still by Delmirez's behaviour. If he'd sprung from the lesser nobility — like the Bishop himself — he could have understood it better. He knew and could sympathise with men who felt the spur of ambition. A poor scholar who was clever and looking to make his reputation might decide to preach dangerous ideas — perhaps even as dangerous as Delmirez's — provided he was prepared to change tack when it was clear they were going to get him into really serious trouble. Thereafter he could show they had been misunderstood and capitalise on his earlier notoriety. But Delmirez had nothing to prove; he wasn't some poor scholar trying to make his way in the world, he was son to one of the oldest Houses in Castile. Dammit! He would have been Count of Soria if he hadn't renounced the title. How in the name of Christ could a man have all that and throw it away?

Try as he might the Bishop could not understand why the man thought as he did — even after sitting for several days at his Inquiry. Listening to him arguing with his examiners — all of them highly respected scholars — that his ideas were right and they, their peers, Popes, all Christendom itself it seemed, had misinterpreted Scripture, the Bishop had wondered whether Delmirez was mad. If that had been the case it would have solved the Bishop's problem. He could have dismissed him from the University, but with sadness and great sympathy and earned kind words from the King and his fellow bishops about the way he had handled it. But the damned old villain had argued so cogently for the truth of his ideas that the Bishop had decided finally that he'd lose face if he showed leniency. He didn't want a trial. God forbid! Soria was a power to be reckoned with, even in the hands of his niece and Delmirez was a highly respected scholar still. If some of his colleagues spoke in his defence it would give credence to the slanders whispered by Palencia's enemies, that its University was a hotbed of heresy.

Some of his fellow bishops had argued that it should be closed and removed lock, stock and barrel to their city. And why wouldn't they? It was Spain's first and only university. But it was his — a legacy from his predecessor — and he was determined to defend it, whatever the cost. Packing Delmirez off to Samos had shown his determination to crush any possibility of heresy and it had blunted his enemies' sting. Now he would use the Congregation to begin the process of re-establishing the University's reputation and it would prosper again, he was sure of it. However, while he was passionate about defending his University the scheme he cherished above all: to commence a new cathedral to compete with Leon's would remain a dream without more money. He had devised a plan that would have given Palencia sufficient to build a new one, but it had come to nought unfortunately.

The Bishop left the remains of his breakfast and went over to his study's window, from where he could see San Antolin's Cathedral, a stretch of city wall and the woods to the south, beyond it. From the first moment he had entered the room he had fallen in love with its view and every time he looked upon it he thanked God for his good fortune. His predecessors too had used it as their study and each had added something to it, such as the collection of small pictures depicting Christ's life on earth that had been painted by an Italian artist and a range of gold wine goblets. His only displeasure was its stifling heat on summer afternoons. He endured it, as all his predecessors had done, because of its private staircase that was secreted behind the wall panelling next to the stone fireplace. Very few people on the Bishop's staff knew of it, or that it enabled him to move through his domain without being observed.

There was a knock at the door and after a moment his private secretary opened it and entered.
"Good morning, Your Grace," he said, bowing low. "I trust you slept well. I'm sorry to interrupt your breakfast but I've just received an important message. The Templar who delivered it insisted you see it immediately."
Taking the scroll that his secretary was offering the Bishop broke its seal and spread it out on his desk. He read the outer letter first. It was written in Latin by an experienced hand and it made no sense. Then he unrolled the second. That too was written in Latin. The beautiful morning was spoiled utterly when he realised that it was the first page of Rolfe Cardiaye's journal. Quickly, he reread the first letter. Sweet Jesus! Now it made sense.

"Who did you say delivered this?" He had not intended to speak sharply, but he was still in shock.

"A Templar, Your Grace."

"Did he say anything else? Is he waiting for a reply?"

"Only that it was very important. Then he left."

The Bishop was on the point of ordering the secretary to call out the guard, but he stopped himself. To act without thought could lead to disaster.

"Did you see him, what did he look like?"

"Tall, very broad. Age? Five and thirty, more or less."

"How did you know he was a Templar?" He realised immediately that it was a stupid question; he would have been in uniform.

"He was dressed in his uniform. You don't look very well, Your Grace. Are you unwell?"

"No, no." He waved his hands to dismiss his secretary's concern. "Just indigestion. Too much bread with the eggs I think. What are my appointments this morning?"

"You're meeting several of the city senori. You wanted to talk to the Archdeacon about the next Council meeting. The architect is coming about the designs for the new University and —"

"Cancel them."

"Your Grace?"

"You didn't hear? Cancel them. And have someone clear up this mess." He pointed at his unfinished breakfast. "And tell them to bring me wine and water. Then leave me in peace, I'll call when I need you."

Once his secretary had closed the door the Bishop sat down and studied the page from Cardiaye's journal. There was nothing incriminating in it. It stated merely his purpose in keeping the journal: to record his pilgrimage to Santiago. But the sender would have no interest in the journal's opening page; it was what the monk had written after leaving Carrion de los Condes that he wanted to trade. He left his desk and went to the window and stared out at the view that had lifted his heart a few moments earlier, before Fortuna had visited this piece of extortion on him. Christ save me! he thought. How could this damned business have gone so wrong? Two concerns were dominant: to protect himself and his Office. And until his desk was cleared of breakfast and wine and water brought, his mind ran hither and thither over what might happen if the facts become known.

Soothed by the mixture of wine and water he began to dissect the problem facing him. A Templar had delivered the message: therefore it was reasonable to suppose that they had the journal. They and he were accountable to the Pope. They might take it to the Legate or even to Innocent himself. And what would be his punishment? At the very least he would be stripped of his Office. On the other hand the Church might hand him over to the King's law. He shuddered at the thought. But if the Templars' motive was his punishment they would not have indicated willingness to trade and he began to see that by doing so they had disarmed themselves. If they sought to expose him he would accuse them of extortion and use it to show they were willing to be complicit in his crime. To act in haste would be taken by the Templars as confirmation of his guilt. Far better to continue with his affairs as if there was nothing untoward. If it became necessary to open negotiations he would not do so until their second or third approach. He snatched the letter from his desk and read it once more. Ring your bells, he thought, God take your impudence! He would do nothing except wait on events. In the meantime it would be well to visit Nico in his quarters and tell him the bare details.

47

Clarini lived in that part of the Palace where His Grace's most senior servants were lodged. His suite of two connecting rooms — one for sleeping, the other for sitting and taking his ease — was large and well appointed and those of similar rank on the Bishop's staff looked on it with envy. When the Bishop knocked, Clarini was following Ibn Nusair's advice and resting on his bed. His face would be scarred, but the wound had almost healed and he had returned to most of his duties. He wasn't surprised altogether to find the Bishop at his door: he had visited regularly when it was thought Clarini might die from his wound and he still came occasionally, to enquire of his progress. Clarini was touched by his interest, for although he had known the Bishop since boyhood His Grace had never shown such concern before.

Clarini knew his noble family had rejected him and that the Bishop, then a young priest, had taken him under his wing. He'd placed him in a monastery where he'd been cared for, loved even at first and taught how to talk and behave with others, to read and write and say his prayers. He couldn't remember precisely when it was he realised he had enough food to eat, he was safe and that he was a human being. But the realisation had struck him like a thunderbolt. From that moment on he'd begun in earnest to watch, listen and learn; and he'd learned quickly. It wasn't long before he'd emerged from his shell and became just another of the monastery's child-oblates: talking, laughing, playing when allowed to by the monks, and many other things that were forbidden. For the first time in his young life he knew what it meant to be happy, although the disciplined life of the monastery sometimes irked him.

It was at about that time when he was struck by three more revelations: life was a struggle that could be won only by the strong; that he was tougher, both physically and mentally than any of his peers; and that there was another world, vastly bigger and far more mysterious beyond the monastery's walls. He was determined to see that world from that time on. In the meantime he began, gradually at first, to test the verity of his first two revelations and when he saw they were true his attitude and behaviour changed. He stopped being the one who was sometimes victim to his fellows' horseplay and, once they'd realised that he'd use fists, feet, teeth or any other weapon that was close at hand, and that he'd keep coming at them, until he was dead, or they were beaten, they all feared him. The bumps, bruises and cuts from the blows that he and his fellows suffered did not go unnoticed by the monks and they sought a cause for this outburst of violence.

In due course they came to the conclusion that it was he. They admonished him — gently at first — with soft words of reason. But in his world he was cock of the walk by then and he knew that if he submitted to a superior force his playmates would believe him weaker and unite as one against him. The monks had expected that he'd take the line of least resistance, he defied them instead and they turned to harsher measures. But his first few years on earth had been a literal living Hell. There was nothing they could do that was worse than what he'd once suffered and he knew it. They beat, starved and worked him hard, made him say prayers in chapel that seemed endless, but he wouldn't bow down and the other children never once challenged his authority over them. In fact, his chastisements served only to strengthen his conviction that the world was divided into the weak and the strong and that he was undoubtedly part of the latter. It was further reinforced when, after years spent on the rack for persistent crimes of unruliness and defiance, he was taken to the Abbot's office. The Abbot had recited his list of crimes and told him dolefully, as if it were the ultimate punishment, that he would be cast into the world beyond the monastery's walls. He could hardly believe it: through his own power and strength of purpose he had achieved his first ambition.

He was less elated when the Abbot left his office and another man entered. He hadn't seen the man for some years, but he recognised immediately that it was the young priest who had rescued him. He saw too that the priest had grown into an important man. Expecting to receive a whipping and shouts of righteous anger he had been astounded by the man's stern, yet kindly words and his sympathetic consideration. He'd called him Nico and spoken of reasons that could excuse his bad behaviour. His rescuer said that he had spoken to the Abbot and thought deeply on the matter and he'd decided that he, Nico, would train as a priest. It was at the end of the man's short speech that he had been visited by another revelation: whether it be God or the Devil, a man must follow a star if he is to prosper. His rescuer was his guardian angel — he had thought of him thus ever since — and he would follow him, honour him, even die for him.

Nevertheless, it was a long time before he had begun truly to honour the promise he'd made to himself in the Abbot's office. He had tried, God knows he'd tried. But everything he'd done in the service of his guardian angel had always seemed to come to an unhappy ending. He'd become a priest and worked as a secretary, but sooner or later he'd get into a scrape. He'd given much thought to the reason for it and come to the conclusion that it was due to the restrictions that beset his life. He had believed that escaping the monastery would set him free. Instead, he'd become prisoner in another world. Its regime was less strict than the monastery, but he still found it vexing and tiresome. What he yearned for was freedom: to take decisions and exercise his discretion, not to follow petty rules and procedures; to roam far and wide in his master's service; and, within his guardian angel's span of authority, to take charge of something.

God had granted his wish eventually when, after yet another scrape — an argument with a colleague that had ended in near fatal violence — his guardian angel had apprenticed him to a senior officer in Castile's military. He found at once that a soldier's life played to his strengths: it was power, expertly applied; strategy and tactics; a sense of 'never say die' and opportunities to practice violence. There was discipline it was true, but he could understand and believe in its purpose and, when the unexpected occurred, initiative was a soldier's sharpest weapon. He had blossomed in the life and the lessons he had learned and now applied had enabled him to fulfil at last the promise he'd made in the Abbot's study.

"How are you Nico?" asked the Bishop as he entered. "Are you still mending well?"
"Getting stronger every day, if it please Your Grace. Won't you sit down?"
"Thank you, no." The Bishop went and stood by the window that looked over the west side of the city. "Ordinarily I would not speak so bluntly. However, it seems that Cardiaye's journal has been found."
"That's not possible, Your Grace. There was a diligent search, I assure you."
"I have its first page and a note to go with it," the Bishop continued, affecting not to hear Clarini's interruption. "Delivered to me by a Templar within the last hour. The note says that they have the rest of the journal and they want to trade for it. They don't say what they want, although I suppose it's gold. The Templars always want gold. They're extorting me, Nico." He pointed a finger at his own chest. "*I'm* being blackmailed," he added incredulously.
"What do you wish me to do, Your Grace?"
"I shall carry on as normal. I'm going to the Congregation at Leon the day after tomorrow. It's on for two weeks and I will decide how to handle the damned Templars on my return. I would like you to attend the Congregation too. Come in a few days when you're a little stronger. A change of air will do you good; you can enjoy yourself, meet people, build yourself up again, the banquets are not to be missed."
"Thank you, Your Grace, I will attend of course. But I can't see how the Templars could have come by Cardiaye's journal. It doesn't make sense. Everyone involved is dead." He pointed to the patch over his left eye. "Even the man who did this."
"Please, Nico!" said the Bishop, who had put his hands to his ears when Clarini had spoken so explicitly. "You know my views: I speak to you only about a problem. How it is resolved I leave to you and unless I say to the contrary I don't want to hear another word about it. Is that clear?"
"Yes, Your Grace."

"Good. Now, I look forward to you joining me at Leon and in the meantime I expect you to observe our understanding: protect my interests at all times but don't overreach yourself. I have given some thought to this business with the Templars; I don't want to rush anything, the longer it takes the more likely it is to come to nothing." He moved away from the window and went to the door. "Take care and follow the advice of my physician. I'll see you in Leon."

Clarini was sure of one thing as the Bishop left his rooms: he would not rest until he had discovered something about the Templar who had visited the Palace. It was the Bishop's city, but he ruled its streets and he'd spend eternity with the Devil rather than let any harm befall his guardian angel. He was at his place of work in the Palace cellars, calling for his lieutenant, by the time the Bishop was entering his study.

As soon as Clarini arrived at his office he sent for his henchman, Enrique Gonzales. Clarini had decided at the outset that he needed a certain type of man as his lieutenant and Gonzales had all the necessary qualities. He wasn't a gentleman; he had a phenomenal memory; he kept his mouth shut and he liked to hurt his fellow creatures.

"Good morning, your honour," said Gonzales, as he entered. He stood in front of Clarini's desk and bowed. "May I enquire after your honour's health?"

"No you may not. What are the reports for the last twelve hours?"

"It's been very quiet, your honour. No one unusual entered the city and nobody we're watching has left. There was some grumbling in one or two tabernas about taxes — nothing more than wine talking though. And there was a brawl outside another; over a woman I'm told."

"Has anyone seen or noted the movements of a Templar?"

"I was just coming to that, your honour. Yes, a Templar entered the city by Sancho's Gate in the afternoon and was observed later in San Antolin Plaza. He was staying at the El Jabali. He walked about, had a drink in a taberna and then we lost sight of him."

"Was?"

"Yes. He left first thing this morning."

"And you say you lost sight of him? What in the name of Christ does that mean?"

"He was being followed by one of the men I've just set on your honour. He's still new to the game. This Templar must have spotted him and thought he was a villain; knocked him out cold and left him in an alley. We thought his jaw was broken, it's not, but he took a bad crack."

"Where is he now?"

"I sent him home sir."

"Not your bloody man! The Templar! You said he left El Jabali. So, where is he now?"

"I'm sorry sir, I don't know."

Clarini sprang from his chair, came around the desk and seized Gonzales by his tunic. "You pile of dung! Is this what I pay you for?" He shoved Gonzales away with such force that the little man fell almost backwards onto the floor. "For your information this Templar came to the Palace not an hour ago."

"Are we sure it's the same one, your honour?"

"How often do we see a Templar in Palencia? You oaf! Of course it's the same one! Now get out there and find him. And try not to make any fuss. I want your report by the end of the next hour," he added, as Gonzales bowed hurriedly and left.

Outside his master's lair, Gonzales leaned against the corridor wall and took a deep breath. In the early days he had cringed before Clarini's rants; now he knew that the time to be afraid was when the Italian spoke softly and fixed you with his icy stare. Gonzales had few illusions about himself: he knew he was a mean spirited little swine and that it was the reason why Clarini had chosen him. For his part he hated the Italian, but it was steady, well paid work and he had a sick wife and six children to feed. His loyalty had been bought and he would do whatever he was told. However, if his opinion had been sought, he would have said that it was impossible to do a quiet job in the time that he had been given.

In his office Clarini was pacing angrily up and down, fuming over the fact that last night's incident with the Templar had not been reported before. Then reason reasserted itself and he calmed down. It was unfair to blame Gonzales; he had made a reasonable assumption given what he knew at the time. If the Templar was still in the city Clarini was sure Gonzales would find him, until then he would have to be patient. After filling a silver cup with wine he sat down at his desk and looked with pleasure at the office that he'd made from an old storeroom. He had worked without one, originally. However as the Bishop's problems multiplied and his own initiative, to create a web of spies across the city, began to bear fruit it became obvious that he needed one. When the Bishop gave him an old store his colleagues had chortled, but he had seen its potential. The project he had in mind needed money of course, but by then he was accepting gifts from citizens who wanted to avoid being questioned in the Palace cellars about remarks they had made against their Bishop. Gifts of money, furniture and tapestry had transformed the dark old store into a brightly-lit nobleman's room, which his peers regarded now with malignant jealousy.

When Gonzales returned he reported only bad news. The ten 'watchers' that were on duty currently had walked around their designated barrios visiting hostals, tabernas, shops and churches. None had seen a Templar that morning, nor had anyone they'd questioned.
"Christ's Blood man!" Clarini yelled at his lieutenant. "He can't have just disappeared. What about the Barrio Judio, have you asked there?"
"Yes your honour, we have and nobody can remember seeing him. The sentries at Sancho's Gate have confirmed a Templar entered the city yesterday after noon, but no one has seen him leave. Mind you it is a market day; there are a lot of people about, especially at the gates. It's possible our people missed him."
"Where's the idiot who was following him last night?"
"Still at home sir."
"Well get him in and make him go through what happened last night again. Then double check everywhere the Templar went. Jesus, Mary and Joseph! I

don't need to explain everything to you, do I? Have you questioned the servants at El Jabali, they might know where he went? And what about the market?"

Gonzales licked the bruised knuckles of his right hand. "The servants know nothing, your honour, I can assure you of that. And I've posted two men in the market."

Clarini drummed on the desktop with his fingertips. The Bishop ate his midday meal at noon and he had wanted to give him definite news by then. The Templar probably had left the city, nevertheless he would have one more try.

"Do it all again."

"Your honour?"

"You heard me, do it again and this time get everyone working on it, the off duties, anyone who's sick; get them out of their beds and onto the streets. That's what the whores' sons are paid for. Report back here a quarter hour before noon."

49

After delivering the letter William had taken the precaution of slipping on the Soria surcoat. Then he'd gone directly to Sancho's Gate and he'd watched and waited for an appropriate moment. The fact it was market day was an unexpected bonus and when the sentries were preoccupied with some peasants, herding their goats into the city, he'd slipped out of the city without being noticed. After crossing the Puentecillas he had set off for the village of Banos de Cerrato that lay to the south of Palencia, to visit the little church of San Juan. It had been built before the time of the Moors and he had been told by many of its simple beauty. The trip, there and back, would take two hours out of the day, but this might be his only opportunity to see it and there would still be ample time to reach Carrion de los Condes by nightfall.

He was certain now that it had been Clarini at the Moor's cabin and that the Bishop was ultimately responsible for Cardiaye's murder. He had restated his vows to the Order however: what to do about it was for Montagnac or his successor to decide. But he was no fool: he knew there wasn't evidence credible enough to arraign either Clarini or the Bishop and he never expected the city's bells to be rung. Nevertheless he thought God would approve of him stirring things up a little. It could do no harm to let Clarini and his master know that their crime had been discovered and if they lost sleep because of it so much the better.

The church was close by a copse of trees, a short distance beyond Banos de Cerrato. There was a stream nearby and after watering his horse he tied its reins to a tree. Then he took off the Soria surcoat, stuffed it inside his saddlebag, which he slung over his shoulder. Dressed now as a Templar he walked across the churchyard and up the two steps to the door. San Juan's principle feature was its unique windows, which consisted of tiny keyholes that had been punched through its stone walls. It was bare of decoration inside and gazing at the tiny beams of light dancing on its small stone altar he wondered at the building's simplicity. As he knelt to say a prayer he sensed loneliness about the church and on the spur of the moment he decided to stay awhile. Sitting in a niche to one side of the door he closed his eyes and listened to the wind sighing in the trees outside.

It was after noon and he had been asleep for three hours when two women opened the church door and came inside carrying buckets and brooms. Hidden behind the door he decided to stay there a little longer so as not to disturb their work. After praying to San Juan they began cleaning. He guessed from their conversation that they were mother and daughter, although he paid little attention until they began to talk about the happenings in Palencia that morning.

"I never saw nothing like it," the mother was saying. "They dragged the servants out of that 'ostal, you know the one I mean, El Jabali, the expensive one in the bottom corner of San Antolin. They were pushing 'em about and the maids was crying and the cook — you know, the big fat woman who always wears that old leather apron — she was cussing them. They soon shut her up though; one of the swine knocked her down. But it didn't end there; they were going round the tabernas asking questions, even stopping people in the street. I was glad once I'd sold me eggs and could get off home."

"Who were they looking for? Had someone escaped from gaol?"

"That's the funny thing. The man who sells the cheeses. You know? The one with the birthmark under 'is eye, he said how he'd 'eard they were looking for a — but I'm sure it can't be right, 'e said —" The church door's hinges creaked and they turned to see the cause. "Oh my God!" she breathed, crossing herself, as she saw William standing in the open door. "Speak of the Devil and He appears."

"God be with you ladies," he said, as he walked out of the church.

"And with you sir," they called in unison after him.

He was in high spirits as he rode away. He had certainly stirred things up in Palencia and he saw it as a sign from Heaven. His visit to San Juan and falling asleep was God's work and now, instead of riding to Carrion, he would wait in earshot of the city to see if the Bishop rang its bells. If they did he would plead with Montagnac to exchange the journal for Clarini; then at least some justice would have been served.

For Clarini to be summoned immediately to the Bishop's study was unusual. If the Bishop wanted to see him it was generally in the evening, once His Grace had finished business for the day. It wanted another half hour 'til noon, Gonzales had not yet reported and Clarini was annoyed because he couldn't give the Bishop definite news. He was a little concerned too by the smirk on the face of the secretary who had conveyed the Bishop's summons. Clarini had seen that smirk before; it betokened bad tidings for someone.

"Come in!" he heard the Bishop shout, a moment after he'd knocked on the study door.

"Make sure you shut it behind you," said the Bishop, as Clarini entered. "Now Nico, perhaps you'd like to tell me what's going on?"

"Your Grace?"

"What did I say to you this morning? I told you not to do anything. Now I'm hearing reports that your men have been turning the city upside down. What in the name of Christ are you doing?"

"I am doing your bidding Your Grace. I'm protecting your interests. I'm trying to find this Templar for you."

"Dear Jesus! Why didn't you go to the Cathedral steps and proclaim it to the world?"

"With respect, Your Grace, I did tell the men to be discreet."

"Discreet!" roared the Bishop. "Your men have beaten a woman in the square outside San Antolin, taberna keepers and customers have been terrorised. All in broad daylight, and on a market day. And you stand there and tell me you've been discreet? God damn you Nico!"

"I'm sorry, Your Grace." Clarini had never seen the Bishop in a mood such as this and for the first time in their relationship he was fearful. "I thought I was doing the right thing. I did it for you sir."

The Bishop shook his head in anger and frustration. Then he went over to the window and stared out at the view, wondering at the way his fortune had changed in only a few hours.

"Have you found him?" he asked, staring still at the view.

"No, Your Grace. He must have left the city soon after delivering the message."

The Bishop turned to face Clarini. "And what would you advise I do now?"

"Nothing; as Your Grace said this morning. Perhaps my men were a little too enthusiastic, but no real harm has been done. The Templar doesn't know what's been happening; he wasn't here."

"God Almighty, and I always thought you were intelligent," said the Bishop, wearily. "Did it ever occur to you that this man might have been impersonating a Templar? It's possible. It certainly helped him get into the Palace without difficulty. But let's assume he is a Templar. Now, I know they're not the cleverest in God's creation but they're not entirely stupid either. Do you not think it conceivable that they could have posted someone else inside the city to see if I reacted to their message? Someone not in uniform, whose job was to sit tight and wait? Can't you see what you've done? Doing nothing gave me the advantage. They wouldn't know whether I'd received it or not and after a while they'd have sent another. Who knows how long I could have played a game with them? Every message they sent would have been an arrow in my quiver, because eventually they would have incriminated themselves to such a degree they wouldn't be able to start a hue and cry. Don't you see? To have the knowledge they claim and do nothing would in itself be judged a crime. And how could they explain it — by saying they were using it to extort me? But now, thanks to what you've done this morning they know they've got power over me and you've forced their hand. They know they can't delay now, either they get what they want or they hand the journal over to the authorities. You've given the Templars the advantage and I'll have to do business with them."

"I'm sorry, Your Grace, I didn't —"

"Think?" interrupted the Bishop. "No, you didn't." He turned away from Clarini and stared at the view from his window once more. "I shall be busy preparing for the Congregation tomorrow, but when I come back I want a full report on your activities. And I mean a full report. I've left you to deal with things for far too long and God has punished me for it. Well, I'm not giving you a free rein anymore, so get your hounds off my streets. And dismiss every one of them, especially that little rat I see sometimes about the Palace. What's his name?"

"Gonzales."

"Get rid of him. And do it before the end of the afternoon. You may go."

Clarini walked to the door in a daze. The Bishop, the man he loved almost as a father, had shattered in a moment the world of power and influence that he had built from nothing.

"And you *will* attend the Congregation, Nico," said the Bishop, as Clarini opened the door. "Until I've had your report I want to know where you are. Be there in time to sup on the day after tomorrow. That's an order."

The Bishop gave Clarini sufficient time to quit the vicinity of his study before going to see his senior secretary.

"Roberto," he said, as he entered the secretary's small office. "I want you to issue instructions to ring the bells of San Antolin, San Lazaro and San Miguel tonight at the second hour."

"Your Grace?"

"Don't question my orders! Do it!"

Returning to his study the Bishop sank to his knees and prayed for God's guidance. He had always tried to do his best for Nico, but he had a streak of wildness in him that seemed beyond control. Had he indulged him too much? Perhaps, if he had ignored the Abbot all those years ago and thrashed the boy and made him buckle to life as a monk he would have turned into a better man. The Bishop knew the fault lay with him, rather than Nico. He was the one who had promised his mother to look after him. Lucrezia Clarini came from one of Rome's oldest and noblest families and her father, who doted on her, was determined that his beautiful daughter would marry a prince. However, when she was sixteen she had fallen in love. Not with a prince, but the man was of noble birth and he had loved her passionately, even though he knew it was wrong. He was a young priest and a rising star and his mentor, a high official in Rome's Curia, had persuaded Count Clarini to appoint his young protégé to the post of family confessor. The priest was seven years her senior and he loved her from the moment he saw her. It took months to seduce her, but she succumbed at last and they loved in secret. Then she found a life, growing inside her.

She was undone. And when she refused to name the father, her own father disowned her and the unborn bastard. Banished from Rome, she was kept prisoner on her father's estate outside the City. Through Fortuna's cruel humour, only the family's confessor — the cause of her fate — was allowed to see her. And in all the times he had visited not once did she blame him. Only at her death — an hour after the birth — did she plead for a favour. He promised to care for their son, but he was young, and his career, as yet uncertain, would have been finished if it were known he had fathered a child. He heard and saw nothing of the boy until, five years after the birth, he had occasion to visit the Clarini estate. What he found almost broke his heart. His child was being kept like a dog: in a pen, chained to a post, a kennel to sleep in and only scraps of food to eat. There and then he had sworn to God that he would never again desert his son. He had ordered the servants to release him and he'd taken the boy back to Rome and placed him in the care of a monastery. Then he'd gone directly to the Count and in a violent rage he'd resigned his post. When his mentor in the Curia asked for his reasons he told the old man what he'd found on the Clarini estate and of his disgust for the Count, although he didn't say the boy was his son. His act of charity was reported widely — even, it was said, to the Pope — and he was praised for his saintliness. His career progressed and no one in the Church was surprised when he was appointed to rule Palencia.

If he had been challenged now some twenty years on — as Bishop of his city — to explain why the son that he dare not recognise, whom he had sworn to bring to righteous manhood was working in the cellars of his Palace, using means he preferred not to hear about, he would have said that he never intended it. Indeed, he would say that until the Abbot had warned him the boy's fiery temperament could not be contained within his monastery's walls, he had expected Nico would become a monk. Guided by the Abbot he had taken the boy away and sent him to be trained in the priesthood. But his headstrong ways and violent temper had soon led him into trouble. Returning from Rome to his native Spain the Bishop had set him to work as a junior secretary. But there had been difficulties in Palencia too and in despair he had sent Nico to learn the art of soldiering. Here at last he found his calling: his strong physique — inherited from the Clarini males — his aggression and fearlessness made him an ideal soldier. Unfortunately he was a priest. However, by the time Nico returned to Palencia from the military the Bishop had realised that the most intractable issues of his government were secular rather than religious and he needed someone with Nico's qualities to take them on. In due course many *administrative problems* — as the Bishop habitually called them — had arisen. He dealt with the great majority, but when they required more radical solutions they became *problems for Nico* and the Bishop left Nico to do whatever he thought necessary.

52

William rode into Ponferrada castle in the fifth hour of the morning. On setting out from Carrion de los Condes five days earlier he had thought to slip by and go directly to Samos. On reflection however he decided that he must call on Bescanson as a matter of courtesy. It had been a hard dusty journey and he was very tired. His stallion was in poor condition too and once inside the gates he walked the beast to the stables and sent for his squire. He was talking to the lad when Bescanson strode into the stable yard and, after telling the squire to attend to his duties, he took William by the arm and steered him purposefully towards a quiet corner.

"God take you, Stanley!" he whispered, fiercely, once he saw they wouldn't be overheard. "I told you to come straight back here. That was fifteen days ago. Fifteen days! Where in the name of Christ have you been?" He crossed himself quickly to ask pardon for his minor blasphemy. "Montagnac's played hell with me; threatening me with God knows what for dereliction of duty. Believe me Brother you've got a Devil of a lot of explaining to do."

"Montagnac's alive?"

"Alive and kicking. And he's been kicking my arse from the moment he got back from Samos."

"When was that?"

"Yesterday; he came in the Abbot's coach. The Abbot's going on to Leon; he gave Montagnac a lift."

"How is he?"

"Don't worry, he's back to his old self," Bescanson said grimly. "And he's waiting to see you in his solar. So move your arse!"

Plodding wearily up the steps in the north tower William reckoned that twenty-two days had elapsed since his last summons to Montagnac's solar. It felt like a lifetime. As he arrived outside he remembered the Abbot of Samos's comment that men like Montagnac didn't die easily. Fortuna had certainly been kind to him. What did she have in store for him, William wondered, praise or punishment? He was fairly sure he knew the answer: Bescanson had just given him a strong dose of reality — it would be punishment. Montagnac would acknowledge that he'd found the journal and fitted together every piece of its puzzle. Then his transgressions over the past twenty-two days would be examined, placed in the balance and he would be found wanting. But perhaps that would be his fate henceforth for committing the sin of pride.

He coughed and cleared his throat as he reached the solar's threshold. "I've come to report to you as ordered, Master."

Montagnac, who was sitting on the window seat, turned and smiled. "Brother William. I thought never to see you again. Are you well? Come and sit with me."

"Are *you* well Master?" said William as he sat down.

"I still have my aches and pains, but I'm recovered from my fall, praise be to God." He noted the tiredness on William's face and his travel stained apparel. "You've had a hard journey I see. Are you thirsty?" He pointed to an earthen pitcher and beaker, on the seat next to William. "There's water if you wish it."

"I'm fine, thank you Master."

"As you like. Well, can I hear your report?"

William nodded and began to speak about the events of the past twenty—two days and, with one or two interruptions from Montagnac, he spoke altogether for over a quarter of the hour.

Since he had heard Palencia's bells ringing at the appointed hour he'd struggled to find solutions to two problems: putting the facts together to decipher Cardiaye's formula and deciding how he could omit Cristina from his report, whilst obediently telling his Master all. He had solved Cardiaye's riddle as he was passing Astorga, but a solution to his second problem had eluded him and it was only as he'd reached the summit of Monte Irago that he'd found the answer. Speaking to God before the altar in San Marcos he had drawn a clear distinction between his vow to the Order and his vow to help Cristina; it would be inconsistent now to take another course. And if God was angry he felt sure that the Virgin would intercede to preserve the honour of an innocent lady.

"To summarise the main points then," said Montagnac, once he'd heard William's report. "After the skirmish at the Moor's cabin you found Cardiaye's journal. You had it translated and in so doing you realised that something happened to him between Carrion and Sahagun that made him fearful. Then, quite by chance, in Leon, you heard the term 'Bishop's man' and that set you on the path to Palencia, where you were able to elicit that it was Clarini who paid the Moor to kill Cardiaye. Finally, you deceived its Bishop into confirming that he's party to it."

William nodded. "Once I heard Palencia's bells I had no more doubts and on the way back I deciphered finally the formula in Cardiaye's journal."

"Can I see this famous journal?"

William passed it to Montagnac who began to scan each page quickly.

"That's the page in question," said William, when Montagnac reached it. "If you look at the dates you can see the record he made in Carrion. Then there's a gap of four days before he arrives in Sahagun when he takes up his record again. The distance between Carrion and Sahagun is less than nine leagues; he could have ridden there in a day easily on his palfrey. But he didn't go to

Sahagun; he went to Palencia instead. Carrion to Palencia is about the same distance — a day's ride. The next day he stayed in Palencia and on the third day he returned to Carrion and stayed there overnight. The next day he went to Sahagun — another day's ride. That's what he was doing for those four days."

"There is another explanation Brother; he could have visited some of the shrines off the Camino. That would account for the missing four days."

"It would, but every time he left the Camino to visit a church or a shrine he made a note of it. He makes no mention of visiting anywhere in those four days. All we have is that formula."

"You mean this strange figure?" Montagnac stabbed it with his forefinger. "It doesn't make any sense."

"Yes Master it does, once you know the Bishop is involved you can set it against the facts and see plainly what Cardiaye has recorded. Palencia's University has yet to appoint a new master. Delmirez was to have been, until he published his criticisms of the War. They've done a lot of damage to the University's standing and it's no secret that the Bishop is trying to rebuild its reputation. Cardiaye was a scholar of some repute. 'One of the finest in Christendom,' according to the Abbot of Samos. And he was ambitious; although I got the impression he hadn't yet made his mark. I think the Bishop invited Cardiaye to Palencia to offer him mastership of Palencia University. That's what 'MUP' on the left-hand side of 'versus' means: 'Master of the University of Palencia'."

"And the letters on the right hand side of the line — what do they mean?"

"Another fact we know is that Cardiaye was on a commission for the Pope. According to Delmirez the journal was a record of every place he had visited on and off the Camino, including notes on easy river crossings, good hostals and clean water. What does that remind you of Master?"

"The Codex Calixtinus."

"That's right, the pilgrim's guide to Santiago, written for Cluny by Aymery Picard and commended by Pope Calixtinus. And fifty years on here's another monk from Cluny, with a commission from the Pope, going over the same ground as the Codex."

"He was revising it?"

"I'm sure of it. The letters, 'RC — DP' to the right of the 'versus' stand for 'Revise Codex — Detour Palencia'. That was the substance of the Bishop's offer to Cardiaye: make Palencia an official stop on the way to Santiago and you'll be Master of Palencia University. All Cardiaye had to do in return was find a reason to divert the pilgrims' trail south to Palencia. It's not an insurmountable problem because there is a road of sorts to it from Fromista. Once the pilgrims reached Fromista they would head south to Palencia, from there they would take the road that goes directly north to Carrion. It would mean a detour of about ten leagues.

The pilgrims' places between Fromista and Carrion would no longer be on the Camino of course. But they'd have some visitors still; the villagers on that stretch who profit from the pilgrims would just have to make do with less. The important thing as far as the Bishop was concerned is that it wouldn't have upset the powerful interests: the Benedictines, our Order, the Knights of Santiago, the bigger towns and cities — their hospitals and hospices wouldn't have been affected at all. Cardiaye was a scholar; I'm sure he could have found good reasons to make Palencia an official stop. He'd have been well rewarded and Palencia's problems would've been solved, no one would have been any the wiser and no great harm would have been done. It's a very clever plan and the Bishop must have thought Cardiaye would seize his offer with both hands. But, according to Delmirez, Cardiaye was a firm believer in scholarly integrity and I think he refused the offer and threatened to expose the Bishop's scheming."

And that explains the 'IwillP' that's written under 'versus'; 'I will punish'. He was going to report the Bishop."

"It could also mean 'Innocent will punish'. Perhaps Cardiaye told the Bishop he would make a report to the Pope. People say that Innocent is determined to stamp out corruption; I can't see him taking kindly to anyone who tries to interfere with Christendom's third greatest pilgrimage. The Bishop must have thought carefully about the likely consequences of Cardiaye's threat and rather than face Innocent's wrath he had Clarini kill him. If it hadn't been for your suspicions he would have got away with it too: Cardiaye would have been just another pilgrim who'd been robbed and killed on the Camino."

"Why does the Bishop want Palencia included in a revised Codex?"

"Oh that's simple. He has great plans for his city but insufficient money. Once Palencia became an official stop on the Camino pilgrims would flock there; the city would grow rich and he'd reap the taxes."

Montagnac leaned back against the wall and closed his eyes. "You've taken my breath away, Brother. I can see now that you've been hiding your light under a bushel. But tell me." He opened his eyes and looked directly at William. "Can you prove any of this? I ask because the only evidence you seem to have is this diagram in Cardiaye's journal. I'm not disputing anything you've said; indeed, the fact the Bishop rang the church bells is powerful confirmation. But it will be almost impossible to convince a court of it. All those who could have served as witnesses are dead, save you, and you can't swear before God that it was Clarini at the Moor's cabin. We can't lay charges against a bishop without incontrovertible proof. The Order in Spain is weak enough as it is; to act on this would be exceedingly dangerous for us."

"With your permission, Master, I have a suggestion. I agree, I don't think we will be able to bring charges against the Bishop but we might convince him to give up Clarini to justice. We have the journal, he's prepared to trade for it, and I suggest we ask for Clarini."

"The Bishop would never agree; Clarini would implicate him at his trial."

"Does he have to go before a court? We could deal with Clarini in the same way the Bishop has dealt with Delmirez. The castle's dungeons are old but they could be made serviceable easily."

Montagnac stared at William for moment or two. "You really have been hiding yourself away haven't you, Brother William? Up until this morning I always took you for a good, honest knight but I see now that you are quite politic."

"I had a good teacher, Master — I was in Richard Lionheart's company for several years. I know well enough how princes play the game they call 'politics'. I'm sure the Bishop will sacrifice Clarini if we can fox him into believing it's the only way to save his own skin."

"I see," said Montagnac softly. "Can I take you up on a name you mentioned a few moments ago? The Abbot of Samos tells me you disobeyed his order that Delmirez be denied writing materials. Is that so?"

William guessed they had reached the point when Montagnac would begin to list and examine all his transgressions.

"Yes," he said firmly.

"Delmirez has also managed to make sense of Cardiaye's formula, which hasn't pleased the Abbot."

"Do you know whether Delmirez is saying the same as me?"

"I think so from what the Abbot said, but that's not the point Brother, you have transgressed against the Abbot and he's asked me to punish you. What would you suggest I say to him?"

"I think finding a murderer is more important than giving pen and paper to Delmirez. All right, he knows the truth about Cardiaye's murder. But what harm can he do? He can't talk about it to anyone: he's a prisoner."

"What do you think of Delmirez? Did he discuss any of his ideas with you?"

"Not really. But he was certainly a Godsend. Without his translation and suggestions I wouldn't have solved the murder. As to his ideas —" He shrugged. "They're just castles in the air. We're committed to fighting this War and nothing he says is going to change it."

Montagnac smiled. "I agree. Well, you have given me a great deal to think about, Brother William and it will take me some time to come to a conclusion. I don't want us to rush into anything. I'll keep Cardiaye's journal, if you don't mind."

"Of course, Master."

"You look very tired. When did you eat last?"

"Yesterday, I think."

"In that case, I want you to go to the kitchen. Tell them I said they were to feed you. Choose whatever you like. Then go to the dormitory and sleep. I don't want to see you at either Sext or Noones, and that's an order. We will talk again when you are refreshed. I will send for you."

"Thank you Master," said William, rising stiffly from the window seat.

"Thank *you* Brother," said Montagnac. "One more thing," he added, as William reached the solar's threshold. "You've done well, very well, and I will see to it that you're rewarded. Now go and get some sleep."

On the way down the tower's steps William could only marvel at his reception. Bescanson's comments had prepared him for an angry tirade; instead he had received a full and sympathetic hearing. And praise and promise of reward — something that Montagnac had never offered before to anyone in his command. Was this a new Montagnac? Alive by a miracle; his nature changed by the fall? Or was there another reason for his sudden change of behaviour?

53

William had gone to the dormitory with a belly full of food and he'd slept until the bell rang for Vespers. Feeling fresher, he donned his knight's robe and walked, in the pinky grey light of dusk, to the chapel where he had taken his usual place among his fellow knights and sergeants. Acknowledging their nods of greeting, he noticed the Abbot of Samos standing at Montagnac's side at the front of the congregation. The chaplain led the devotion and at its conclusion Montagnac beckoned William.

"Attend on me after supper. We'll meet here in the chapel; it will be easier than going to my quarters," said Montagnac. He turned towards the Abbot who was standing beside him. "You know Brother William of course."

"Indeed I do," said the Abbot coldly, glowering at William. "He disobeyed my orders."

"In a good cause, Abbot," said Montagnac soothingly, "in a good cause."

"So you say," said the Abbot grimly.

"Shall we go to the refectory?" Montagnac bowed to the Abbot and gestured towards the chapel's open door. "I told the kitchen to prepare something different from our normal fare in honour of having you sup with us."

As Montagnac and the Abbot made their way to the refectory, William walked behind at a respectful distance. Montagnac seemed to have damped down the Abbot's wrath but he sensed that his close attendance could easily re-ignite it.

Supper, like every meal, was eaten in two sittings; knights ate first; sergeants, squires and serving brothers entered only when their betters had finished. The Rule required meals to be eaten in silence while the chaplain read to them from Holy Scripture. In large commanderies, this task was shared generally between chaplain and those knights who could read Latin. In smaller houses however, like Ponferrada, the chaplain performed the ritual and, at the meal's conclusion, he ate alone. While every brother had an allotted place at table, the Master could choose his. The previous Master had taken a seat in the company of his fighting men. Montagnac, in contrast, had chosen from the beginning to eat by himself at a separate table.

Knights were standing beside their benches when Montagnac entered with the Abbot, who was to share his isolation. Grace was said and the company sat down to eat in the glow of flames that rose from the lamps of oil on the tables, highlighting faces and casting long shadows onto the walls. The meal that Montagnac had ordered was especially good: a portion of chicken empanada, roasted goat and peaches preserved in wine. William, in common with the rest, could only wonder at the change in their Master — for him to show an interest in their victuals was new entirely. But to judge him was unfair, some whispered, because the previous Master had also taken care to treat an eminent outsider.

After supper, William and Montagnac walked together to the chapel and once inside Montagnac bid him take a taper to the flame that burned on the altar and light the chapel's small oil lamps. There were two chairs only. Montagnac sat in the Master's and invited William to take the chaplain's.

"I have thought all afternoon about what you told me," said Montagnac, as William sat down, "and I have decided to go to Leon to see our Provincial Commander. The Abbot has agreed I can ride with him in his coach, which will certainly make it an easier journey."

"Do you want me to come too?" asked William, sure that Montagnac would want him by his side in Leon.

"No. I shall take Bescanson and two sergeants as escort." He could see the surprise and disappointment on William's face. "I'm sorry but there are good reasons for leaving you behind. For a start, you are still tired from your journeying, but the main reason is that I don't want you appearing before the Commander. He dismissed your story out of hand before and I don't think it's a good idea to present you again. I shall see him on my own: I know Pelet; I'll have a better chance of convincing him."

"What if he doesn't believe you either, Master?" William was certain that Montagnac was ignorant entirely of Pelet's opinion of him.

Montagnac smiled. "I have more powers of persuasion than you, I think. But you're right. He may not. Nevertheless, it is politic to present the matter to him in the first instance. If he accepts your theory — and without proof it is only a theory — then I shall have his endorsement when I approach the Bishop. If he rejects it I shall have to tackle the Bishop on my own and I confess that at this moment I have no clear idea of how to go about it. But he's in Leon for the next two weeks at the Bishops' Congregation so it will be easy to find him. And it started today so there will be plenty of time still for us to do business. The Abbot's going to the Congregation too. Perhaps he'll know the best way to approach the Bishop; I'll ask him on the journey."

"You won't tell him the reason? He's cousin to the Bishop by the way."

"Of course not! Do you take me for a fool?"

"Will you ask for Clarini as I suggested?"

"I will ask certainly, but we don't always get what we want, as well you know. Clarini will be punished though, one way or another. Does that satisfy you Brother?"

"Yes Master," said William, although he wanted desperately to argue against it. It was he who had solved the case and he knew the detail, not Montagnac. How could the man hope to convey the whole story without him being there? But he could not contradict. At San Marcos he'd vowed that henceforth he would obey his superiors' orders and he realised that part of his desire to face Pelet again was pride.

"Good. The Abbot and I will set out at dawn. We should be in Leon the day after tomorrow. I can't say when I'll return, probably sixteen or seventeen days from now. You'll be in charge while I'm away. I gave the order this afternoon." He rose from his chair and started towards the door. "There's nothing special I want you to do, just keep the command running smoothly. And blow out the lamps when you leave," he added, as he opened the door. William liked the idea of command, although he realised with regret that he would not be able to visit Samos to see Delmirez, as he had planned, until Montagnac had returned from Leon.

54

It was sixteen days later, in the hour after Noones, when the lookout on the castle's east wall spied a column of soldiers coming down the trail from Foncebadon and by the time William was climbing the steps to the rampart the sentry was calling out their disposition.

"Eleven knights, a small group — maybe four or five — that look like clerics, squires and about twenty foot soldiers bringing up the rear, sir."

"What are their colours?" asked William as reached the rampart.

"White surcoat with single red cross, sir. Templars, or Santiagos."

"Let me see," said William, peering over the wall at the approaching troop. "They look like — They're Santiagos," he said, once he could see that the upright of the red cross on their surcoats was in the form of a sword. "But the one leading is a Templar."

"Two in the column are wearing black sir."

"It's our two sergeants and Bescanson," said William, catching sight of that knight's golden beard.

"Sergeant Lorca! Call out the guard!" he shouted down to the duty sergeant on the gate. "You better challenge them when they get within hailing distance," he said to the sentry on the rampart beside him, another long-serving sergeant. "You know what a stickler young Bescanson is," he added, before starting down the steps to the yard.

When the company came clattering through the gates he stood ready to greet them. They pulled up their horses, Bescanson nodded to the captain of the Santiagos who shouted an order for both knights and their squires to dismount. The grizzled old sergeant of foot roared at his men to stand easy, and they broke ranks immediately and ambled over to the courtyard's west wall to sit in the shade. As Bescanson eased himself stiffly out of his saddle William took the opportunity to look the visitors over. He knew none of the Santiago knights, nor any of the clerics, who were standing in a group with their backs to him. Then one of them turned and William saw the crimson eye patch and livid scar on his face. Even though they had never met he had no doubt of it. It was Clarini! What in the Name of Christ was he doing here? "Has all gone well?" asked Bescanson, once both his feet were on the ground.

"No problems to report," said William, looking still in Clarini's direction.

He had enjoyed being in command: within the daily constraints of chapel, inspections and garrison business he had been able to please himself and most days he had found an excuse to sneak away to bathe in the Sil.

"What is this all about?" He nodded over his shoulder at the crush of soldiers. "And why are the clerics here?" he added, glancing again at Clarini as the priest happened by chance to look simultaneously at him.

Their eyes met for a moment and he returned Clarini's impassive stare without blinking. Clarini too turned away without a hint of recognition. But given the circumstances of their meeting, William would have been surprised if Clarini had recognised him. What was the whore's son doing here? And where was Montagnac?

"Never fear, Brother," said Bescanson, oblivious to the fact that William was as tense as a drawn bowstring. "All will be explained. Now, I want you to tell all our knights and sergeants to muster in the hall as soon as possible; the clerics want to speak to them. Once that's over we need to have a chapter meeting. You!" he shouted, as he spotted a senior serving brother. "Go tell the cook we need fifteen extra meals at the first sitting and another thirty out here in the courtyard." He took hold of the brother's habit and pulled him closer. "And tell cook not to lavish too much attention on this scum," he added, confidentially, nodding towards the squires and foot soldiers. The brother ran off and Bescanson turned back to William who was overflowing with questions. "God damn it Brother! Are you still here? I gave you an order. And see to it that these squires know where to take their horses."

Knights and sergeants were drawn up on three sides of the hall's great table, standing to attention, when Bescanson and the clerics entered. Bescanson strode directly to the top of the table and stood by the Master's chair while the clerics took their places beside stools that William had thought to place alongside it. The chaplain said the customary prayer as prescribed by the Rule and Bescanson ordered knights and sergeants to take their places. However, because it was customary that only the Master could sit in the Master's chair he continued to stand. Once the company had settled Bescanson announced that two meetings would be held in the course of the after noon. Their guests would lead the first; a chapter meeting would follow. William was deaf to Bescanson's words. Bewildered by the events of the last quarter hour, his thoughts were upon what Clarini's presence betokened and, as Bescanson began to introduce the clerics, he took the chance to study the man he'd disfigured.

He saw immediately that Clarini's appearance was in sharp contrast with his fellows. The crowns of their heads were shaved entirely, with only a narrow surrounding fringe. Clarini's tonsure was tiny and almost hidden by his thick, raven hair. His fellows' beards were long and unkempt. His was tidy and trimmed short. They were wearing clerical habits, of black. He was dressed in a tailored riding tunic of deep blue. Their soft bodies and pallid faces told of lives with ample food, sweet wine and long hours spent in prayer. He was tall, lean and muscular, his face was tanned and he seemed to glow with robust health. His age was no more than five and twenty and seeing his right profile, with Roman nose, strong jaw and chiselled features

William thought him handsome. Then, in turning to whisper in the ear of a fellow, he offered a view of his left side and William stared, transfixed by the sight of the vivid red scar that ran from jaw to eye.

William's attention returned to the meeting the moment he heard Bescanson call on Francisco Cee, Archdeacon of Palencia, to speak. Cee rose from his stool, thanked Bescanson and went directly to the reason for his presence at Ponferrada. In the course of their annual Congregation the bishops of Spain had convened a special hearing to consider charges against a priest and teacher called Diego Delmirez, heir renounced to the Count of Soria. After listening to Delmirez's defence they had charged him with heresy and ordered him to be given into the custody of his bishop at Palencia, who would be responsible for his trial and execution. Charges had been made also against his niece Dona Cristina Delmirez, heiress to the Count of Soria. The bishops had found her complicit in his crime. But since she was a woman, unable to understand truly the full import of her uncle's ideas, the bishops favoured clemency. She was to be detained indefinitely in the convent of Las Huelgas Reales at Burgos in the care of its Abbess and, on the present Count's death, the King of Castile would exercise his right to reclaim the lands and title of Sorria and do with it as he wished.

During his imprisonment at Leon, Delmirez had revealed the existence of a settlement in the Valle del Silencio whose people had dedicated their lives to his heretical ideas. He also confessed that in pursuit of his heretical teachings they had committed foul murder on a respected Christian teacher and scholar, one Rolfe Cardiaye of Cluny. They were to be arrested and taken to Astorga where they would be tried in the Bishop's court for heresy and murder. Their settlement was to be razed. Cee and his fellows had come to Ponferrada on the authority of the Congregation in order to supervise the heretics' removal to Astorga. The bishops recognised that the Valle de Silencio was in lands vouchsafed to the Templars by the King of Leon and that it had no power to command them to make the arrest. However, Ponferrada's Master had promised his full support while asking for knights from the Order of Santiago to supplement his own meagre force. This had been agreed and the Bishop of Astorga had provided foot soldiers to ensure sufficient men for the task.

Bescanson thanked Cee, and knights and sergeants sat in silence as the clerics filed out the hall, but the moment its doors closed they began to murmur animatedly. William sat quietly however, staring at the table, trying to make sense of what he had heard and willing himself to appear composed. In an instant of time he had heard the people of Nueva Vida declared guilty of Cardiaye's murder — a lie of such magnitude that he wasn't sure still whether he had misheard. Delmirez was set for execution and it was likely that Cristina would remain, locked up, in Las Huelgas for the rest of her life. Clarini on the other hand — the arranger of Cardiaye's death and murderer in his own right — was as free as a bird. And Montagnac was nowhere in sight. It was beyond all contemplation: he was in despair and he felt as if he would sink under the weight of unanswered questions. How could bishops — men who represented God on earth — commit such sin?

"It's important I have your attention brothers," said Bescanson, who had remained standing beside the Master's chair throughout Cee's address.

William raised his eyes from the table and tried to concentrate on the chapter meeting.

"I have something of utmost importance I have to tell you," Bescanson was saying. "Robert Montagnac is Master of Ponferrada no longer, he has been posted to the Court of His Majesty Alfonso VIII, King of Castile."

Knights and sergeants sat in silence for several moments, stunned by the thunderbolt that Bescanson flung at them. Then, ignoring the Rule's insistence that chapter meetings be conducted in an orderly manner, they exploded into excited chattering. For William however, it was another body blow as he realised that Montagnac must have set out for Leon with the idea of making a profit from Cardiaye's journal. What had the scheming bastard offered in exchange for a place in Castile's Court?

He was deaf suddenly to his brethren's gabbling. He felt hot and then deathly cold: on the verge of fainting for the first time in his life, he gripped the edge of his bench, forcing himself to conquer it. His discipline held; the sounds of the meeting returned and Bescanson was banging on the table again and again calling for order. Knights and sergeants fell silent and Bescanson continued.

"We would have met before the clerics addressed us, if it had been my choice, but I was ordered to let Cee speak first. The first thing I have to say is that the Provincial Commander wants you all to be clear that arresting these heretics is a Templar operation — the Santiagos will be acting under the command of our new Master, which brings me to the reason for this meeting."

Fresh tension filled the hall as knights and sergeants looked at each other, each bursting to know the answer to the obvious question.

"By the authority of Brother Henri Armand Pelet, Provincial Commander for Leon and Castile, it is my happy duty to report that from this moment the Master of Ponferrada is our Brother Knight, William."

55

William believed that without the Virgin's help he would have lost all self-possession at that point in the meeting. His mind had been floundering already in the flood of revelations from Cee and Bescanson: his unexpected promotion to Master had all but sunk him. He had heard Bescanson's words and his brethren's spontaneous cheer and then, as if in a dream, he had watched Bescanson bow and beckon him take the Master's chair. Sitting at the head of the table, looking at the faces around it, he knew they expected their new Master to speak. But he could think of nothing to say and for a long moment his only thought was to flee. It was then that he called on Her help and in an instant a saying of Richard Lionheart's came to mind — 'If in doubt, say it short.' Finding his voice at last he thanked Bescanson and all the brethren for their support. Then, after calling for another meeting at the end of the hour, when he would speak about the situation at hand, he nodded to the chaplain to say the closing prayer and, leaving the hall, he asked Bescanson to attend him in the Master's solar.

Sitting in the solar's window seat, listening to Bescanson climbing the steps of the tower, William rehearsed the questions he wanted to ask.
"Come and sit with me," he said, as Bescanson arrived.
"I'm sorry for the dramatic way I announced your promotion Master," said Bescanson, as he sat down. "It's not my way as I'm sure you know, but the Commander gave me strict orders."
William dismissed the apology with a wave of his hand. "Forget it. I'm more interested in what happened in Leon. Tell me, did you see much of Montagnac while you were there?" he asked, casually.
"Hardly saw him at all. We dropped off the Abbot and Delmirez and —"
"Delmirez?" interrupted William, trying still to sound unconcerned.
"He was travelling with the Abbot. Didn't you know? He was here in Ponferrada when you got back. Montagnac had him locked up in the south tower."
"You mean he came in the coach from Samos with the Abbot and Montagnac?"
Bescanson nodded. "And of course, we left for Leon while the garrison was at Prime: that's why you didn't see him, you were in chapel. But I'm surprised nobody told you."

"And where did the Abbot take Delmirez once you got to Leon?"
"To the Bishop of Leon's palace." He shrugged. "I presume they locked him up in its dungeon. We went on to the commandery and Montagnac told me and the sergeants to get billets there, whilst he went to see the Commander. They were together for a long time. I know that because I had to see the clerk later to order food and he told me. Anyway, that was the last time I saw

Montagnac. I understand from the clerk that the Commander found quarters for him at Court."

"So you don't know whether he saw the Bishop of Palencia?"

"Oh yes, he saw him quite a bit, I think. I don't know whether you've spent any time at the commandery, there's nothing to do, I hate it. Anyway, I could tell by the clerk's attitude that something was going on, so to pass the time I used to go and talk to him." Bescanson smiled. "He chatters away like an old woman if you speak kindly to him. It was he who told me that Montagnac was going to and fro between the Bishop and the Commander."

"Did he say why?"

"Something to do with that dead monk's journal. He didn't know what exactly but he said the Commander was excited at the prospect of having a Templar attached to Castile's Court. I got the impression it was something Pelet had wanted for a long time. I think it was the Bishop of Palencia's support that did it. He's very close to the King of Castile apparently."

"You know I caught the man who murdered the monk don't you? Didn't you say anything when they accused these people at Nueva Vida? Didn't you think it strange even?"

"Of course I did Master. But the whole business was beyond belief: for instance the clerk told me that in the hearing Delmirez had accused his own bishop of killing the monk. I mean, how mad can you be? I know you found the murderer and I was dumbfounded when the Pelet told me different. But what could I say? I can't argue with the Provincial Commander."

"What precisely is Delmirez accused of — do you know?"

"Yes. Oh God. What is it called?" Bescanson drummed slowly on his knee with his fist. "It's a strange word. Pris — something. *Priscilianism*, that's it, Priscilianism."

"What in the name of Judas is that?"

"You don't know Master? I thought it was on everyone lips," said Bescanson facetiously. "It's the ideas of an early Christian, a holy man called Prisciliano. He came from Galicia. Had a big following across northern Spain apparently. He believed that monks and nuns should live together and that people should follow some of the old pagan ways. His followers couldn't eat meat and they had to walk barefoot and go naked in the sun. Or so the clerk said."

"Never heard of him."

"I'm not surprised: he lived a very long time ago. I think the clerk said he was executed by a bishop sometime around the year 400, long before the Moors conquered Spain, anyway."

"I thought Delmirez was in trouble because he'd argued against the War in Outreamer and here?"

"Had he? I don't know anything about that." He shrugged. "Perhaps that's part of this Priscilianism thing as well."

"But —" William hesitated: showing that he knew something of Delmirez's ideas was dangerous. But for the bishops to link Delmirez's views of the War with the ideas of this Prisciliano — a holy man who'd lived hundreds of years before the Moors invaded Spain — was absurd. "So what are these people at this Nueva Vida place supposed to be doing? Going round naked, tupping each other?"

Bescanson smirked. "That's what the bishops say. Whether it's true or not I don't know. I'm a soldier: I do as I'm told."

Now where have I heard that before? thought William. "Where is Nueva Vida precisely? The Valle de Silencio covers a large area."

"That's the problem. Nobody knows except Delmirez and he's not saying."

"He told them of its existence. Why stop there?"

Bescanson sighed. "I think his interrogators forgot he was an old man in their rush to get it out of him. They didn't kill him, but damn near. He's in a bad way I understand."

"This village falls under the ecclesiastical jurisdiction of the Bishop of Astorga, but two of these four clerics represent Palencia. Do you know why that is?"

"Francisco Cee is part of the Congregation's secretariat, I think," said Bescanson. "Clarini — the one with the scar — can identify Cristina Delmirez."

William had almost flushed at the mention of her name and he willed himself to appear unconcerned. "I'd have thought Cee could have done that. He is Archdeacon of Palencia after all: he must have seen her when she visited the city from time to time. Anyway I thought she'd been taken to Las Huelgas."

"She'll go there once they find her, but she's disappeared. The word is that she's fled to France, but she might have gone to ground at Nueva Vida. It's certainly possible: she won't know Delmirez confessed its existence under torture."

"I see. Is there anything more I need to know Hugh? This is my first task as Master: I don't want anything to go wrong."

"Only to say that Montagnac sent a message for you via the Commander."

"What is it?"

"He says to tell you that: 'Now you are Master you can punish the accused.' I suppose he's wishing you good luck on the operation."

"That's kind of him. Did he know that Delmirez had confessed this village by the way?"

"I can't see any reason why he wouldn't: the Commander's clerk did."

"Thank you Brother, that's been most helpful. Now, we're due to meet again very soon, but there are a couple of things to do before then. I've decided to lead the round up of these heretics myself. I want you to stay here and take charge while I'm away. And so as not to surprise you at the meeting, I'm telling you now that I'm appointing you as my deputy."

"Thank you, Master."

"There's no need to thank me. You're the best man for the job. I'm taking eight men — all sergeants — with me. It's more than we can afford but it's a big search area. I think it's important to get there tonight so we can start as soon as the sun gets up. We'll leave at dusk — there's plenty of moonlight still — and be there by midnight. I'm going now to speak to the Santiagos' captain and the sergeant of footmen and tell them to muster for food in the courtyard at half an hour before Vespers. I want you to tell the kitchen to have food ready to serve. And tell the cook I'm sorry I've changed the orders." He smiled at Bescanson. "It's never a good idea to upset cook. And make sure this priest — what's his name?"

"Clarini."

"Right. Clarini. Make sure he knows to muster in the courtyard too. I'll need to keep him close by if he knows Delmirez's niece."

The Santiagos' captain was in the courtyard, sitting in the late afternoon shade, when William found him. He grasped William's plan quickly and was already calling his knights together for a briefing as William hailed the sergeant of footmen. His words to the tough old soldier were brusque: his men would muster in the courtyard and march out of the castle at dusk, after they had been fed. Disobeying orders would merit a whipping.

The last sliver of the sun's rim was sinking below the horizon and the waning moon was rising in the darkening sky to the east when William rode into the courtyard to address his company. They were drawn up in three ranks. The Bishop of Astorga's foot soldiers were in front; dressed in thick broignes and iron caps they certainly had the look of professionals. The knights of Santiago and his sergeants made up the second and third ranks. The Santiagos were young: with the exception of their captain the oldest looked no more than two and twenty. None of them had seen combat, although they appeared to have the ardour of knights who had offered their lives to God. In contrast, William's eight sergeants were mature. Indeed he had taken care to chose the most experienced: men who would keep their heads and who would obey orders in a fight. Standing some distance behind him in a group were the clerics, with Francisco Cee, holding a staff with a crucifix atop, to the fore. Clarini, astride his black stallion, was a little way off. He was attired still in his blue riding habit to which he had added accessories: armoured mittens, a dagger and sword.

William cleared his throat: "Our task is to search out and arrest people who are living in a village somewhere in the Valle de Silencio," he said, his voice echoing off the courtyard's walls. "This will require stealth and discipline: if we alert them to our presence they will melt away into the forest. We will camp at the mouth of the valley tonight and begin the search at dawn. I'll give more detailed orders at that time."
He was on the point of giving the command to march when Cee's voice rang out: "You fight for the Faith!" he bellowed. "Rid us of these heretics. Send them to God's judgement and save your souls!"
William's fervent wish at that moment was to ride Cee down. Instead he nudged his stallion gently around and asked Cee to bless the company. The Archdeacon duly obliged and if his previous exhortation had left any doubt the words of his blessing made it plain to all — the Church was ordering William's company to put the people of Nueva Vida to the sword.

57

William's company reached the Valle de Silencio some two hours after leaving Ponferrada and bivouacked by the trail that led up to Penalbra. It was late September now and the mountain air at night was chilly and dank. Nevertheless, he refused the request to light fires and he insisted on a silent camp. Sergeants and knights accepted his orders stoically. Astorga's soldiers grumbled, as William knew they would, but they too were soon huddled inside their blankets and, exhausted by their long day's march, quickly asleep on the cold, damp ground. His sergeants were in better condition and he divided sentry duty between them; one to guard the horses, another to patrol the perimeter on a roster of two hours on, four off, 'til dawn.

Wrapped in his blanket, William lay on his back wrestling with questions that denied him sleep. Bescanson's answers had made clear that Pelet and Montagnac had connived to agree a bargain with the Bishop in which each had gained something that was precious to them and in so doing they had devised a foolproof plan. The more he thought about it the greater his despair: two senior Templars and a bishop had conspired to bear false witness against their neighbour and the Congregation had cynically exploited it. An idiot could see that that the charge of Priscilianism had been cooked up between them so that Palencia's Court could condemn Delmirez without reference to his ideas about the War. He was shocked and outraged, not because he was naïve — he knew something of statecraft's falsities — but because princes of the Church were willing to break one of His commandments to silence a misguided old man. They had committed a mortal sin and he wondered that God allowed it.

And what was his part in this conspiracy? he wondered. He was no longer an ordinary knight of the Temple, free from blame as long as he followed his superior's bidding, but an officer who bore the guilt of those under his command. Francisco Cee had called on him to murder women and children, but to obey orders you knew to be wrong was to deny your responsibility towards your fellow creatures: a responsibility that he had sworn personally to God when Philipe's father dubbed him knight. Did obedience to the Order override his knightly vows? But how could it? He was a knight first and foremost and knighthood was the essence of his being. How did other officer knights in the Temple — the highest officials who answered to God for the sins of all — how did they distinguish between right and wrong? Or was the secret of command the refusal to distinguish right from wrong? And was that why Pelet and Montagnac had promoted him — because they believed he could be relied upon to follow orders? He knew them now for godless villains and Montagnac's cunning message about Clarini was another example of their deceit. He wasn't offering up Clarini to rough justice; the reason the Italian had come to Ponferrada was to kill Cristina if she was hiding at Nueva Vida. A month or two earlier, William would have been proud to accept command of Ponferrada; he wished now that he could refuse it. But it was another penance for his sins of pride and he would endure it. He would not serve willingly under sinful men however and once he'd finished his sentence he would leave the Order and Devil take the consequences.

There was no debate in William's mind about Cee's call to kill the people of Nueva Vida. He didn't care whether Cee was speaking for Palencia alone or the whole damn Congregation of bishops: he wouldn't do it. The problem was how to stop it. He would have to lead a search and if it wasn't done professionally the Santiago's captain would soon become suspicious and, once they began a systematic sweep of the valley, it would be only a matter of time before they discovered the village. And then what? His command was a mixed bag and Cee had held out the hope of salvation if they did murder. Once they found the village it might be impossible to restrain them. And if Cristina was there — what then? He prayed she wasn't. But he was sure she would have realised that nowhere in Spain was safe for her and that she'd have fled to France.

She was always in his mind. He even dreamed about her — wooing her and winning her love, standing together against the world and defending her honour. He knew it was fantasy, nothing could come of his longing. He had restated his vow; he was a Templar, sworn to be chaste and his thoughts of her were an offence to God. And even if he wasn't a Templar — what could possibly come of it? He had betrayed her and she despised him, she might spit in his face but she would never take his hand. Even if, by some miracle, he could redeem himself in her eyes — what then? She would still deny his suit. What Philipe had said was right: he was a poor, ragged arsed English knight, whereas she was the daughter of a Count. His love for her was hopeless. But what if she was at Nueva Vida? The question persisted. Well, if she was and if Clarini or anyone else tried to harm her, he would cut the swine down in front of the whole company. Her life would be saved, but unless he could find a way for her to escape she would be made prisoner. What would she think of him, when they took her to Las Huelgas in chains?

He threw off his blanket and got to his knees. The Virgin would not let evil men murder innocents, even if they were bishops: She would guide him. At first he thought She was deaf to his prayers until he realised suddenly that there was only one way to save them. He thanked Her. He didn't like Her solution, but he could see the sense of it and there was time, it could be done. Taking care not to wake his squire he got to his feet and, after gathering his blanket, he made his way quietly to the horses' picket line.

"Sleep won't come tonight, Brother," he said, quietly, handing his blanket to the sergeant on sentry. "Cut that into pieces and muffle my horse's hooves, will you? I'm going to scout around while the moon's still up, see if I can find any signs of this village."

"Do you want one of us to come with you, Master?"

"No, I'll make less noise on my own. I'll be back well before dawn."

As he led his stallion away from the camp in the moonlight a voice inside kept saying that deserting his men in the field was a betrayal of his most fundamental duty as a soldier. And that it had nothing to do with justice and mercy: he was doing it out of pride. He argued with the voice: he wasn't deserting, he was saving lives and he would return by morning after he had set a wrong, right. On reaching the first trees of the forest that covered the floor of the valley he mounted his stallion and urged it along the path at a gentle trot. Guilt about leaving his men and breaking his newly made vows to the Order still nagged at him, but he carried on, with the wind moaning in the trees, fearing to look over his shoulder lest he saw the Devil at his back. And if Cristina was at Nueva Vida — what then? The question repeated and repeated. He told himself to stop thinking and concentrate on keeping to the track. He had chosen to follow his knight's vows to God rather than his vow of obedience to the Order: his fate now was in His hands.

It took more than an hour to find the old bridge. Once across it he walked with his horse through the ruin and set off down the narrow path that led to the village. A faint scent of wood smoke told him it was near and a few moments later the path opened out into the clearing. He had expected to be challenged, but no one was on guard and after tying his horse's reins to a tree he crept to the priests' hut.

A lamp stood on the ground between their rough wooden beds and he could see in the glow of its flame that both were asleep. Putting his hand over the priest's mouth he shook him gently. He awoke with a start and William had to force him back down on the bed.

"Don't worry, I'm not going to hurt you," whispered William, his hand clamped tightly over the priest's mouth. "Do you remember me? I came here with Dona Delmirez a few weeks ago. I'm here to help you; you're in great danger. I'm going to take my hand away from your mouth and let you up so that you can wake your friend. Do you understand?"

The priest nodded and William released him and once he had woken the imam William knelt on the floor between their beds.

"My God, you're a Templar!" hissed the priest, as he saw William's surcoat clearly. "You were in Soria's colours when you came before. Who are you?"

"What do you want? Have you come to kill us?" asked the imam in a loud voice.

"Shush!" whispered William. "It's important we don't frighten the village. There's a company of soldiers down the valley and they're coming for you. Wait!" He seized the arm of the imam to prevent him rising. "You've got three or four hours yet, there's time to save everyone as long as we don't start a panic. I want both of you to go round the huts and wake all the families. Tell them to collect their belongings — only what they can carry comfortably — and get the women to pack food on your donkeys. Then everyone should go and wait in the refectory."

"What about the rest of our animals?" asked the priest.

"Cut their tethers and run them off, they'll slow you down, you'll be safer without them."

"But they're all we have!"

"Then you'll have to get more!" hissed William. "You're going to lead everyone up the trail to Penalbra. You've been there before, I take it?"

Both men shook their heads.

"Neither has anyone else in the village," said the priest.

"Well then, listen carefully, once you're across the bridge just follow the river, the trail to Penalbra runs alongside it. Not long before you get there you'll see a little shrine to Our Lady. There's a path beside it that will lead you through the woods on the eastern side of the village. It runs close by it in places so tell everyone to keep quiet. It's quite steep but it will lead you to the mountain's eastern ridge. You should get there by first light."

"And what do we do then?" asked the priest.

"You climb it of course. Don't worry: you won't have to climb the mountain itself, only the slope that goes up to the start of the rocks. It's covered in grass and stones; it's not especially tough. And remember to keep on the east side of the ridge once you're clear of the trees, so you can't be seen from the village. It's a couple of thousand paces from the end of the woods to the start of the rocks that go up to the summit. You'll see it immediately you come out of the wood — a huge lump of rock that rises almost vertically from the ridge. Once you get to it, turn left and follow it until you're on the other side of the mountain. It's probably best to head south from there."

"You talk of climbing mountains, but we have children and babies," said the imam.

"You can do it, believe me, it's not that difficult. You'll see what I mean once you come out of the woods above Penalbra. If there were another safe way out of here, I'd tell you. Now, you must make sure that people don't take too much. I don't want them dumping stuff when they find they can't carry it. Everything that's left behind must be hidden, everything. The soldiers must believe you left here days ago, so make sure the women douse the fires and spread the ashes."

"Where shall we hide the things we leave behind?" asked the priest.

"The children have a secret place: we'll hide everything there. I'll make sure the soldiers don't find it."

"How can you do that?" asked the imam.

William had decided on his way from the camp that there was no point in lying to them. "I'm their commander."

The priest and imam looked at him in disbelief.

"It's not a trap. I'm trying to save you. Please trust me and believe it when I say that if you don't leave here, the soldiers may kill you. I might not have the power to stop it."

"Why are you doing this?" asked the imam.

"I made a vow to God when I was still young. Now will you please go and get your people moving. And tell them to do it as quietly as they can."

They stared at him in silence for several moments; then they nodded to each other, got off their beds and left the hut.

On his way to the refectory, William could see signs of people lighting tapers inside their huts and a few moments later he heard them moving about. He sat on a bench and watched their progress, impatiently clasping and slapping his mittened hands together. The moon was past its zenith but the stars were bright and it was light enough to see people scurrying to and fro across the clearing. Time passed and villagers began to gather in the refectory, whispering together and looking at him. Everyone had a bundle and some were carrying earthen oil lamps, which they set down on the tables. One or two smiled; most were hostile. Only the boy Abdul greeted him and after volunteering to keep lookout he ran off down the path to the bridge before William could say it was unnecessary. On William's count, everyone was present except the priest and imam. He was getting anxious, he had planned to see everyone safely away before returning to his men; precious time was being lost. He asked if anyone knew where they were and when no one answered he decided to go and look for them. He was on the point of doing so when they emerged out of the darkness in the company of Cristina. At any other time he would have been overjoyed to see her, but not here, not now.

"What are *you* doing here?" she asked.

He nodded towards her two companions. "I'm sure they've told you that already."

"I want to hear it from you."

"Please, lady, we haven't much time. We have to get these people out of here. Now!"

"Why should we trust you? You're our enemy. Have you betrayed us?"

"No! I give you my word."

"You gave me your word once before."

"I know I failed you and I'd cut off my hand if it would set things right. But please, my lady, for the love of God, don't let what's happened stop you listening to me now."

He glanced over his shoulder at the villagers who looked as if they were enjoying his tussle with her. Time was running away, but he didn't want to tell her about her uncle in front of these people.

"There's something I have to tell you Cristina and I'd prefer to do it in private, if I could."

"You're the one who's turned up in the middle of the night frightening everyone. If you've got something to say you better spit it out."

She'd left him no choice. "As you wish lady," he said grimly, before turning to face the villagers. "In the last few days Diego Delmirez has been tortured — almost to death." He heard her small cry of pain, but he carried on. "He's confessed your existence, he's marked to die and so are you if you don't leave this place."

"It's good advice lady," a man's voice called from the direction of the path, silencing the hubbub that had erupted at William's news.

William turned on his heel to see Clarini, sword in hand, entering the clearing. Christ help me! he pleaded, I've lead him straight to her!

"I found this on the path, I'm sure someone will want to claim it," said Clarini casually, tossing an object that landed with a solid thud onto one of the refectory tables.

The villagers uttered a collective cry of horror; a woman screamed, another sobbed. It was Abdul's head. William grasped the hilt of his sword.

"I'll kill her!" cautioned Clarini, pressing his blade's point to Cristina's throat before William's was clear of its scabbard.

"And how are you my lady?" he continued urbanely, as he watched William sheath his sword. "I confess, finding you here is an added prize. Everyone thought you had fled to France."

"You betrayed us!" Cristina hissed at William, her voice thick with hatred.

"Tush lady," said Clarini, his eyes on William still. "You're too harsh. Did you not hear? Your uncle betrayed you; this brave knight came to rescue you. I watched him leave the camp and I knew then what he intended. That was your plan wasn't it, Master?" he said to William. "To help this rabble escape, then rejoin your men and lead them on a wild goose chase? Or were you going to run away too?"

"And what's your plan?" replied William. "To kill us all?" He nodded towards the families clustered behind him in the refectory. "There's too many of us."

"Diego Delmirez is dead," Clarini said loudly to the villagers. "His heart gave out under torture." He smiled as Cristina began to sob. "It was simpler than a trial," he added, quietly. "We both know these people are harmless," he said to William, "but God puts each of us on earth for a reason and when Astorga hangs them they will have served their purpose. I take no personal interest in their deaths however. My purpose here is to kill you, that's why I came to Ponferrada." He touched the crimson patch over his sightless eye. "To give you full measure for this."

"But you didn't recognise me in the castle yard."

"Why do you think Pelet promoted you Master? So I would know you of course. As to the number of these people, do you think I care for that?"

He swung his blade across the imam's throat and returned its point to threaten Cristina with such accuracy and speed that William couldn't believe it, until he saw the imam fall.

"Stay where you are or I'll kill you all!" Clarini shouted over the villagers' screams. Women sobbed and children cried in fear, but nobody moved.

"You see?" he gloated. "A wolf takes no fear from the size of the flock."

"I'll kill you!" said William, but a tiny part of him wondered whether he could. Clarini's ability with a sword was breathtaking.

"No, you won't. You'll try and I'll welcome the sport. Pelet says you could match Richard Lionheart. Is that true?"

"Why don't you stop clacking and find out?"

"Why not indeed." Clarini punched Cristina suddenly in the face with his mittened fist, knocking her to the ground. "Draw your sword Master."

The villagers fled into the shadows the instant their blades clashed. They fought in the glow of the stars and setting moon and the lamps that were burning still on the refectory's tables. With sword and dagger they cut and thrust, blocked and parried as they attacked and defended, each probing to find the other's weakness. William circled constantly to attack Clarini's blind side, Clarini countered with thrusts to William's left. It was an even match: one would advance, forcing the other to retreat, then the one in retreat would force back his attacker. The duel continued on and on, to and fro, steel ringing, the pair grunting and panting as they swung their blades until gradually, blow by blow, Clarini began to gain the upper hand. His attacks forced William to retreat further than before and William's counter attacks were soon repelled by his superior speed. William fought on, but Clarini was ten years his junior and unencumbered by armour, his wind was good and he was fresh still. William on the other hand was losing the power to swing his sword, his legs were beginning to buckle, and he was gasping for breath. He was finished and he knew it. Perhaps, if he could shed his hauberk and chausses he could beat Clarini although he doubted, even then, whether he could match the man's extraordinary speed.

Now he was in constant retreat, parrying and blocking, parrying and blocking, fending off blows of increasing ferocity.
"Come on old man, you're losing," taunted Clarini, as he pushed William further and further back, past the village oven and the church, out of the village centre until they were at the edge of the clearing. William stepped back from a blow that would have sliced through his throat, his heel caught an exposed tree root and he staggered, missed his footing, his guard dropped and Clarini's sword thrust pierced his hauberk and passed through his left side with searing pain. He fell heavily onto his back and Clarini swept the sword from his hands with a blow that sent it spinning away. Defenceless and whooping for breath, William lay across the tree roots with Clarini, standing over him, one booted foot trapping the dagger in William's left hand, his blade's point resting in the hollow at the base of William's throat.

"I had planned to make your death seem like an accident," said Clarini panting heavily. He took half a dozen deep breaths and his breathing eased. "But I owe you the honour of a worthy opponent and I shall say now that you died defending the Faith. You stumbled on the village by chance and fought to the death: that will be the story. My bishop will say a Mass for you: William Stanley the hero, martyred by the heretics of Nueva Vida. Has a nice ring to it, don't you think? In time you might even become a local saint. I

salute you Templar, you fought well. I would like to have seen you fight in your youth. Is there anything you want to say before I kill you?"
William tried to speak, to pray that he'd spare Cristina, but without the breath, he could only shake his head. "Very well, make your peace with God."

"No!" shrieked Cristina, emerging suddenly out of the darkness and hurling a knife at Clarini's head.
Surprised, he ducked instinctively. William sucked up a lung full of air and grabbing Clarini's sword blade with his right hand he wrested his left free and lunged forwards to thrust his dagger into the Italian's crotch. Clarini screamed; his legs sagged and William caught hold of his tunic, pulled him down and stabbed him in the heart.

"Oh Jesus! Are you hurt badly? Please God, tell me you're not," said Cristina as she helped him push Clarini's body away.
"I don't know, it hurt's like Hell. But we need to get the people moving."
"They've gone already. Once I came round, I sent them off with the priest. You were fighting still. Sweet Mary! I thought it would never end."
"Are you all right?"
"The swine bloodied my nose and split my lip, but I'll live."
He pointed at Clarini. "Do you know him?"
"Nicolo Clarini, I met him once, in the church of San Antolin. Come on, let's get you where there's some light."
With her help he struggled to his feet and made his way to the refectory.

"Once we get your hauberk and shirt off I want you to lie on this table so I can see how bad it is."
"First let me see your face."
"For God's sake man, my face isn't important."
"It is to me. And please my lady, must we always fight?"
She tilted her face so that he could inspect her wounds in the dim light. Her lip was cut, the right cheek was swollen badly and her nose had bled, but it wasn't broken: she would soon mend.
"Satisfied?"
"Thank you. You saved my life you know."
"What did you expect me to do? Stand there and wail like a ninny while he killed you? Anyway, I'm sure you would have thought of something."
"No, lady, I was a dead man."
"Well, he's dead now so come on, I need you out of that shirt."

Clarini's blade had passed clean through his side, both entry and exit wounds were bleeding and bruised and it throbbed unceasingly, but it seemed to have missed his vitals.

"It's difficult to see in this light," said Cristina. "But I'd say that it needs to be sealed with a hot knife."

"There isn't time for that."

"I know. I'll have to stitch it. It's a good job I bought my needles and thread. Mind you," she said, examining his chest, "I did a good job the last time."

He smiled. "Indeed, the physician who removed your stitches praised the skills of my doctor."

They talked as she washed and stitched his wounds. He told her the gist of his story and she spoke of an old family friend — a senior churchman — who had brought early news of her uncle's arrival in Leon and the Congregation's plan to charge him with heresy. A day or so later he had learned that she would be charged too and detained in Las Huelgas: she had left Leon immediately.

"Why didn't you go to France?"

"There was only Pilar and I. Two women, alone on the road, all the way to France? I might have done it once, but not now, not after —" She hesitated.

"I understand," he whispered.

He had thought to tell her of his anguish at her fate and beg forgiveness, but he saw that any mention of it would cause her pain.

"This was the only place I could go and I couldn't desert my uncle's people."

"Where is Pilar?" he asked, to change the subject.

"I sent her off with the villagers. She'll wait for me above Penalbra."

"And what will you do now? Start another community?"

"No. It's over, I could tell that by the way they said goodbye. I thought we might carry on without him, but we can't. Poor uncle Diego, I never believed they would kill him."

"You know the charge against him?"

"Yes. How can men do such things and call themselves Christians?" She swallowed on her tears. "Was Clarini right about your plan?"

"Yes, he was a clever villain."

She finished bandaging his wound and he swung his legs slowly off the table and stood.

"We'd have gone back to Ponferrada empty handed, everyone would have blamed everyone else, but it would have soon died down. I would have served out my sentence, and then I'd have quit the Order. I'm not sure what my company will do once it discovers Clarini and I are missing. They'll look for us, that's sure, but it'll probably be days before they find the village."

"Why did you come here tonight, William?"

"I wasn't prepared to do murder on behalf of evil men. They say that God gave man free will; I decided it was time I used mine." He hesitated, fearful of how she might react. "And I wanted to make sure you were safe."

"What about Clarini? Would you have killed him?"

Had she understood the import of his words? he wondered, or had she understood and decided to ignore them?

"I'd promised myself I would, but once the villagers had escaped and I'd rejoined my men I might have decided it was better to let things settle. It didn't occur to me that Pelet had promoted me Master so that Clarini would know who blinded his eye. I don't know why, perhaps because it never entered my head that my Commander would betray one of his own knights. I don't know whether he wanted me dead on his own account — to shut my mouth — or perhaps the Bishop demanded it. It doesn't make any difference now: I'm dead if I go back to Ponferrada." He paused, hesitating to ask his question. What would he do if she spurned him?

"I know what you think of me and I deserve it. And I have no right to say this, but would you come with me, if I asked you? I think France would be the safest place."

"What exactly was your crime? You never did tell me."

"I killed a knight in a tourney. He was son and heir to the Count of Flanders. It was deliberate: he was going to marry a girl I loved. I repent it now, truly, before God. The Bishop of Bruges gave me twenty years. Now that I'm a deserter — ? Who knows?" He shrugged. "According to the priests I'll burn in Hell for not finishing my penance. But after everything that's happened I don't think I believe what the priests tell us anymore."

"You mustn't say that William. You mustn't doubt God because men are evil."

"I don't doubt God, only priests."

She hadn't answered his question, but with her he had no pride; he would ask it again and pray to Her for an answer.

"So will you come with me, Cristina? I have no money to buy the things we'll need on the journey, I'm afraid. I'm as poor as a church mouse," he added lamely.

She stared steadily into his eyes. "What *can* you offer?"

Disarmed by her directness, he wilted under her gaze as he fumbled for the right words. Every fibre of his being wanted to say: "To love and cherish you." But he held back; it was presumptuous and, in light of what he'd visited on her, it was dishonourable too. God had answered his prayers: he'd been given a chance to redeem himself. He must gain her respect and affection before he could win her heart: he would be wise, he wouldn't push his suit. But at this very moment he was standing before her and she was expecting an answer. What could he say that wouldn't sound foolish? Help me Lady! he prayed silently to Mary.

"I see," Cristina breathed softly, ending the silence between them.

"My sword for your protection and a promise to be a faithful companion," he blurted.

She regarded him carefully for several moments. She had despised him for failing to protect her, but tonight he had risked everything, even his life, to save her and the villagers. Uncle Diego had chosen him and, before the attack on her, she too had started to think of him as an honest and gentle knight. She would have to flee Spain and she quailed at the idea of her and Pilar journeying alone to France; however the thought of him by her side gave her fresh courage. And he wouldn't leave her unguarded again, she was sure of it.

"In that case sir, I accept your offer. And I agree. We should go to France; the Languedoc is best I think. My family has blood ties with the Counts of Toulouse."

She paused. She'd guessed from the look on his face a moment ago that he cared for her and she didn't know whether she should acknowledge his feelings. He had redeemed himself in some measure, she owed him something for that. He was handsome enough, but she had never thought of him in that way, not in the least. Still, honest words could do no harm and they might make for a more harmonious journey.

"I sense you care for me William," said quietly, "and I'm not sure how I feel about that. To tell you the truth, I'm not sure how I feel about anything anymore. A lot has happened since first we met. Now —" She sighed. "Uncle Diego is dead and I shall never see my grandfather again and our family will no longer be Counts of Soria. I've lost everything. I need time to think; I have to find out who I am. Do you understand?"

He'd expected a forthright rejection, instead she had been gracious: it was better than he'd hoped for and a lot more than he deserved. He'd live with his love unrequited. All he asked for was to be by her side.

"Yes, lady, I understand," he said, softly.

"Thank you. What you did for us tonight took great courage. Uncle Diego did well when he chose you — you are a *good* knight, not a Templar." She smiled, briefly. "What a pair we are, I shall never be Countess of Soria and you're a deserter, but I daresay we'll get by." She took his hand and squeezed it briefly. "Now," she said in her brisk tone, "put on this shirt and cloak while I get the horses. Once we're clear of the valley we can collect Pilar and head for France."

oooOOOOooo

ISBN 141206317-5